Karlsruher Beiträge zur wirtschaftspolitischen Forschung

Karlsruhe Papers in Economic Policy Research

herausgegeben von Prof. Dr. Rolf Funck und
Prof. Dr. Werner Rothengatter

I W W   Institut für Wirtschaftspolitik
und Wirtschaftsforschung
der Universität Karlsruhe (TH)

Band 4

Niklas Sieber

Rural Transport and Regional Development

The Case of Makete District, Tanzania

Nomos Verlagsgesellschaft
Baden-Baden

Die Deutsche Bibliothek – CIP-Einheitsaufnahme

Sieber, Niklas:
Rural Transport and Regional Development : The Case of Makete District, Tanzania /
Niklas Sieber. – 1. Aufl. – Baden-Baden : Nomos Verl.-Ges., 1996
   (Karlsruhe Papers in Economic Policy Research ; Bd. 4)
   Zugl.: Karlsruhe, Univ., Diss., 1996
   ISBN 3-7890-4507-1
NE: Karlsruher Beiträge zur wirtschaftspolitischen Forschung

1. Auflage 1996
© Nomos Verlagsgesellschaft, Baden-Baden 1996. Printed in Germany. Alle Rechte,
auch die des Nachdrucks von Auszügen, der photomechanischen Wiedergabe und der
Übersetzung, vorbehalten.

Table of Contents

List of Tables

List of Figures

9

List of Abbreviations

DANIDA	Danish Volunteer Organisation
FAO	Food and Agricultural Organisation of the United Nations
GDP	Gross Domestic Product
GNP	Gross National Product
ILO	International Labour Office (Geneva)
IMF	International Monetary Fund
IMT	Intermediate Means of Transport (Intermediate between motorised vehicles and walking; i.e. bicycles, wheelbarrows, pack animals...)
IRP	Integrated Roads Programme (World Bank Programme in Tanzania)
MIRTP	Makete Integrated Rural Transport Project
NGO	Non Government Organisation
Pkm	Passenger kilometre: One passenger transported one kilometre
SIDA	Swedish Volunteer Organisation
Tkm	Tonne kilometre: One tonne transported one kilometre
Tsh	Tanzania Shilling
UNCTADA II	Second United Nations Transport and Communications Decade
UNECA	United Nations Economic Commission for Africa
USAID	United States Volunteer Organisation
VOC	Vehicle Operating Costs
WHO	World Health Organisation
WTP	Willingness to Pay

Unit-Conversion

Exchange Rate (May 1994)	1 US $	518 Tsh
Area	1 Acre	0.4047 ha
Weight	1 Debe	20 kg

Acknowledgements

I want to thank the following persons for the support of my study:

- ✍ Prof. John Howe, Prof. Rolf Funck and Prof. Werner Rothengatter for their scientific consultancy,
- ✽ Morris J. Roche and Cree Oliver for their language corrections,
- ✎ Robert and Naomi Mamba for their Swahili translations of the questionnaires,
- ☞ Andrew Mbiling'i, Meshack B. Kyando, David Mtenzi and Moses Tweve for their enumeration during the field study,
- ✉ the ILO and the Karlsruher Hochschulvereinigung for the financial support of my field study,
- ☎ Tom Strandberg for the supply with information about the MIRTP,
- ☞ Christian Dierks and Meike Müller for their diploma thesis,
- ❀ The members of the Institut für Wirtschaftspolitik und Wirtschaftsforschung (IWW) for their patience and for their general aid concerning all kinds of problems,
- ♡ Julia for her love, patience and support during times of difficulty.

Foreword of the Editors

Poor transport conditions are regarded as one of the major constraints for rural development in Sub-Saharan Africa. The actual focus of donors on 'roads and cars' is criticised, since, as a result of this, the transport needs of rural households are widely neglected. Several recent studies show that mobility of the rural population in many Developing Countries consists mainly in walking trips on footpaths and trails, distant from the rural road network, and that very few motorised trips are undertaken. The majority of transport time and effort is spent on transport activities necessary to secure the households' subsistence needs: carrying of water, and burning materials. The largest share of the transport burden is carried by women. The effort, drudgery and the excessive time requirements to be devoted to transport purposes, significantly hamper the growth of agricultural production: According to the International Food Policy Research Institute's judgement "Africa's poor record on food production is largely due to labour constraints" which are, in turn, to a large part the result of poor traffic conditions.

Based on these considerations, the International Labor Organization conducted a pilot study in Makete District, Tanzania, in the second half of the 1980s, following a household survey: footpaths, tracks and roads were improved, intermediate means of transport promoted, and transport avoiding measures implemented. In 1994, the author carried out a similar survey in the same district, employing a methodological approach comparable to that of the ILO study. Thus, the author is able to compare the transport patterns of rural households before and after the improvements, and from that comparison, it becomes, for the first time, possible to assess, on a household level, the benefits of appropriate transport improvements.

He establishes an econometric model based on a systems dynamics approach. The model simulates the feedback processes between agricultural production, income, time budget and transport activities, and assesses the regional economic impacts of various transport investments in several scenarios. The model shows that the strongest impacts can be achieved as a result of the construction of a low-cost road to the regional centre, combined with the setting up of a credit fund for the purchase of intermediate means of transport. The model also demonstrates that a low-cost road can be entirely financed on the basis of local road pricing.

As a conclusive scenario, an optimal investment strategy to be financed by a Regional Transport Fund, is designed: in the initial phase, while the region is not accessible by motor vehicles, a local footpath to an external market is improved, and credits are distributed for the purchase of intermediate means of transport. Then, a low-cost feeder road to the regional centre is constructed, and a road user charge levied on regionally exported products, as a percentage of the producer price. The growing market production will enable the road users to repay the debt within a decade, and, during the second decade, sufficient amounts of user charges have been accumulated to finance the construction of motorable tracks to every village. This investment then entails another production expansion, so that the fund re-accumulates faster, so that transport avoiding measures can be financed.

The author has invested a large amount of empirical work on location, of sound theoretical reasoning, and of personal involvement in the task of improving the living conditions in a developing country. Our knowledge about the relationships between transport infrastructure, means of transportation, agricultural production and income development in rural regions in developing countries is greatly improved, well beyond the specific situation in the case region. The editors trust that the book will be well received in the academic, and planning community as well as among development agencies.

Professor Dr. Rolf Funck
Professor Dr. Werner Rothengatter

1   Introduction

During the last decade per capita incomes and food production of most Sub-Saharan African Countries declined. The FAO estimates that chronic undernutrition and hunger currently affects 180 million people world-wide and anticipates that this amount will probably increase to 300 million by the year 2010. Because $^2/_3$ of the African population live in rural areas, a solution to the crisis must be found in the countryside. "Such development as there is for most Sub-Saharan African economies, for at least the next decade, is therefore likely to be 'agriculture led'."[1]

Poor transport conditions are generally regarded as one of the main constraints against rural development. Therefore since 1940 the World Bank spent more than $ 62 billion world-wide in over 1000 transport projects. Since 1970 transport investments comprised 13-16 % of total expenditure. The presidency of Robert McNamara directed the bank's bias towards the construction of rural roads.

The exclusive focus of donors on roads and cars has been criticised since the 1980s, because the transport needs of rural households are neglected. In his famous World Bank Paper "Rural Poverty Unperceived" Robert CHAMBERS (1980) linked rural indigence firmly to lack of mobility. Four years later another World Bank Paper by EDMONDS and RELF concludes that 'plans, projects and existing policies in the transport sector do nothing or little for the rural poor'. This group of 'transport disenfranchised' can be conservatively estimated at world-wide to the order of 700 million people. A number of recent studies show that the rural population of many Developing Countries moves mainly by walking on paths and trails away from the rural road network and undertakes very few motorised trips. The majority of time and effort is spent for transport purposes which secure the household's subsistence needs. These transport constraints can significantly hamper rural development. The understanding that "Roads Are Not Enough"[2] to stimulate economic development in rural areas was grasped by the World Bank, thus launching the Rural Travel and Transport Project for Sub-Saharan Africa.

A variety of appropriate measures are available to improve the rural transport system: construction of low cost roads, tracks and paths, the introduction of Intermediate Means of Transport[3], installation of rural transport services and transport avoiding measures. The questions arise which of these transport interventions have the strongest effects and which the highest efficiency? Which transport interventions are most appropriate for which phase in development?

---

1 HELLEINER (1992 p.58); compare as well TIMMER (1988).
2 Title of the book by BARWELL and DAWSON (1993)
3 Intermediate Means of Transport are appropriate technologies which are intermediate between motorised vehicles and walking; i.e. bicycles, wheelbarrows, pack animals...

15

How can rural transport investments be financed and the maintenance secured regarding the poor financial situation of governments and rural households? Which assessment methodologies can be used to estimate future effects of appropriate transport interventions?

This thesis tries to find answers to these questions with an empirical study and an econometric model. In the following Chapter 2 an overview of the state of research on rural transport in Sub-Saharan Africa is given. Chapters 3 and 4 present the results of a field study, which was carried out in the Makete District in the South West of Tanzania. The study observes the effects of a pilot project which was conducted by the International Labour Office (ILO) in order to improve the transport of rural households. Before the project started a household survey was undertaken, which was repeated at its end. The data base gives rise to a number of conclusions concerning the effects of the appropriate transport interventions. Chapter 5 contains an econometric model, which simulates the regional economic effects of rural transport interventions and especially their impacts on agricultural market production. A system dynamics approach is applied and the model is calibrated using the data observed during the field study. The new approach towards rural transport necessitates different assessment methodologies for transport investments, which are roughly described in chapter 6.

2 Rural Transport in Sub-Saharan Africa

2.1 Transport Theories for Developing Countries

The high share of transport investments in the public expenditure of Sub-Saharan African Countries and in development aid from international donors gives rise to the question about the impacts of these expenditures for the regional development. Until today no general theory which assesses the economic and social impacts of transport investments, could be developed.

Since the beginning of economic theory, transport has been judged as a crucial element for the increase of welfare in society. Both Physiocrats and Mercantilists as well as classical and neo-classical economists demanded the dismantling of transport constraints. In 1837 Friedrich LIST described the impacts of steam trains as follows: "The more people are able to communicate and conduct actions complementing one another, the faster the progress of mankind accelerates" (§1). LIST forecasted that the introduction of steam trains would reduce transport costs and travel time, expand markets, increase production and consumption, enhance the division of labour and enlarge productivity.

These statements were verified one century later by empirical studies conducted by Walt ROSTOW (1960) and in Germany by Fritz VOIGT (1959). The latter explains the wealth of Industrialised Countries mainly by means of the autonomous development caused by shipping, railways and improved communication technologies. The author examines the impacts of the introduction of a modern transport system into a homogeneous pre-industrial region, in which, due to the isolated situation, no autonomous development takes place. A 'Big Push' caused by the introduction of an efficient modern transport system overcomes the stagnation by increasing the marginal productivity of capital in central locations, which gives incentives for new investments. These locations are the development poles which contribute to overcome subsistence economy. The following spillover effects have stronger impacts than the transport infrastructure itself: the attraction of purchasing power in the centres induces an expansion process with increasing demand, rising income, population growth and rural exodus. VOIGT judges the negative effects by the growing spatial disparities smaller than the benefits from this growth process. The following effects are generated by transport investments:
* Reduction of operating, maintenance, time and accident costs,
* increase of production due to reduction of transport costs,
* enhanced communication and diffusion of innovations and
* depletion of the peripheries.

VOIGT concludes that the transport system itself is able to create special impulses for an economic growth process (p. 306). Therefore transport investments in Developing Countries should be undertaken even if they are not economically viable (p. 312).

The optimism of the modernisation theories culminated in the statement of CHRISHOLM (1962): "...if you drive a road or railway through a cultivable area, you automatically stimulate economic development."

HIRSCHMAN (1958) could not share this optimistic view. He classifies investments into directly productive activities (DPA) and into social overhead capital (SOC) under which transport investments can be subsumed. Two unbalanced strategies can be pursued: in the first strategy the investments are channelled in DPA and the existing infrastructure is simply used more intensively until bottlenecks occur and investments in SOC have to be undertaken. The second strategy favours the provision of infrastructure by investing in SOC which is expected to induce directly productive activities (DPA). HIRSCHMAN decided that the first strategy, called development by shortage, is more likely to succeed, because the second strategy, development by excess, favours investments which are essentially permissive.

In the beginning of the 1960s the research of COOTNER (1963) and FOGEL (1964) contradict LIST regarding the strong effects of the steam engine for development. They claim that industrialisation would have occurred without the invention of the railways.

During the following discussion[1] the optimistic view was replaced by the statement that transport investments are a 'necessary but not sufficient' precondition for development. WILSON (1973, p. 208) distinguishes between "(1) the creation of economic opportunity and (2) the response to economic opportunity. The first depends upon the quality and quantity of resources in the regions served, the actual change in transport rates and service and commodity price levels". Various studies show that when prices were falling and yields not increasing, the key to development lay in declining transport costs. If both were not the case the transport investments were permissive rather than causal. "The main factors influencing the response to new transport capacity are: (a) awareness of its potential, (b) the availability of finance, and (c) the magnitude of possible benefits relative to alternative investment options" (p. 210). WILSON states that next to the direct economic impacts spillover effects occur, which are much stronger than the direct reductions in user costs: "The unlimited access of roads in the early stages of development of any region has an awareness effect that serves to induce a larger number of people to take advantage of new economic potential" (p. 211). These changes in attitude are much more strongly influenced by roads than by other modes of transport[2].

---

1 HEINZE (1967), FRITZ (1975), GAUTHIER (1973), JÄGER (1972), HOYLE (1973), BARON (1980), HOWE (1980)
2 WILSON does not include Intermediate Means of Transport in his argumentation.

According to WILSON (1973) markets which had been protected by high transport costs, would be exposed to competition with cheap international products after the opening of the region by transport infrastructure. This process could even entail a decline in real incomes. A survey of 50 road projects in Africa conducted by FISCHER (1983) verifies that the effects of roads in the sphere of consumption are stronger and visible earlier on here than in the field of production. The problem of growing regional disparities already mentioned by VOIGT was picked up by MYRDAL (1974): the regional disequilibrium caused by the concentration of the investments on the development poles will be amplified in a circular cumulative process and will not even out as the neo-classical theory claims.

The intensive discussion of the 1960s and 1970s calmed down and gave way to the insight that it is difficult to verify the theories empirically because the nexus between transport investments and regional development can seldom be proved. General theories only make sense if they are spatially and temporally differentiated[3]. HOYLE (1973) differentiates between two phases, one following on from the other: while the "initial transport provision" stimulates the economy[4], induces spatial disparities and forms the future regional structure, the "transport elaboration" has a primarily permissive character and might lead to spatial inequalities if no regional planning measures follow[5]. HOYLE proposes a spatially differentiated observation of
- densely populated regions with good transport endowment,
- rural growth regions with basic endowment,
- rural indifference regions without transport endowment and
- rural depletion regions with basic endowment.

The appearance of the New Growth Theories reignited the discussion about the macroeconomic effects of transport investments again. After ASCHAUER (1989) observed a high productivity of public infrastructure investments in the USA, a number of international studies[6] followed. The studies used multivariant regressions in order to estimate the impacts of different public investments on production. They reveal that infrastructure investments have the biggest production

---

3 One of the most popular studies is on the historical development of the transport infrastructure in Ghana, which was researched by TAFFE, MORILL and GOULD (1970).

4 A good example of the positive impact of a new road is the Andapa-Savamba Road in Madagascar, because the frame conditions were extraordinary: Household income grew significantly, income disparities were reduced and the mobility of people increased.

5 A study of nine projects of rural road construction by ANDERSON and VANDERVOORT (1982) concludes: "The new road projects were followed by a substantial and sometimes dramatic increase in agricultural production..."(S. 13), while the growth was bigger than after an improvement of an existing link. An empirical research by LEE and VONNAHME (1985) about the regional development in South Korea confirms these statements.

6 An overview of these studies is given in Chapter 1 of the World Development Report 1994.

elasticities[7]. EASTERLY/REBELO (1994) computed world-wide country data on infrastructure investments since 1960 and observed a production elasticity of 0.16. The growth was achieved by increasing the social return on private investment, but not raising private investment activities themselves. The authors admit that the crude country data only allows the observation of "suggestive evidence". BINSWANGER/KHANDKER (1992) observe an elasticity of 0.07 for roads in rural India, but other variables like education (0.08), market regulations (0.04), commercial banks (0.03), rural electricity (0.02) and producer prices (0.02) also showed significant effects. JIMENEZ (1994, p.10) criticises these studies because variations in quality or utilisation are not considered and none of the studies could exclude that a common factor influences both infrastructure and growth. In addition, they could not determine whether the investments were the cause or the consequence of the growth.

2.2 Empirical Evidence of Transport in Rural Areas

HOWE's (1984) comprehensive review of 50 evaluation reports during the last decades shows that the assessments were very much dependent on the regional conditions, on the methodologies and criteria of the evaluation. Project impacts were hard to measure, because they show up with a long time delay, they are difficult to separate from the effects of other complementary investments and they are subject to fluctuations (migration, climatic fluctuations etc.). Effects resulting from the transport of persons were bigger than the effects from the transport of goods. In general the access to social services improved, but only small effects could be established in regard to income and its distribution and especially to poverty alleviation (pp. 79). Land tenancy often determines who benefits most from the project. Road investments reinforce the existing social and economic stratification because "it will help wealthier and better informed producers to expand faster than others." HOWE cites the biblical situation that "to whom that has more will be given". A study from West Malaysia confirms these findings: "...55 % of the poorest people were getting only 10 % of the project benefits..."[8]

Economic impact assessments of rural transport interventions are primarily undertaken with the perspective of improving the marketing channels. Rural transport expands the catchment areas of local and regional markets and forms the link to the international markets. Fig. 2.2-1 shows the classification of a national road network under the marketing perspective. The agricultural products are transported using tracks from the field to the farm-stead and are carried from there on earth roads to the local markets or to the central delivery post.

---

7 Growth of production in percent related to the change of infrastructure in percent.
8 Quoted according to BARTH (1989, p. 27).

From there the crops are transported on gravelled roads to the district town and on tarmac roads to the capital or the export harbour.

FEEDER & DISTRICT ROADS		INTERURBAN ROADS		CITY ROADS
On Farm, Farm to House	Farm to Market	Rural Road	National Road	City Roads
Track	Earth Road	Gravel	Asphalted	
< 6 Veh. / Day	6 - 35 Veh. / Day	35 - 150 Veh. / Day	> 150 Veh. / Day	
2 km	5 - 20 km	40 - 100 km	60 - 160 km	

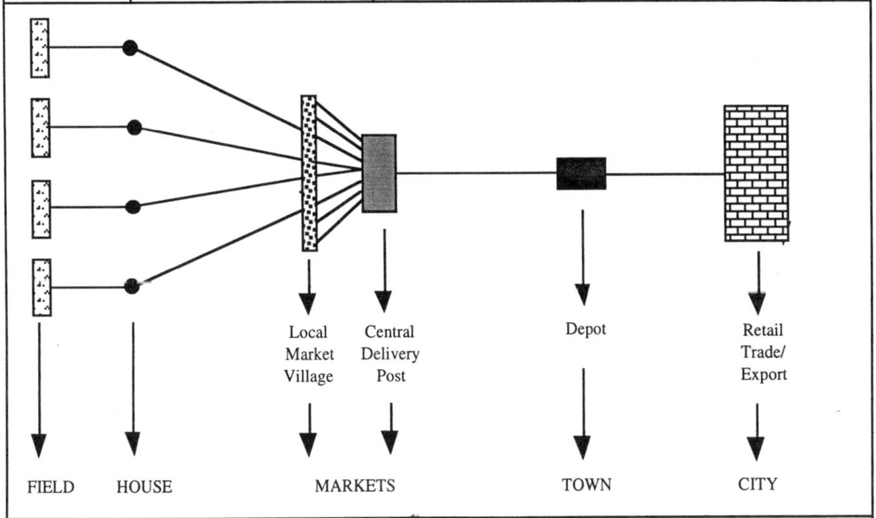

Local Market Village   Central Delivery Post   Depot   Retail Trade/ Export

FIELD   HOUSE   MARKETS   TOWN   CITY

Source: METSCHIES, GTZ in: ABRAHAM (1993), S. 210

Fig. 2.2-1   Classification of a national road system under marketing perspective

The Producer Surplus Theory (Chapter 6.2.1) is often applied to assess the effects of road improvements in rural areas. It is assumed that road improvements entail reduced transport costs which cause an increase in agricultural producer prices and thus generate rural growth. A study of 33 villages of the Ashanti Region in Ghana by the Transport Research Laboratory (HINE 1993) found little evidence that agriculture was adversely affected by bad road access. The improvement of existing road surfaces had negligible impacts on producer prices, while the conversion of a footpath into a road entailed benefits to the order of hundred times greater.

A study by the International Food Policy Institute undertaken by AHMED and HOOSAIN (1990 and 1993) in Bangladesh contradicts HINE by stating that the marketing of agricultural products increased very quickly under the influence of infrastructures. The producer prices were not higher in the easily accessible villages, but the lower prices for inputs were causing higher production. The roads were favourable as well for the non-agricultural income, the composition of employment and the market integration. HOWE (1994) contradicts this with the argument that Bangladesh already has an excessive network compared to its neighbouring countries. Missing funds for maintenance will cause a fast deterioration of the roads and will limit the positive effects over a short period. The benefits might not be warranted by the long run maintenance costs for the excessive network. On top of this the disadvantages for the poor like loss of agricultural land and water logging have to be taken into account. A regional survey revealed "a number of strong biases against asset-poor villagers' realisation of benefits from road investments compared with the wealthier strata of the village population. This was related to the limited use that asset poor households could make of the roads given their restricted demand for and means of transport..." (pp 22). HOWE judges large scale road investments in rural areas of Bangladesh to be "a huge waste of resources" (p.24)

A number of studies have observed changes in spatial structures due to road construction. The location theory by THÜNEN (1783-1850) can be witnessed nowadays in many Developing Countries. More than a century ago THÜNEN had already observed circular structures of the agricultural land use around the market towns; with increasing distance the intensity of agricultural production will decrease. HOWE and RICHARDS (1984) discovered Thünen's circles in Bolivia[9], HOFMEIER (1970) perceived an intensive landuse along the trunk roads in Tanzania and MILLARD (1973) observed that the total arable land within half a mile from the road was under cultivation, while five miles away this share declined to only 5 %. In the Ashanti region of Ghana, 98 % of the inhabitants were living within two km of the roads (HINE 1993). A study by KOCHENDÖRFER-LUCIUS (1989) observed the influence of transport infrastructure on historical migrations in the Côte d'Ivoire; along the roads the market production was higher, innovations diffused faster because the access to agricultural services and inputs was better than on remote farms. In easily accessible regions land became a scarce resource causing shorter fallow periods, which entailed a decreasing soil fertility and increasing degradation of the vegetation. Therefore the highest productivity was observed in farms with medium accessibility, where the net profits per labourer were twice as high as on remote farms. Thus the locational advantages can be described as a combination of accessibility and agroecological frame conditions. This insight is confirmed by WAGNER (1993) who states that transport investments might entail severe ecological damages, e.g. by overgrazing in semi arid regions. The same holds true for humid regions, where road construc-

---

9 In the inner circle sugar cane is grown, which has the highest share of transport costs; in the second ring bananas follow and the peripheral regions produce rice, which is easy to store and has low transport costs.

tion entails the migration of farmers into the rain forests, which are often more strongly degraded by agricultural activities than by commercial logging (SIEBER 1988 p. 50).

Some **general conclusions** can be drawn from the theoretical and empirical studies about rural road projects:
- Project impacts are very much dependent on the local frame conditions and are generally overestimated.
- Initial transport provision has stronger effects than transport elaboration.
- Without accompanying measures rural road projects will favour those social groups, which are already better off than others.
- Rural road projects might entail severe ecological damage, especially if the agroecological potential is exceeded.
- It is problematic to select user cost savings as the only criterion for ex-ante evaluations, because spillover effects might have much bigger impacts.

Therefore HOWE (1992, p.13) declares that predictions of the effects of transport investments are rather speculative due to the unpredictable multitude of reactions. Instead of bringing possible benefits to few locations it is preferable to spread the risk. He therefore proposes a cheap strategy of trial and error by building and upgrading as cheaply and extensively as possible. If a response follows further upgrading would have to be undertaken.

2.3   The Role of Non-Motorised Transport in Rural Areas

Next to the road system for motorised transport shown in Fig 2.2-1 a huge network of paths and tracks for non-motorised transport exists in the rural areas of Sub-Saharan Africa. The motorised system did not develop in an organic manner as in the case of Europe, or in hierarchical way as in America, but it was juxtaposed on to the existing network. Nowadays the modern system gives only restricted access to limited areas: transport links to rural areas are either nonexistent or are often in a miserable condition. During the rainy season in particular, many rural regions are cut off from motorised access. Persons and goods can only be transported by walking, causing high transport costs in terms of time and money. The limited time budgets and the physical condition of the travellers (especially on the way to medical facilities) are the main restrictions. However, even in the dry season the overwhelming majority of trips are undertaken by walking. The most simple reason for this is that Africa is too poor to afford motorised transport. In 1988 in Sub-Saharan Africa[10] an average of only nine motor vehicles per 1,000 inhabitants were registered (UNCTADA II, pp 52). This ratio had not increased significantly during the preceding eight years due to

---

10 The Republic of South Africa is excluded.

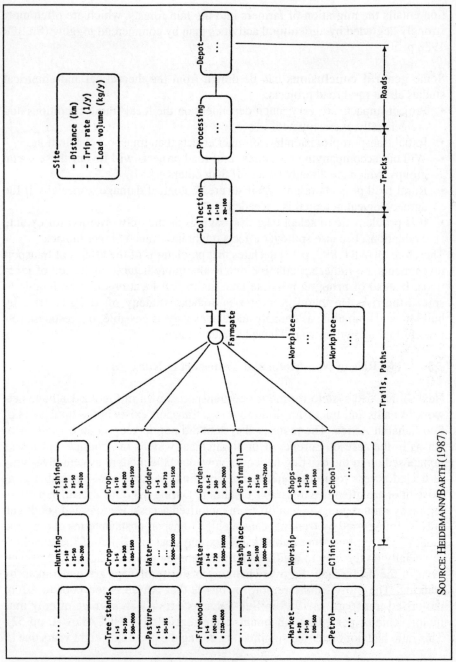

Fig. 2.3-1 Local perception of the rural transport system

the steady economic crisis and the foreign exchange shortage. A transport evaluation on rural roads in Uganda estimates that 75 % of the trips were undertaken by walking, 22 % by bicycle and only 2 % with motorised vehicles. An evaluation in Ghana on rural roads with less than 25 vehicles per day revealed that 90 % of the goods were transported by headload (BARWELL/DAWSON 1993, pp 35). Studies and Projects which only take motorised transport into account neglect the majority of the transport activities of rural households, which EDMONDS and RELF (1984) call the 'transport disenfranchised'.

Box 2-1: Classification of the Rural Transport Network:

Path: A narrow cleared way used for walking, sometimes by bicycles and motorcycles.
Trail: A wider path also passable by pack animals.
Track: Narrow road with a single cleared lane, dry weather standard, can be used by 4-wheel-drive vehicles and animal carts.
Feeder Road: Access road to the national trunk road network, often dry weather standard.

Box 2-1 shows that rural transport infrastructure consists of paths, trails, tracks and feeder roads which are predominantly used by non-motorised means of transport. While Fig. 2.2-1 shows the motorised transport system from the viewpoint of a national administrator or expatriate Fig. 2.3-1 emphasises the perception of a farmer whose transport occurs mainly on footpaths and trails between the farmstead, the fields, the water supply, the pastures, the garden, the washing place and the communal centre with market and church. Only a small share of trips are undertaken to the collection points for agricultural produce.

A very detailed study about transport patterns of rural households was conducted in the Makete District (Tanzania), which is described in detail in the Chapters 3 and 4. More than 90 % of the trips and 80 % of the tkm can be regarded as internal transport in and around the village, during which 80 % of the time devoted for transport is spent[11]. A relatively small share of the transport is conducted on roads, which are suitable for motorised vehicles. Transport for water and firewood collection, to the fields and to the grinding mills account for 86 % of the trips, 81 % of the time and 98 % of the tkm. The remaining transport consists of trips to the village centre, to health facilities and to markets. In 1986/87 most of the agricultural products were marketed in the villages, from where they were carried by motor vehicles[12].

---

11 A study by DAWSON (1993, p. 2) in Ghana confirms the outcomes from Makete: The share of internal transport comprises 91 % of the trips, 76 % of the tkm and 73 % of the transport time.
12 Chapter 3 shows that meanwhile the situation has changed in favour of external marketing.

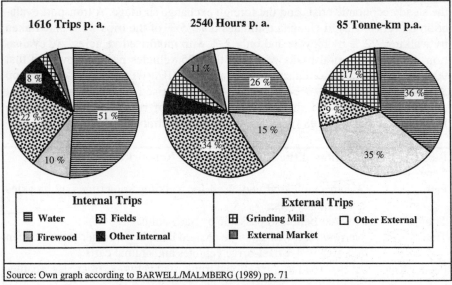

Source: Own graph according to BARWELL/MALMBERG (1989) pp. 71

Fig. 2.3-2   Transport activities in Makete District 1986/87

A research by KAIRA (1983) in the Kirinyanga District of Kenya confirms the primarily internal transport patterns of the households. In contrast to Makete, the farmers are marketing their products externally: 80 % of the households transport less than half a ton to the markets using animal carts and headload. Nevertheless, the remainder of the transport takes place in and around the village.

The transport tasks of rural households necessitate enormous transport loads: a rural household needs 40-60 m³ water (110-150 l/day) and 8-10 m³ wood annually (KAIRA p.34). BARWELL and DAWSON (1993, p.17) estimates the annual transport of a rural household in Ghana at 216 tkm. In Makete this amount[13] comprised 87 tkm, with 72 % being carried by women, 9 % by men and 5 % by children (BARWELL/MALMBERG 1989, p. 81). A comparative study in three African countries (BARWELL 1993) states that at least 65 % of the household's transport time and effort is contributed by women. It is for this reason that Ursula BARTH called her dissertation "Frauen gehen lange Wege"[14].

What is also remarkable is the amount of time needed for transport purposes. In Makete an average household uses seven hours per day (50 hours/week) for transport activities. Fig. 2.3-2 compiles the average walking time for one way trips of different study areas in Tanzania and Ghana. The average time used for a return trip to the water supply comprises 45-60 min, an activity which is ful-

---

13 The big difference stems from the smaller size of the average household in Makete.
14 (1989): Women Have to Walk A Long Way.

26

filled in a few seconds in Industrialised Countries. Tab. 2.3-1 gives a comparative overview of the household time devoted for transport in 5 study areas in Sub-Saharan Africa. The total time devoted to transport ranges from 1,100 to 2,700 hours per year or 0.8 to 2.5 hours per adult per day. Domestic transport accounts for 44 % to 64 % of total transport time. The high number of external trips in Rural Lusaka can be explained by the location of the study area i.e. close to the Zambian Capital, where employment and services can be obtained.

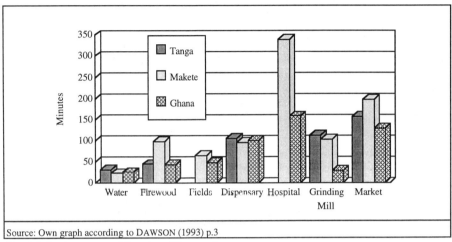

Source: Own graph according to DAWSON (1993) p.3

Fig. 2.3-3   Average walking time (One way)

The time burden for domestic transport tasks reduces the remaining time for welfare increasing activities. In labour intensive economies this allocation of time is a drain on the households labour resources. Time constraints may have severe negative impacts on productivity, especially during peak working periods, e.g. in the harvesting season. JENNINGS (1992, p. 29) reports that many women in the Makete District "indicated that they had additional shambas (fields) which they could cultivate if they had additional time". RIVERSON et al (1991, p. 82) argue that "female labour availability in terms of quantity, seasonability, location, labour quality and incentives, is therefore the key to agricultural improvement." According to the International Food Policy Research Institute, the lack of labour is the salient reason for the low agricultural production: "Africa's poor record on food production is largely due to labour constraints ... These serve to reduce labour input into agriculture, slowing the expansion of area cultivated as well as the yields per acre."[15]

---

15 MELLOR (1985) quoted according to BARTH (1989) p. 14

27

	Zambia		Uganda	Burkina Faso	
	Kasama	Rural Lusaka	Mbale	Kaya	Dedougou
Domestic Transport	1,120	1,201	1,508	669	624
Agricultural Transport	330	75	197	197	456
Services and Social Purposes	287	1,435	633	258	179
Total Transport Time	**1,737**	**2,711**	**2,338**	**1,124**	**1,259**
Hours per Adult per Annum	695	717	899	296	279
Hours per Adult per Day	1.9	2.0	2.5	0.8	0.8
Source: BARWELL (1993) p.7					

Tab. 2.3-1 Annual transport time per household

Conclusion:

In his famous book "Rural Poverty Unperceived" Robert CHAMBERS (1980) linked rural indigence firmly to isolation. BARWELL[16] explains the term isolation as follows: "If a rural area cannot be easily reached, if people living in the rural area cannot easily travel, if the flow of goods and services in and out of that area is physically difficult, unreliable or expensive ... these are the characteristics of isolation." Isolation reduces

- the productivity because the access to agricultural extension services is hampered,
- the educational level due to lower school enrolments,
- the access to public health services,
- the access to external markets,
- the producer prices due to high transport rates and
- the access to non agricultural income.

Following the "vicious circle" theory, lower education and health standards will entail a lower level of productivity and thus generate smaller incomes, smaller savings and lower capital formation.

2.4   Towards an Appropriate Rural Transport Approach

RIVERSON et al (1991) evaluated 127 rural transport projects conducted by the World Bank between 1965-1990 and comprising 160,000 km rural roads. They state that rural transport bottlenecks have contributed to the failure of structural adjustment programmes. Therefore the authors stress the "urgent necessity to develop a coherent Rural Road Strategy":

---

16 Ian Barwell's introductory speech at the First Africa Meeting of the Forum for Rural Transport and Development in Lilongwe, Malawi November 1993.

- Low cost design of rural roads to provide essential access.
- Labour based construction and maintenance of the infrastructure.
- Creation of a decentralised unit taking care of the planning, financing, construction and maintenance of the infrastructure.

In addition the transport policy should be adapted to the needs and economic means of the rural population through:
- Promotion of affordable Intermediate Means of Transport (IMT).
- Implementation of a network of paths, trails and tracks, which can be used by the IMT and which complement the existing road network.
- Realisation of transport avoiding measures.
- Provision of transport services.

An Appropriate Rural Transport Approach combines motorised and non-motorised transport interventions. The following four chapters present the salient features of this approach.

2.4.1 Promotion of Intermediate Means of Transport

Intermediate Means of Transport (IMT) "are defined as those means of transport which are intermediate in terms of initial cost and transport characteristics ... between the traditional methods of walking and headloading and conventional motor vehicles... (and) ... intermediate in time, i.e. they are a stage in the process of developing a traditional to a modern transport system." (HOWE 1994, p. 5). A number of studies concerning IMT[17] have been carried out in many Developing Countries. They emphasise the economic role which IMT can play in the development process. Intermediate Means of Transport are more appropriate for local transport, because they
- are relatively cheap to purchase,
- have a low level of maintenance,
- can operate on paths, tracks and trails, which are inexpensive to construct and maintain,
- are designed for small and medium loads,
- can often be produced locally and thus
- need less foreign currency.

Tab. 2.4-1 gives an overview of the available means of transport in Developing Countries. An optimal combination of IMT and motorised vehicles can be found by taking the regional frame conditions into account: cash income, transport needs, endowment with infrastructure, distance to markets, climatic and morphological conditions, etc. While motorised transport can carry bigger loads over longer distances, the IMT are appropriate if many trips with shorter dis-

---

17 AIREY (1992), BARWELL (1993), BARWELL et al (1985), BARWELL/DAWSON (1993), De Veen (1991), DENNIS/HOWE (1993), EDMONDS/DE Veen (1993), HEIERLI (1993), HOWE(1994), MALMBERG (1994).

tances have to be undertaken. Wheelbarrows and handcarts are suitable if bigger loads have to be moved on a flat terrain and on short trips around the farm stead. Bicycles are able to transport medium loads up to 40 km with a reasonable speed of 10 km/h. Sidecars or trailers can augment the load on flat terrains up to 150 kg, and animal drawn carts up to several tons. Pack animals are more appropriate where the morphology is accentuated or the tracks are not suitable to be passed by the above mentioned vehicles. Also motor cycles can be appropriate because they are able to pass on narrow footpaths and are comparatively cheap. Tractors can be used for different tasks (ploughing, pulling, transport) mainly on shorter distances, while pick ups or trucks are unbeatable on long distances.

Vehicle	Load [kg]	Speed [km/h]	Range [km]	Terrain
Carrying Pole	35	3-5	10	Unlimited
Improved Chee-ke	70	4-5	10	Unlimited
Western Wheelbarrow	120	3-5	1	Reasonably flat, smooth surface
Chinese Wheelbarrow	180	3-5	3-5	Reasonably flat, tolerates rough surface
Handcart	180	3-5	3-5	Reasonably flat, smooth surface
Bicycle	80	10-15	40	Reasonably flat, paths
Bicycle and trailer or sidecar	150	10-15	40	Reasonably flat: wide paths
Tricycle	150-200	10-15	40	Reasonably flat: wide paths
Pack Animal	70-150	3-5	20	Unlimited
Animal drawn cart (oxen)	1000-3000	3-5	50	Reasonably flat: wide track
Luggage on bus	15	30-60	>100	Wide track
Motorised bicycle	100-150	20-30	50	Reasonably flat
Motorcycle: 125cc	150-200	30-60	100	Moderate hills
MC 125cc & trailer or sidecar	250-400	30-60	100	Moderate hills: wide path
Motor tricycle: 125cc	200-300	30-60	100	Moderate hills: wide track
Single-axle tractor and trailer	1200	10-15	50	Moderate hills: wide track
Tractor	10 000	10-15	50	Moderate hills, wide track
Pick Up	1000	30-60	>100	Wide track
Truck	10 000	30-60	>100	Wide track
Source: BARWELL/HATHWAY/HOWE (1982) and METSCHIES (1986)				

Tab. 2.4-1 Performance characteristics of basic vehicles

A salient criterion for the choice of the transport mode are the Vehicle Operating Costs (VOC), which are plotted in Fig. 2.4-1 for Kenya and Malawi. Heavy trucks are cheapest if they operate on tarmac roads and have a high capacity utilisation. Due to the low transport volumes and the bad road conditions many rural areas are only served by pick ups, which have comparable VOC to animal drawn carts and bicycles. Restrictions for the latter vehicles are not the VOC, but the lower speed and the smaller range. Transport around the farm stead has to be undertaken by the expensive headload due to missing infrastructure. Pack animals and bicycles can reduce the transport costs significantly if paths are widened and the surfaces smoothened.

30

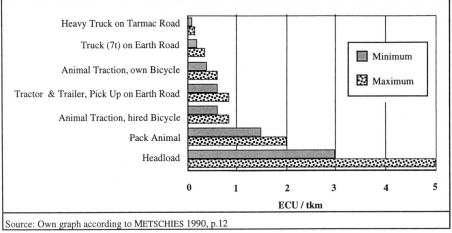

Fig. 2.4-1 Transport costs in Malawi and Kenya

The economic effects of IMT have rarely been researched until today. Five field studies in Zambia, Uganda and Burkina Faso lead AIREY (1992) to the following conclusion: "In economic terms these benefits of IMT can be considered as releasing latent factors of production, principally land, and increasing the efficiency with which the existing labour endowment is utilised. IMT enable the household to extend the distance over which agriculture is practised" and they release the household's time requirements, which can be used for productive activities[18]. The households are able to expand their agricultural production by putting more plots under cultivation. The enlarging distance to the fields and the increasing transport loads entail growing transport in terms of tkm and pkm. The use of IMT can reduce these constraints, because they

• shorten the time required for trips to the fields,
• increase the efficiency with which loads are carried,
• reduce the effort and drudgery involved in human porterage,
• reduce the pest damage and spoilage at crop harvest time and
• increase the use of fertiliser.

The use of IMT involves an expansion of agricultural production combined with an increase in productivity. IMT, especially bicycles are often used for commercial purposes, particularly for trading and transport services for persons[19]. BARWELL (1993) summarises the effects of IMT as follows: "Thus IMT alleviate the task of moving large quantities of agricultural inputs and outputs, facilitate local crop marketing, support small enterprise activities and provide access to employment and are used for social travel by men."

---

18 See as well the discussion in the following Chapter 2.4.2 about the effects of time saving
19 The study of MALMBERG (1994) gives a good impression about the use of bicycles in Uganda.

The question arises why these means of transport were not purchased by the farmers. The reasons are (i) natural restrictions, (ii) lack of awareness and education, (iii) missing production and distribution capacities and (iv) most importantly, missing affordability.

(i)   Natural conditions might restrict the use of IMT. The use of bicycles, animal carts, wheelbarrows and handcarts is hampered by steep terrain, while the tzetze-fly, which spreads the sleeping sickness prevents the keeping of pack animals in the low lands.

(ii) Someone who has never seen a bicycle pulling a trailer will hardly know of its advantages, while traditional behaviour can restrict the use of existing IMT. Cattle are often kept for saving purposes and not used as a means of transport. The gender division of roles restricts the use of bicycles by women, while men regard them as social prestige objects. However, "modern" ways of thinking also restrict the proliferation of IMT; because western ideals are penetrating the most remote areas, government officials do not favour these 'primitive' transport systems and the planning still favours motorised transport. Bicycle imports are often charged with an import tax for luxury items.

(iii) The industrial capacities in many African countries do not allow production of IMT, especially bicycles. The production of carts and wheelbarrows could be undertaken by small scale enterprises if the knowledge could be spread. The production and distribution is hampered by the low demand for IMT.

(iv) Missing affordability is probably the main reason why IMT are not purchased. In the Makete District 60 % of the households would purchase a bicycle, 30 % a donkey and 6 % a wheelbarrow if possible. 80-90 % of the households did not purchase their desired IMT, because it was too expensive. In Malawi a rural household would have to spend 19 times its monthly income to purchase a wheelbarrow, 27 for a bicycle and 113 for an oxcart (DEGWITZ 1992, p. 53). Tab. 2.4-2 shows that the price of IMT lies within the range of the annual per capita GNP. Thus, IMT seem to be mostly available to the wealthier classes.

IMT	Country	Cost [$]	GNP [$ per capita]
Animal Cart	Zambia	150-450	450
Animal Cart	Tanzania	150-450	110
Animal Cart	Malawi	up to 1000	200
Bicycle	Tanzania	77-120	110
Bicycle	Burkina Faso	210	330
Source: Dawson/Barwell (1993), p.48			

Tab. 2.4-2 Price for IMT and GNP per capita

There are a few measures which could be taken to promote the use of IMT. A credit system for the purchase of IMT could probably be an efficient means to proliferate the IMT. West Kenyan experience[20] of a credit system demonstrates that farmers were able to repay their debt for an ox cart after only one harvesting period. The existing credit systems usually make it almost impossible for anyone other than relatively well-off business men, who are mainly urban biased to purchase an IMT (CARAPETIS et al 1985, p. X). The experience with rural credit facilities for IMT in some African and Asian countries shows that credit schemes for IMT can be successfully operated[21]. The example of the Grameen Bank in Bangladesh shows how the borrowing arrangements can be efficiently organised. In chapter 5.3.2 the basic concept of a credit system for IMT is described in further detail.

2.4.2   Transport Avoiding Measures

Time constraints hamper the production of rural households. Time can be saved if a part of the household's domestic transport is avoided. Avoidance means the reduction of distances, time, tkm or pkm due to non transport interventions. Households in Industrialised Countries are supplied with water and energy, while African women have to walk long distances to cover these basic needs. In rural areas of Developing Countries, capital is missing to undertake these enormous investments into the infrastructure, not only because of the general poverty, but also because of the scattered settlement structures. In order to reduce these costs central installations like water supply points can be installed. Biogas supply can be used only if animals are kept in stables. Electricity is often used for lighting and not for energy intensive cooking, which is still done with firewood or charcoal. The promotion of low energy stoves and the installation of woodlots can efficiently reduce the transport of firewood. The decentralised location of public service units like grinding mills, health centres, input distribution- and marketing points also reduces travel distances. The efficiency of these investments depends on the number of households living within the catchment area.

---

20 IT Transport (1989), ITDG Kenya Animal Cart Project
21 In Burkina Faso credits are distributed by the Caisse Nationale de Credit Agricole to village groups and the repayment rates are close to 100 %. In India the Integrated Rural Development Programme provides credits and a 25 % subsidy for the purchase of IMT. In 1992-93 loans of $ 331 million were distributed. In 1993 the Bangladesh Rural Advancement Committee distributed credits worth $ 3 million mainly for the purchase of rickshaws through village associations. A 96 % repayment quota was achieved. In the decade following it's inception in 1976 the Grameen Bank funded the purchase of 15,212 rickshaws, animal carts, and bicycles. Here the repayment quota is 98 %. In Sri Lanka loans were given by the Intermediate Technology Group through farmer societies, while in Zimbabwe credits are only given to farmers who did not receive any loans before. Most of the credit schemes do not demand any collateral and the nominal interest rates range between 11 % and 21 % with a repayment time of 3-7 years. Further information: International Forum for Rural Transport and Development, Forum News, Vol. 2, June 1994.

The Tanzanian Government tried to decrease the costs of rural infrastructure supply by forcing the households to move into compact settlements. This enabled the farmers to shorten their travel time to the rural facilities, but increased the distance to their fields. The acceptance was low and many people moved back to their old homesteads, even if their houses had been destroyed. A strategy of population concentration can only work if IMT facilitate the transport to and from the fields and if the village services are substantially improved. If population densities are low it might be cost efficient to offer mobile services or promote cheap facilities, which can be used in the household (low consumption stoves, hand grinding mills etc.).

The question arises whether the time savings stemming from reduced transport will be used for production increasing activities. A theoretical consideration about the use of the household's time budget is shown in Fig. 2.4-2. The farm households can use 16 hours of their daily time budget[22] for labour on the fields, for leisure and for the households' domestic tasks like water and firewood collection. The amount of time used for household tasks determines how much time is left for leisure and for labour. In the initial situation, household tasks **restrict** the maximum available time for leisure and for labour to L_{maxR}. The production frontier P_R indicates how much output can be produced with different inputs of labour time within the given time restriction L_{maxR}. The decision of how much time is used for crop production and how much leisure time remains can be visualised by a set of indifference curves I_1, I_2 ... I_n, each of them symbolising a different level of utility of a given utility function. The farmers will choose the indifference curve I_R in order to find the optimal production O_R, which necessitates a labour input of L_{maxR} - L_R and leaves leisure of L_R. The point O_R is an optimum because any other point of the curve P would be on an indifference curve with a lower utility: a further growth in the labour input would not increase the production enough to compensate for the reduced leisure time. On the other hand an increased leisure time would entail lower production which reduces the utility. Thus the household chooses the optimal point O_R according to its own preference.

The above mentioned initial situation shows the individual choices of farming households under time restrictions. A different situation occurs after transport **avoiding** measures have reduced the time requirements for household tasks; the maximum labour time moves from L_{maxR} to L_{maxA}, the production frontier shifts from P_R to P_A and a new indifference curve I_A is chosen resulting in an output of O_A. The graph shows that the saved time will be partly used for leisure, but the remaining time is used to increase agricultural output. The inclination of the indifference curves determines how much of the 'saved time' is used for additional labour. Thus a reduction of the household's transport time will entail a production increase.

---

22 The remaining eight hours are spent with sleeping.

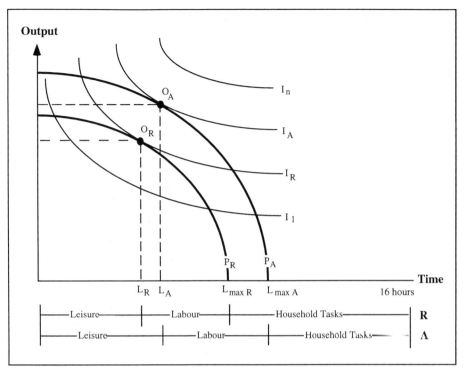

Fig. 2.4-2   Effects of reduced time requirements for household tasks

A study in Bangladesh by AHMED et al (1995, p.10) on the effects of a hypothetical introduction of IMT corroborates these theoretical assumptions: rural households would use 44 % of the saved time to increase their working time and only 18 % for social activities or leisure. 27 % would be used for additional domestic activities, which can not otherwise be carried out due to time constraints. The more the households were engaged in commercial activities, the more time they spent on work.

As women are subject to the most severe time constraints transport avoiding measures should concentrate on the reduction of female transport tasks. JENNINGS (1992 p.24.) states that women face substantial economic constraints, "that their investment in other economic activities will be only feasible if such activities enable them to meet basic needs such as food, clothing, shelter in a more efficient manner." Women will not necessarily use the saved time and energy to increase agricultural production: MALMBERG (1994, p. 38) states that women would enhance the welfare of their family by using more time for household tasks such as child care, cooking etc. Therefore transport avoiding measures can also be warranted by the increase in the family's welfare. How-

35

ever, more recreation time or the reduced drudgery in transport may contribute to a rise in productivity of field labour, because physical energy is less depleted or more quickly restored.

In addition, other non-transport effects such as improvement of the health and environmental situation by the installation of water supply and reforestation occur. BARWELL (1993) observed that the level of utilisation of health facilities increases significantly if it is less than one hour's travel time from the homestead. A review of studies on agricultural productivity concludes that "...there is growing evidence of positive effects of health and nutrition on labour productivity of at least poorer individuals in Developing Countries"[23].

2.4.3 Construction and Maintenance of Rural Transport Infrastructure

The majority of rural transport activities are undertaken on local paths and trails, away from the motorable network. Their bad conditions can hamper the mobility, the load carrying capacity and the trip duration (DIXON-FYLE/FRIELING 1990). The salient restrictions are the crossing of rivers, steep terrain and bad conditions of the paths and trails. Especially during rains the paths become very slippery making trips in steep terrain a dangerous undertaking. The improvement of paths by the construction of simple bridges, drainage systems and hand rails can remove many of these problems through simple and cheap measures; transport security thus increases, bigger loads can be carried and trip duration shortens. The paths can be widened to trails if pack animals or bicycles are available or widened to tracks if the terrain allows the use of animal drawn carts. This network should be a complement to the road system and should secure transport in and around the village. In addition, it should be easy and inexpensive to construct and to maintain.

Sub-Saharan Africa has lower road densities than other Developing and Industrialised Countries[24]. Therefore the UNITED NATIONS Transport and Communications Decade (UNCTADA II, p.4) states that "the need to provide reliable access to all economically productive areas and the demands from fast growing populations require selective upgrading and expansion of both the international and the national road networks." The World Bank estimates that the present rural road network needs to be increased up to tenfold if the full agricultural potential of the region is to be realised[25]. RIVERSON et al (1991) criticise the fact that the expensive construction of rural roads has hindered a

---

23 BEHRMANN (1990) quoted according to JIMENEZ (1994)
24 Sub-Saharan Africa: 5 km/100 km². Latin America: 12 km/100 km², Asia: 18 km/100 km², USA: 67 km/100 km², France 149 km/100 km², Germany 178 km/100 km², Japan 297 km/100 km² (UNCTADA II, p.4, Statistisches Jahrbuch für das Ausland 1993). If the road length is set in relation to GNP then Africa has ratios 10 times higher than France and 20 times higher than Germany.
25 MELLOR quoted in RIVERSON et al (1991) p. 1

further expansion of the rural network. Road planning has often focused on route selection and determination of design standards, rather than optimising the given resources. "This has fostered an overdesign and undue emphasis on investment."[26] Most of the benefits of rural roads can accrue without year-round vehicle access as long as service can be ensured during harvesting periods. The cheap design of new rural roads or tracks, spot improvements of existing roads and the installation of effective drainage structures are appropriate measures. "The prime considerations in defining rural road improvements should be reliability and durability rather than width and speed" (RIVERSON et al p. X). The MIRT-Project described in Chapter 3 will show that the construction of low cost roads and tracks can be an appropriate measure to introduce motorised access to remote areas.

Choice of the Construction Technology

Regarding the financial constraints of public budgets, shortage of foreign exchange, low rural income and high unemployment, labour based construction and maintenance of roads can be a rational solution. The World Bank recommends consciously considering labour based road works if the minimum salary is below 4 $ per day[27]. Above this limit a mix of capital intensive and labour extensive works should be chosen. Tab. 2.4-3 lists various labour based road projects and compares them with capital based investments. The first are much cheaper[28], need less foreign currency and create more wage income. HERTEL (1991) reports that labour based projects created 240 % more employment in Rwanda and 320 % more in Ghana. DE VEEN (1984) states that the labour based Rural Access Programme in Kenya needed half of the amount of foreign currency as comparable conventional projects. EDMONDS and DE VEEN (1993, p.7) affirm that in eight Developing Countries labour-based road construction was less expensive than capital based projects, whereas the quality of the results was in every way comparable.

The capital based construction operates with heavy machinery according to the technical standards in Industrialised Countries. Labour-based methodologies try to use as much labour as possible and as little machinery as necessary; this means not to maximise the labour input, but to optimise the employment, which is supported by machinery. Instead of using an expensive grader the labour based works use hand tools, which can be produced in the country. Therefore foreign exchange spendings, which typically range between 70 % and 90 % (HERTEL 1991) of total capital intensive project costs can be more than halved.

---

26 RIVERSON et al (1991), pp 11. The authors report that some rural roads were planned with a 7m wide carriageway for traffic of 20-30 vehicles per day.
27 Price level 1986.
28 Labour based construction in Kenya is 50-60 % and in Zimbabwe 42 % cheaper than capital intensive works.

Country	Organi-sation	Project	Share wages	Reduction compared to capital intensive approach		Source
				Financial Costs	Foreign currency	
Kenya	World Bank	7,800 km unclassified roads	60-71%*	40-50%	-	Riverson, Gaviria, Thriscutt 1991
Tanzania	ILO	Kilimanjaro	25 %	36 %	-	ILO, Dar Es Salaam
7 coun-tries	ILO/ IBRD		30-50%	15 %	40 %	Riverson, Gaviria, Thriscutt 1991
Rwanda	ILO	Earth and laterite roads		30 %	60 %	Hertel 1991
Ghana	World Bank	900 km feeder road rehabilitation		10 %	50 %	Hertel 1991
Zimbabwe	ILO	18 km rehabilitation	40 %	31 %		ILO (unpublished)

* Since 1980, in the initial phases high costs where caused by consultancy by expatriates

Tab. 2.4-3 Comparison of labour and capital based road construction

While some authors (HERTEL, RIVERSON et al 1991) regard the involvement of women in labour based road work as generally positive, because income can be generated for asset poor women, BRYCESON and HOWE (1993) are rather scep-tical: "Most women are already coping with extremely full work days and earn-ing cash in the low-paid, often arduous work conditions of road sites is not allur-ing." The female involvement in labour based road works might, in addition entail a reduction in agricultural production.

One of the main features is the involvement of the local private sector in labour based road works. Small contractor capacity can be promoted by training, creating appropriate contract procedures, assistance during the establishment of enterprises and securing constant cash flow during the project (EDMONDS/DE VEEN, 1993). For maintenance works the 'lengthman system' has proved to be efficient, where road agencies contract one individual who is directly responsi-ble for a road segment (COOK et al 1986). During the Kenya Rural Access Roads Program 7,800 km of rural roads were successfully maintained by 'lengthmen' recruited from the villages along the roads.

Some of the construction and maintenance works in Africa are done with unpaid volunteer labour (Self Help). The participation can be regarded as a local development tax. Chapter 5.5 shows that Self-Help labour is often inefficient, the participation is enforced and the social and gender distributions are unequal. It may be used to construct new infrastructures if the participants benefit directly from the improvements, but maintenance works using volunteer labour are not sustainable in the long run (COOK et al 1986).

During the 1960s the African road network was rapidly expanding with the assistance of international donors. Unfortunately, less care was taken with regard to maintenance, which caused a rapid deterioration of these infrastructures. In 1988 more than 70 % of the unpaved roads were in poor to fair condition (Tab 2.4-4). "Hence, while Africa is underequipped in relation to its potential it is overburdened by the little infrastructure that it possesses" (RIVERSON et al p.5). The consequence is an isolation of many rural areas especially during the rainy season. The World Bank estimates that in 1987 Somalia could not evacuate one third of its bumper crop due to bad transport conditions.

1988	Good	Fair	Poor
Paved Roads	52 %	25 %	23 %
Unpaved Roads	29 %	32 %	39 %
Source: MASON/THRISCUTT 1991, p15			

Tab. 2.4-4 Road conditions in Sub-Saharan Africa

One of the major consequences of this lack of maintenance are higher vehicle operating costs (VOC) on the resulting poor roads. In personal transportation the fares on a badly maintained road can be up to 50 % higher than on a good road (KROH 1987 p. 37). Every dollar which is saved on maintenance causes three dollars of higher user costs (SANDHU 1992, p.23). Furthermore, the costs for road rehabilitation could have been prevented by regular maintenance. Therefore "preventive maintenance ... generally has a higher economic rate of return than reconstruction, mainly because of the cost savings from not having to reconstruct deteriorated roads at a later date" (MASON/THRISCUTT 1991, p.22). As an answer to these problems UNECA and the World Bank have launched a "Road Maintenance Initiative" which is aimed at raising the conscience of policy makers and designing policy action programs.

A World Bank Study (MASON/THRISCUTT 1991) estimated the annual costs until the year 2,000 for the rehabilitation and maintenance of the whole Sub-Saharan African road network at $ 1.8 billion, an amount which is probably not affordable. Therefore the authors selected an 'economically justified' priority road network for every country and compiled a number of maintenance strategies (Tab 2.4-5): a continuation of the existing maintenance practices would leave all unpaved priority roads and 80-90 % of the paved priority network in a bad condition - a strategy, which is clearly not desirable. The authors therefore push for the rehabilitation and the maintenance of the whole priority network, which can be financed by reducing the costs for new construction of roads to 20 % or less of total road expenditure. They emphasise (p.23) that the non-priority network "would remain in fair or poor condition unless or until traffic or other factors warrant rehabilitation". Without external aid about one third of the African Countries will not be able to restore even their priority network to an adequate condition.

Strategy until year 2000	Priority Roads in bad condition		Annual Costs	
	Paved roads	Unpaved Roads	Mill $/a	Share GNP
Continuation of routine and minimal maintenance	78-91 %	100 %	228	0.2 %
Only roads now in good condition correctly maintained	47-50 %	72-81 %	409	0.3 %
Maintain good roads and restore fair condition roads to good condition	17-29 %	42-47 %	680	0.5 %
Restore the priority network of roads to good and fair condition	0 %	0 %	1,147	0.8 %
Source: Mason / Thriscutt 1991, pp 24				

Tab. 2.4-5 Maintenance strategies for the priority network in Sub-Saharan Africa

Using this perspective it will be difficult to fulfil the demand of the UNCTADA II for the new construction of rural low volume roads. Thus the isolation of many rural areas will probably continue or even increase. However, the creation of low cost infrastructure using labour based methods for construction and maintenance might allow the extension of the 'economically viable' road network.

HEGGIE (1994) regards institutional constraints as the root causes for bad road maintenance in Sub-Saharan Africa. Road administrations can be characterised as follows:
• They lack a clear organisational and management structure,
• qualified staff are missing,
• domestic revenue mobilisation is wholly inadequate,
• financial and management systems are not up to the task of controlling large sums of money,
• the channels to the road administration are fraught with difficulty and funds are frequently diverted.
A reform of African road administration seems to be unavoidable. The World Bank (HEGGIE 1994) proposes the "commercialising of African roads" by 'bringing roads into the market place, putting them on a fee for service basis and managing them like any other business enterprise'. The salient feature of the reform is the installation of independent road agencies on the various administrative levels. Four basic building blocks should shape the reform:
• Creating ownership by involving road users: installation of a board of directors with representatives of road transport industry, contractors, consultants, farmer's associations and concerned government departments.
• Stabilise the financial flows by mobilising revenues and linking revenues and expenditures e.g. by the installation of a road fund.
• Clarify the responsibilities among different government departments and road agencies.

- Improve the management by creating a more business-like environment: pay the staff adequately, install effective management structures, where managers can act commercially, introduce auditing procedures, create contracts between the government and the road agency.

HEGGIE proposes a general deconcentration of the road agencies at the national level and a greater aggregation at the local level. Experience (RIVERSON et al 1991, p. XI) has shown that three principals secured a successful planning and implementation of rural roads: (i) Programmes were effectively launched and implemented if road departments had relative autonomy and separate funding. (ii) The participation of agricultural officers and local communities at the planning stage led to better road selection and maintenance and (iii) simple and well established planning procedures encouraged participation and resource mobilisation at the local level. A small centralised agency responsible for regional planning, which is allowed to raise its own funds and receives technical advice and matching funds from the central agency seems to be most effective. These demands were partly implemented in Tanzania. Box 2-2 describes the main features of the reform of the Tanzanian road sector.

Box 2-2: The Reform of the Tanzanian Road Sector

In 1987-88 only 41 % of the total collected revenues from road users was devoted to road maintenance the remaining part being contributed to the general tax revenue. Nevertheless, the actual maintenance expenditure only covered 31 % of the necessary amount to keep the national road network in an acceptable condition. Maintenance received a lower priority than new construction. In 1990 only 15 % of the trunk roads and 10 % of the regional roads were in a good condition, while two thirds were impassable or not maintainable.

The World Bank organised seminars to which public and private sector stake holders were invited in order to raise consciousness about the maintenance backlog; the user groups bluntly said that they would be willing to pay more for roads if they were better maintained. Besides numerous activities in the transport sector, one of the salient results of the Integrated Roads Project, which was initiated by the World Bank, was the set up of a National Road Fund in 1991. Government funding for road maintenance increased by more than three times mainly due to an increase in fuel tax. 10 ¢/litre of fuel are earmarked for the fund, which together with other road charges is exclusively used for the maintenance of roads. 20 % of this fund is allocated to rural roads.

The creation of a semi autonomous Road Agency is envisaged. On top of that a Central and a number of Regional Road Boards are planned. The central board is to include the Chamber of Commerce, Organisation of Engineers, Automobile and Roads Associations.

Missing maintenance mainly stems from an insufficient provision of funds. Fuel prices are often subsidised or kept at a low level for political reasons and no or few revenues can be obtained. The collected revenues from vehicle licence fees are not necessarily used for the roads' sector. One of the salient points of reform is to allow each road agency to collect its own charges and pay them into a fund outside the finance minister's control. SMITH (1991) lists the different possible revenues of national road agencies: (i) general fuel tax, (ii) taxes on vehicles, spare parts and tyres, (iii) distance tax levied on passenger fares and freight charges, (iv) road tolls, (v) non variable vehicle charges, e.g. vehicle registration fees and licences and (vi) non-user taxes, e.g. a sales tax on agricultural produce. Decentralised rural road agencies are only able to levy road tolls (v) and non-user taxes (vi). The remaining cash requirements have to be transferred from the national road fund. The question arises whether under the financial constraints, an adequate funding of rural roads stemming from the national road fund can be possible. Additional local revenue collection to finance the road expenditures seems to be necessary. In chapter 5.5 an example is given of how the low cost construction of a rural road can be entirely financed with a local road toll.

2.4.4 Provision of Motorised Transport Services

Motorised transport services in rural areas are a necessary complement to the improved rural road network. They enable farmers to carry their products to the markets, to purchase farm inputs, to consume centralised services or to travel for leisure purposes.

In general it can be stated that the quality of the transport services decreases with worsening road conditions with overloaded buses, uncomfortable "seats" on the back of pick ups or trucks, low reliability and service frequency, high accident rates, slow average speed and excessive prices being the salient features of rural passenger transport services. According to World Bank research (CARAPETIS et al. 1984, p.14), state owned companies are performing badly: they have no incentives to change the quality of services, are often working inefficiently, are producing financial deficits, have a low capital endowment, are frequently subsidised, have a bad management system, and poor morale due to low salaries. The Bank states that private companies are working efficiently, are more flexible and show higher motivation due to better payment of the employees. Regulations of the transport market like market entry restrictions, control of routes and the setting of rates, often below the profit margin, hamper the proliferation of private companies. Next to deregulation the provision of credits could promote the operation of private companies, which could also operate with IMT[29].

---

29 BARWELL and DAWSON (1993, p. 63) report on a milk company in Bangladesh using rickshaws to collect milk from its farmers and cooperatives in India providing bullock carts for

A comparative study by HINE and RIZET (1991) between three francophone African countries and Pakistan demonstrates that Vehicle Operating Costs (VOC) are not only influenced by the quality of the infrastructure, but also by the efficiency of the transport services: the costs in Africa are four times higher than in Pakistan, where the trucks run twice the number of kilometres, register less empty trips, have lower maintenance costs due to low speeds and the responsibility involvement of the driver. While in Pakistan a competitive environment favours the purchase of cheaper appropriate vehicles, in Africa sophisticated vehicles are bought, which run at low utilisation levels.

This example shows that a privatisation of transport services does not necessarily improve the transport quality if a competitive environment is missing. In Sub-Saharan Africa private companies operate mostly on profitable routes, because the low transport volumes and the bad road conditions in rural areas lower their profits. If they are servicing the countryside they more often than not have a regional monopoly which enables them to charge excessive tariffs, even ignoring state regulations. In these cases the state has an important role in controlling how regulations are met and offering transport services in areas where no private company is present.

2.5   Conclusions

In regard to economic theory transport investments have long been regarded as a direct stimulus to development. This optimism faded away in the 1960s and gave way to a judgement which emphasises the permissive character of transport infrastructure: how the economic opportunities created by the transport investments are used, depends very much on the local conditions. Even though recent macroeconomic country studies emphasise the strong impacts on production, the empirical evidence of regional case studies gives a very heterogeneous picture, where various positive and negative effects of transport investments occur. Road projects often generate a production increase, but they favour these social groups, which are already better off than others. Initial transport provision generates stronger effects than the upgrading of existing infrastructure and rural road projects may entail severe ecological damage. Therefore, the prediction of future effects of transport investments involves strong uncertainties. Thus, a cheap and extensive construction strategy of "trial and error" is recommended in order to reduce the unreliabilities of forecasting.

After the independence of Sub-Saharan Africa massive investments in transport infrastructures were undertaken which were not adequately maintained. In

---

the transport of agricultural produce. In San Salvador a 5-ton truck for the distribution of soft drinks by Pepsi-Cola was replaced by a bicycle with a trailer. The distribution was so efficient, that the company decided to test specially built tricycles. (HEIERLI 1993, p. 121)

the 1990s the discussion arose as to how the rehabilitation of the deteriorated road network could be financed. Preconditions are new institutional and financial arrangements, which entail a decentralisation of the road administrations, the integration of the road users into a board of directors and financial independence from recurrent government budgets. The right to collect their own revenues can also be important for the financial performance of rural road administrations. Low cost and labour based technologies should be used for construction and maintenance purposes.

The bias towards the 'road & car' approach[30] neglects the needs and abilities of rural households. Recent research demonstrates that households carry a considerable transport burden which requires substantial quantities of time and effort. The majority of trips are undertaken in and around the village by walking on local footpaths and trails. Women carry the biggest transport burden for the household's domestic purposes. Rural households possess practically no motor-vehicles and undertake very few motorised trips. Transport constraints can significantly hamper the growth of agricultural production. Therefore a rural development strategy should not only take care of the road infrastructure but also improve paths, trails and tracks, promote Intermediate Means of Transport, implement transport services and conduct measures which avoid transport.

The following chapters will show that this strategy can improve the economic performance of rural areas. The next two chapters will give an example of the effects of an integrated rural transport project in Tanzania, which took account of the transport needs of rural households.

---

30 Focus of donors and national decision makers on the provision of infrastructures for motorised vehicles.

3   Framework of the Field Study

The Makete Integrated Rural Transport Project (MIRTP) was carried out by the International Labour Office in Makete District in the south-west of Tanzania. Its principal aim was to reduce the transport burden of rural households. This was to be achieved by improving footpaths, tracks and roads with labour-based technologies, by making donkeys available for the local population and by reducing trip lengths by repairing local grinding mills. Before the project started a survey concerning the transport patterns of rural households was conducted in 1986 and 1987. In 1994 a second survey was carried out (by the author) using a methodology comparable to the previous research. This chapter will show the outcomes of the field studies which were designed in order to estimate some of the effects of the different transport interventions.

During the period under consideration, from 1986 to 1994 Tanzania has experienced severe political and macroeconomic changes, which probably have had considerable impacts on the development of the Makete District. Therefore a brief review of Tanzanian history since independence will first be given.

3.1   Tanzania: General Framework

After independence in 1961 Tanzania registered a moderate per capita growth of the economy. Six years later President Nyerere declared a Pan African Socialism (Ujamaa): private enterprises were nationalised, prices, wages, interest and exchange rates controlled, marketing and trade were organised by parastatal enterprises and all economic activities were planned in Five-Year-Plans[1]. The government invested in human capital formation and improvement of the health system and succeeded in meeting the subsistence tasks[2], which brought strong sympathy from western donors. In the 1970s economic performance weakened and by the beginning of the 1980s the economic crisis had reached unprecedented proportions: the per capita GDP and the real income had declined since 1977, inflation reached annual rates of 30 %, the public finance deficit rose to 20 % of the GDP, the external balance of payments deficit proliferated rapidly (BAGACHWA/MALIYAMKONO 1990, pp 1), and the population could not be nourished by the national agricultural crop production. BRYCESON (1990, p 229) states: "Had it not been for the large increase in per capita food imports, some parts of the population, notably those in urban areas would have experienced life threatening shortages of food". The government claimed mainly

---

1 These plans were elaborated by western consultants, not by the national planning commission.
2 The country's literacy rate rose from 10 % to 60 % between 1961 and 1977, while the life expectancy increased from 43 to 52 years.

external reasons for the crisis: the soaring terms of trade, the oil price shocks[3], the military spending for the war against Idi Amin's Uganda, the break up of the East African Community and severe droughts. But many internal factors contributed substantially to the economic crisis:

- Neglect of the agricultural sector, i.e. low producer prices, little investment in infrastructure, poor marketing arrangements and bad input distribution.
- The Villagisation Programme, which forced most farmers to move to communal centres causing an immense disruption of agricultural production.
- Emphasis on large scale and import intensive industries.
- Excessive growth of public administration and bad management of public enterprises, thus producing severe deficits in government budgets.
- Strong government interventions regulating all economic activities as mentioned above.

The rural households reacted by retreating from the official economy, production was decreased to almost subsistence level and the small surplus was often marketed through illegal channels; the second economy proliferated. The steady economic decline forced the government to announce a Structural Adjustment Programme (SAP 1983-1985), in order to receive new international credits. Because the SAP was not actually a revision of the socialist economic policy, an agreement with the IMF could not be achieved and the international donors retreated. The volume of external aid declined from 1980 to 1985 by 30 %, while foreign debt continued to grow. The lack of foreign currency was becoming the main bottleneck in the Tanzanian economy, as essential raw materials and spare parts could not be imported any more. Finally the retreat of president Nyerere in November 1985 gave way to an agreement with the IMF, which financed the Economic Recovery Programme (ERP I 1986 to 1989) followed by the Economic and Social Action Programme (EASP 1989-1992). The programmes contained the usual IMF market reforms: devaluation of the Tanzanian Shilling, deregulation of the internal market and external trade, privatisation of parastatal companies, reduction of government budget deficits, rise of real interest rates and the abatement of inflation. Some measures like the currency devaluation were introduced in a "shock manner", others were implemented gradually. The economic transformation process was still underway in 1994.

The economic reforms first showed macroeconomic effects, when the real growth rates of the GDP reached positive values in 1984 and overtook the population growth in 1986, which is estimated at 3,2 % p.a.[4]. The agricultural sector

---

3 "In 1978-1982, the loss of income purely on account of terms of trade movements amounted to 12 % of GDP. Furthermore, the oil import bill, as a proportion of total export earnings, rose sharply from 26 % in 1978 to 56 % in 1982, with quantities remaining fairly constant" (BAGACHWA/MALIYAMKONO 1990, p.3)
4 1978-1988: new surveys estimate the population growth at 3.8 % (HOFMEIER, 1993, p 178).

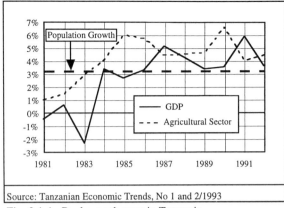

Source: Tanzanian Economic Trends, No 1 and 2/1993

Fig. 3.1-1   Real growth rates in Tanzania

was growing stronger than the rest of the economy. Similarly, real per capita incomes increased and real interest rates were adjusted to almost positive levels. The inflation rate, which reached 36 % in 1984, stayed at an unsatisfactory high level of 23 % in 1994. The export earnings, which stem mainly from the sale of agricultural produce, did not rise partly due to the stagnation of production and partly due to the deterioration of the terms of trade. Only one third of imports were covered by exports. The resulting balance of payment deficits could only be compensated for by the growing transfers from national and international donors. In 1990 the foreign debt reached 260 % of the GNP. Economic growth in Tanzania was only partly due to internal reforms; a big share was externally financed.

Special emphasis in the economic recovery programmes, was laid on the promotion of the agricultural sector, in which 82 % of the active population is engaged. Before the reform the Primary Co-operative Societies[5] had a legal monopoly on crop purchasing at the farm level. Unions assembled the commodities from the primary societies and then processed and handed them over to the state owned marketing boards. "This system was grossly inefficient and resulted in lower producer prices, untimely delivery of inputs, poor quality of exports due to processing problems and shipping delays" (BAGACHWA 1992 p.35). Although the government set up the agricultural producer prices, they only rose in nominal terms and not in real terms, due to inflation and the growing margins of the national marketing boards. Therefore the government abrogated the marketing monopolies of its parastatals. In 1989 private traders were allowed to buy grain from primary societies and in 1991 farmers were given the freedom to sell to any buyer[6]. By 1992 producer prices were almost completely liberalised; only the prices for maize, wheat and paddy were still under government control. Private traders could also participate in the distribution of agricultural inputs.

---

5 Parastatal marketing boards
6 The 1986/87 survey in Makete (Barwell/Malmberg 1989) shows that many farmers sold their produce to private traders, which were operating illegally.

47

According to AMANI (1992, p 51) the market reform entailed mainly positive effects, causing both an increase in food production and urban supply. BAGACHWA gives a more detailed picture: the production of food crops rose from 1986 to 1988 for maize and wheat (34 %), beans and cassava (16 %) but the growth slowed down until 1992 in such a way that the overall increase could not keep up with the population growth. The production of traditional food crops like cassava stagnated and that of sorghum and millet declined. Rising imports of food crops were necessary to secure the food supply of the population. The production of most export crops with the exception of sisal increased from 1985 onwards, often exceeding 1981 levels before 1992. However, the soaring terms of trade[7] did not entail a growth in the export earnings. The prices for inputs, which were rising sharply in the last years due to cutbacks in government subsidies, had negative repercussions on the agricultural production.

The cutback in government expenditures[8] had far reaching consequences for the provision of social services. During the socialist period external observers admired the high standard and the free access to public services like schooling and health services. During the crisis in the 1980s it became clear, that this standard could not be maintained without giving up the principle of free charge services. Today schooling fees are a significant hurdle for school enrolment.

A critical study on behalf of SIDA of the social, economic and cultural changes resulting from the structural adjustment process in Tanzania, in which 600 people in 12 villages were interviewed, concludes with the remark: „We think that there are good grounds for reporting, that import and domestic trade liberalisation has been good for rural people, including those locally regarded as relatively poor and perhaps especially poor women as well as the better off and those living in towns." (BOOTH et al 1993, p. 118). According to the villagers the availability of goods more than compensated for their higher prices. Agricultural production was improved by the better transport situation, but higher prices for agricultural inputs gave rise to new restrictions on traditional food and export crop production. However, new production activities like brewing local alcohol, quarrying, collecting sand and supplying local urban markets with food crops became possible. On the other hand the social services built up since independence seem to be in jeopardy due to insufficient public funds.

During the 1980s and 1990s the transport situation has deteriorated rapidly in Tanzania; in 1990 only 15 % of the trunk roads and 10 % of the regional roads were in a good condition, while two thirds were impassable or not maintainable.

---

7 Especially the price of coffee, which in 1981 comprised 33 % of the total Tanzanian export earnings, fell rapidly in the beginning of the 1990s. Sisal prices showed a steady decline since 1981.
8 Not all of the cutbacks had negative social consequences. For example 16,000 "ghost workers" were removed from the public payrolls.

This resulted in high road vehicle operating costs, thus entailing low producer prices, delayed evacuation and damage to crops. The national railways and ports could not meet the transport demand, causing significant stockpiles of crops and diverting bulk transport to roads. The potential transit traffic from Zambia, Zaïre, Rwanda and Burundi could not be handled and the transport parastatals made losses or generated low returns. The World Bank estimates (1990, pp 3) the total losses produced by the inefficient transport sector at annually more than $ 300 million.

In 1990 the World Bank started the Integrated Roads Project (IRP I) with a budget of $ 871 million for the coming five years, 91 % of which was financed by foreign capital. The project planned the rehabilitation and upgrading of the trunk and regional road network, the institutional strengthening of road management capacity, the enhancement of the road maintenance capacity and management assistance to public transport services (WORLD BANK 1990). Up to 1994, the proportion of trunk and regional roads in good condition has at least doubled. In 1992 and 1993 the traffic volumes on the rehabilitated road sections doubled or tripled (WORLD BANK 1994, pp 2). The Kilimanjaro Region experienced an increase of average daily road traffic by a factor of five, of passenger traffic by a factor of 20 and a reduction in vehicle operating costs by about 31 % in real terms. An impact survey stated that the access to markets, agricultural inputs and to public services like health facilities and schools has improved substantially.

The government created a road fund[9], in order to finance maintenance and upgrading activities, using the revenues from a road toll which was introduced in 1991. The percentage of transport sector expenditure on development and recurrent budget increased from 13 % to 39 %. Until 1995 road maintenance will be financed completely by the road fund. The institutional settings were changed in favour of better management and the funds are distributed to the institutions concerned: national roads are under the supervision of the Ministry of Works, regional roads are managed by the Regional Engineer and district roads are maintained by the District Councils. In 1992/93 the flow of budgeted funds to the Regional Engineer were considerably delayed and many regional roads were not maintained adequately. On the district level the maintenance of roads is often conducted by the local population with self-help labour due to the shortage of funds. From 1996 to 2001 the World Bank plans a Second Integrated Roads Project (ERP II) with $ 650 million including 75 % foreign participation. Less than 1 % of the financial means will be used for a Village Travel and Transport Programme, which would promote inter alia low cost means of transport and path construction.

---

9 Compare Box 2-1.

The economic liberalisation brought very strong impacts for the transport sector: during the socialist period, practically no private ownership of motorised vehicles was allowed and the importation of bicycles was highly taxed. After the liberalisation the ownership of motor vehicles was permitted and the taxation for imported bicycles eliminated. As a result, the yearly imports of motor vehicles nearly tripled between 1984 and 1990, while the total value of vehicles and parts[10] increased by 470 %. Compared to the importation of motor vehicles, the number of bicycles showed an explosive development between 1988 and 1989, with the number of imported bicycles[11] rising from 100 to 73,000. The imports for transport equipment comprised 24 % of the total Tanzanian imports in 1992. These imports were only possible with the support of the international donors, who covered the external debt by making fresh money available.

3.2   Description of the Makete District

3.2.1   Geographic and Economic Basis

The Makete district is located in the south west of Tanzania close to the lake Nyassa, 900 km away from the biggest town Dar-Es-Salaam and 400 km from the regional centre Iringa. The district stretches over a mountainous plateau with an altitude of 1,500 to 2,400 m containing mountains, hills, ridges, valleys and steep escarpments. Makete has a moderate tropical climate with annual rainfalls of 1,300 to 2,000 mm mainly in the rainy season from November to May. In the central and southern part of the Makete district, live the Wakinga people, while in the north dwell the Wawanji, who speak a different language. In 1988 the official census reported that the number of inhabitants in the Makete district was 100,000. Assuming an

1988	Makete District	Iringa Region	Tanzania
Population	102,617	1,193,074	23,174,000
Population density	18 P/km^2	21 P/km^2	27,5 P/km^2
Female/male ratio	1.26	1.18	1.04
Population growth	1.3 %	2.7 %	2.8- 3.3 %
Households within 400 m from water supply	26 %	42 %	
Households with electric supply	0.13 %	2.38 %	
Literacy rate (>5 years)	68.4 %	57.5 %	85 % (>15)

Tab. 3.2-1 Characterisation of Makete District

---

10 The biggest growth is registered in imported chassis with engines and bodies, which are assembled in Tanzania.
11 The government reduced the import tax for bicycles and the Netherlands conducted a programme to import bicycles from India.

annual growth rate of 1.3 %, the population can be estimated at 111,000 inhabitants[12]. The population growth is much lower than the regional and national growth rates as well as the ratio of female to male inhabitants. These are two indicators of the high outward migration from the area. Local experts estimate that 60 % of the working age population and 80 % of the active males leave Makete to find income outside the district. The people from Makete are generally well known as hard labourers and skilful in the art of pit-sawing. Some businessmen are very successful outside the district.

The population density figure for 1994 is reported at 18 persons/km^2, which is less than the regional and national average. The population lives in villages with an average of 1,100 inhabitants, often in scattered settlements. Makete, the administrative centre of the district, has more of a village than a town of the character. In the 1970s the Tanzanian government undertook a large re-settlement scheme, in order to concentrate the scattered population in more densely populated villages[13], where the endowment of infrastructure and services would be better. In Makete 85 of the 96 villages were required to resettle. Despite the Villagisation many of the villages are still very scattered today. This makes the provision with piped drinking water and electricity costly and could be one reason besides poverty, for the low endowment-ratio in Makete.

The macroeconomic changes already mentioned in Chapter 3.1 also had their impacts in Makete: general economic growth, (temporary) increasing producer prices, changes in the marketing system, private ownership of cars and cutback in public expenditure, brought with them a lot of changes. On top of this, a steady development took place due to the opening up of the district, and the increasing activities of international donors.

A MIRTP document of July 1985 states: "There is nowhere locally to obtain equipment, spare parts and administrative material. Private sector facilities are minimal. There are few shops or other services and only the most basic commodities can be bought ..." Today, Makete village where the district headquarters are located gives the picture of a slowly but steadily developing area. A regular market takes place twice a week. A number of shops have been established, a wider range of commodities is available, a telephone link was established, the postal services have been improved, a bank opened a branch, and the infrastructure for the district authorities has been expanded.

---

12 Other reports estimate the total population in 1993 at 117,000 assuming a growth rate of 2.7 %.
13 In many cases the Villagisation Programme was not planned carefully; more often than not farmers did not receive proper compensation for their lost plots and were forced to move. Consequently some of them returned later to their homes. In addition the resettled farmers often had to walk much further to reach their fields.

Changes at the household level can be assessed by comparing a survey conducted in 1986 and 1987 by BARWELL and MALMBERG with a similar survey[14] from 1994. The latter survey was undertaken in two study areas[15]: the study area **Bulongwa** is located in a peripheral part of Makete; situated close to the escarpment, which forms the western border of the district and which can only be crossed on foot. Here the terrain is very steep and the agricultural activities are restricted. The second study area, **Matamba,** is located in the north western part of the district. It is the region with the best external access, because 24 km of road leads down the northern escarpment, where a tarmac road leads to the capital, Dar Es Salaam and Mbeya, a nearby and major regional centre. The northern area is very active in agricultural production, because of its favourable agroecological conditions and the traditional market orientation.

		Bulongwa	Matamba	Total * Survey area
Monthly Expenditure (May, June)	1994	$ 37	$ 20	$ 28
[$/Household]	1986/87	$ 20	$ 11	$ 14
Households possessing	1994	44 %	28 %	38 %
Radio	1986/87	34 %	26 %	29 %
Households possessing	1994	36 %	27 %	33 %
Tin Roof	1986/87	29 %	22 %	24 %
* Including Ihela, which does not belong to Matamba or Bulongwa Region				

Tab. 3.2-2 Indicators for living standard

The average household in Makete has 4.9 members of which 2.3 are children and 0.7 persons older than 45 years. 46 % of the inhabitants have primary and 2 % secondary education. In Matamba the situation is better than in Bulongwa. Official statistics, as listed in Tab. 3.2-1, give a more optimistic picture about the educational situation; Makete's literacy rate is higher than the average of the whole Iringa Region. Two indicators show a decreasing tendency for out-migration; while in 1986/87 19 % of the households were headed by women, the percentage decreased in 1994 to 13 %. In the same period the ratio of female to male adults changed from 1.35 to 1.13.

The household income was estimated by assessing the household cash expenditure[16], which amounts in May and June 1994 to 28 $/month. The monthly expenditure rises by $ 1 if barter trade is included[17]. Since 1986/87 the

---

14 A description of the conduct of both surveys is given in Chapter 3.4
15 The location of the study areas is given in the map in Fig. 3.3-1.
16 This methodology was chosen, because a direct question about income might give false results. Still the income might be underestimated, because expenditures like agricultural inputs and savings are not included.
17 Some authors describe the economy of Makete as predominantly relying on barter trade. In the survey villages only 3 % of the monthly expenditure was bartered.

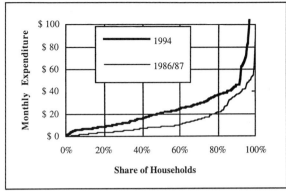

Fig. 3.2-1 Income distribution in the survey villages

average household expenditure[18] doubled. This is an indication of the rapid changes in Makete. The household endowment is another indicator that the standard of living has generally risen. The possession of radios and tin roofs was in particular more common in 1994. Household expenditure, income and endowment show significant regional disparities. In general, households in the Matamba Region are worse endowed and have a smaller expenditure[19]. There is a gap between expenditure and marketing revenues, which seems to indicate that many households have other sources of cash income, e.g. cash remitted by relatives[20].

Fig. 3.2-1 shows the distribution of the monthly expenditures in Makete during the two surveys. The changes were favourable for all income groups of the society; no household was worse off in 1994 compared with 1986/87. While the mean value increased from $ 14 to $ 28, the median rose from $ 9 to $ 21. The analysis of the personal expenditure distribution shows that the inequalities were reduced; the Gini-Coefficient decreased from 0.51 in 1986/87 to 0.47 in 1994. This seems to indicate that the strong developments taking place in the survey area are not based on growing inequalities; quite the reverse happened.

If households are asked about main source of cash income, most of the households (77 %) indicate sale of agricultural produce, 8 % are craftsmen, 7 % receive cash from relatives and 4 % are in regular employment. Other sources of income are sale of livestock, trading and brewing beer. The situation did not change significantly during the observed period, with the exception of an increase in artisan and timber activities. In Bulongwa more households receive their main income from agricultural activities than in Matamba, where more

---

18 In general all values given in Tanzania Shilling are converted into US$ with the May 1994 exchange-rate. The 1994 value of the 1986 Shilling is calculated by multiplication with the national consumer price index. A rural price index was not available and the national index including price changes for urban households was used. Because urban inflation is assumed to be higher than rural price variations, the above mentioned changes in the expenditure are most probably an underestimation.

19 This seems to completely contradict the observations of marketing activities and the income derived from them. On top of this more households in Matamba receive cash remitted by relatives.

20 Because only the main source of cash income was asked, no indication about the magnitude of the other sources can be made.

cash is received from relatives. An exception is the village Ihela in the centre of the Makete District, which is not listed separately in the tables. The village has always been a source of migrant labour. Therefore only 38 % of the households receive their main income from farming, 29 % from artisan or timber work and 28 % receive cash remitted by relatives or from salaries.

If households were asked about their main occupation the picture is comparable: 87 % of the heads of household state that their main occupation is farming, 6 % are craftsmen and 5 % employees with regular salaries. Since 1986/87 the number of craftsmen increased, while the share of farmers decreased.

3.2.2 Agriculture

The economy of Makete basically relies on agriculture. The agroecological conditions are in general favourable for the rainfed cultivation of crops. Problems occur at the slopes of steep hills where erosion can often be noticed. The agricultural potential is seen in two contradictory ways: while some experts state that problems "cannot be attributed to the low inherent capability of the natural resources or the unavoidable pressure of population" (Howe 1987, p.13) others see limitations because of population pressure and thin soil layers (ibid. p.27). The Regional Agricultural Development Plan (1986) states that nowhere in Makete is the population pressure very high, but 27 % of the population live in wards with high pressure and 60 % with medium pressure. Especially in the vicinity of the villages the pressure on arable land forces the farmers to shorten fallow periods, which are necessary for the natural regeneration of the soils[21]. Because of the relatively low pressure on land there is no "landless class" in Makete. Since livestock is not very important, there is no competition between pastoralism and farming.

Smallholder farms dominate the farming-system and the farm sizes within a village do not differ significantly. The average agricultural area per household is 5.2 acres and consists of 6.9 plots. Between the two surveys 1986/87 and 1994 the agricultural production was extensified: the average land under cultivation nearly doubled, while the use of fertiliser decreased. A reason might be the strong rise in fertiliser prices after the state gave up its subsidies. Only 4 % of the farmers in Bulongwa purchase fertiliser compared to 80 % in Matamba, where the relative small size of the plots is compensated for by the use of fertiliser. Another reason might the better road access to Matamba and the possession of IMT.

The average household harvests 2 t of crops per year, which is 38 % more than in 1986/87. This shift is due to the change from light to heavy crops and to

---

21 This situation will change in future with the rising population density, but the use of agricultural inputs could increase the productivity and reduce the pressure on land.

		Bulongwa	Matamba	Total Survey area[*]
Land under cultivation/household	1994	6.6	3.9	5.2
[acres]	1986/87	2.9	2.7	2.7
Households purchasing fertiliser	1994	4 %	80 %	50 %
[%]	1986/87	16 %	85 %	56 %
Fertiliser/household purchasing fertiliser	1994	18	135	125
[kg]	1986/87	no data	155	-
Harvesting of crops	1994	1.9	2.3	2.0
[t]	1986/87	1.1	1.6	1.45
Marketing of crops	1994	0.42	1.24	0.77
[t]	1986/87	0.16	0.47	0.31
Marketing of ulanzi	1994	50	450	250
[l]	1986/87	no data	195	-
Revenues from marketing	1994	48	121	79
[$]	1986/87 [**]	28	87	55

[*] Including Ihela, which does not belong to Matamba or Bulongwa Region
[**] Estimate

Tab. 3.2-3 Basic agricultural data per household

a general increase in agricultural production. The crop production must be distinguished between Bulongwa Region, where subsistence is dominating and 1.9 t are harvested annually and Matamba, where the harvest reaches 2.3 t and bigger quantities are marketed. In Bulongwa the cool climate allows the production of cereals such as wheat and maize, which comprise two thirds of the weight harvested and Irish potatoes and vegetables (each 10 %). In Matamba wheat accounts for only 1 % of the harvest, while maize and potatoes each claim 40 % of the production. Other products are sweet potatoes, beans, peas and fruits. Due to the diversity of crops grown, harvesting and marketing occurs throughout the whole year.

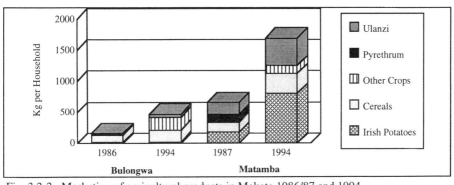

Fig. 3.2-2 Marketing of agricultural products in Makete 1986/87 and 1994

Agricultural products grown in the moderate climate of Makete are traded with the tropical lowlands. During the observed period the marketing increased substantially; while in 1986/87 only 21% of the crops harvested were marketed, this amount rose to 39 % in 1994. The quantity marketed in Bulongwa is much lower than in Matamba. DIERKS (1995) found out that the increased marketing did not cause a reduced subsistence food production measured in calories per capita. In 1994 the average household in Bulongwa received revenues of $ 48 and in Matamba $ 121 by the marketing of agricultural products. The increase in marketing and the changing prices caused a rise in revenues in Bulongwa of $ 20 and in Matamba of $ 34 per household[22]. Even thought the absolute growth is in Matamba much higher, the percentage increase was stronger in Bulongwa. The marketing increase did not change the distribution of the revenues among the Makete households as represented in Fig. 3.2-3.

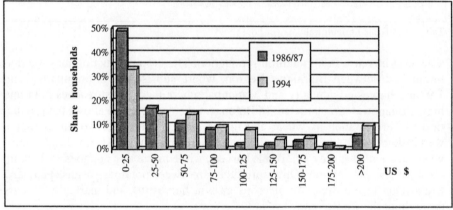

Fig. 3.2-3   Revenues from marketing of agricultural products in the Makete District

In 1987 the Matamba Region produced 85 % of the pyrethrum[23] exported from the Iringa Region. Due to the falling prices of pyrethrum the production declined by 50 % between 1976 and 1986 and stopped completely in 1994, after the state owned pyrethrum boards did not pay for the collected harvest[24]. Pyrethrum was replaced in Matamba by cereals and potatoes, whereas in Bulongwa other crops like vegetables became more important. Many farmers sell other agricultural products such as the alcoholic bamboo juice ulanzi, which is marketed in considerable quantities in the Matamba Region, where annually 450 l per household

---

22 The revenues for 1986/87 had to be estimated, because the data were incomplete.
23 Pyrethrum is harvested from flowers and used for the production of biological insecticides.
24 The director of the Matamba Pyrethrum Board left the country with a couple of million Tanzanian Shillings after collecting the harvest from the farmers and not paying them.

are sold to traders, at local markets or to other members of the village[25]. Quite often the ulanzi is transported with four-wheel drive-vehicles to the big towns of Mbeya and Iringa.

	Bulongwa 1986-1994		Matamba 1987-1994	
	Prices (Njombe) [Tsh]	Marketing [t]	Prices (Mbeya) [Tsh]	Marketing [t]
Beans	+81 %	+256 %	+154 %	+294 %
Irish Potatoes	-30 %	+136 %	-15 %	+381 %
Wheat	-22 %	+94 %	-20 %	+186 %
Maize	+135 %	+50 %	+55 %	+122 %
Source: Dierks (1995) p. 30				

Tab. 3.2-4 Change in real agricultural producer prices in Makete

The increase in marketing was partly due to the changing producer prices, which was a result of the liberalisation of the agricultural markets. While the real prices for beans and maize were submitted to large increases, the producer prices for wheat and Irish potatoes decreased moderately. The decrease might have been smaller if a rural consumer price index could have been used[26]. Even though the prices of some products were decreasing the market production increased. This augmentation cannot only be explained by price incentives. Other factors must have influenced the agricultural production: the permission of private traders and private ownership of vehicles, the changes in the transport system and the general opening of the district.

	Bulongwa	Matamba	Total Survey
1994	22 %	69 %	57 %
1986/87	56 %	89 %	71 %

Tab. 3.2-5 Share of crops marketed in the village

---

25 A considerable amount (45 %) of the ulanzi harvested is consumed by the households themselves. Nearly 300 l are annually drunken by adult household members from their own harvest, not including the ulanzi bought in the local shops. Excessive consumption of alcohol seems to be a serious problem in Makete.

26 The 1986/87 producer prices were adjusted with the national price index. Distortions might occur, because the index is dominated by the patterns of urban consumption. An index of rural consumer prices does not exist in Tanzania. The devaluation of the Tanzanian Shilling was one of the major reasons for the consumer price increase, because imported goods became more expensive. Assuming that the urban consumption has a higher share of imported goods, the devaluation of the Tanzanian Shilling has increased the price of the urban basket of commodities considerably more than the rural consumer prices. Therefore the (moderate) reduction of producer prices for Irish potatoes and wheat might not have occurred if a rural consumer price index could have been used to calculate the price changes.

As previously mentioned, the marketing monopoly of the parastatal marketing boards was broken and private traders were permitted. This had severe impacts on the marketing of crops in Makete, which changed from primarily marketing in the village to external marketing. Farmers from the Bulongwa Region, where motorised access to the villages is difficult, market $^4/_5$ of their crops outside the village while in Matamba, which has good external access, only $^1/_3$ of the products are sold externally. The latter region has to be analysed more carefully, because the village Mpangala dominates the results with the marketing of heavy crops. Here 70 % of the crops (mainly potatoes) are sold on the fields or on the street to private traders, because the heavy crops cannot be transported to the lowland markets. In the remaining two villages the weight of the products marketed (maize, sorghum) is lower and some farmers prefer to walk to the lowland markets where the prices are higher than in the village. In these villages 75 % of the crops are sold externally.

One of the main restrictions for agricultural production is not only marketing, but also the transport of the products from the fields. While the amount of products harvested varies between 1.6 t and 4 t per household, the amount transported from the field only alternates between 1.4 t and 2.6 t. The remaining amounts are either sold directly on the field or consumed right away. Although the Matamba Region registers bigger harvests, the amount transported home is not significantly higher than in Bulongwa. In Matamba a good road passes by the fields of two villages and allows the marketing of products directly from the fields[27]. Even though the amount harvested is much higher in Matamba, less tkm are transported from the field to the farm than in Bulongwa. In general the transport burden caused by the evacuation of products from the fields is higher than from marketing activities. The former imposes restrictions on the agricultural production, which cannot be solved by motorised transport, because the fields are often not accessible by roads.

Tons per household	Bulongwa	Matamba	Survey Villages
Products Harvested	2.08	3.17	2.57
Transported home	2.03	2.22	2.10
Not transported home	0.05	0.95	0.47
Tkm (Field-Home)	8.2	6.7	7.5
Tkm (Marketing)	3.5	6.8	4.7

Tab. 3.2-6 Transport of Crops

3.2.3   Transport Activities

Transport in Makete is restricted by the steep terrain and poor road conditions. The dominant mode is walking. The average household uses 45 hours per week for transport activities which comprise a transport volume of 83 tkm per annum.

---

27 These products are mainly potatoes which are transported from the fields directly to the street. A considerable amount of ulanzi is harvested from the bamboo bushes in or beside the village and transported directly to the street, where it is collected.

The main features of the rural transport system as described in Chapter 2 remain untouched. Half of the time is used for the collection of water and firewood and 18 % for trips to the fields. 21 % of the transport time is devoted to trips to external markets of which less than 2 % is used to market one's own produce. The marketing of agricultural produce amounts to less than 5 % of the total tkm of an average household, while the collection of firewood and water comprises 80 %. A detailed listing of the transport patterns is given in Tab. 3.2-6, Fig. 3.2-4 and in the appendix.

	Trips/Annum	Trip Distance [km]	Hours/Annum	Tons /Annum	Tkm/Annum
Water	1,055	2	811	18.2	28.2
Firewood	276	5	370	6.9	37.3
Village Centre	206	2	138	-	-
Grinding Mill	36	4	71	0.7	5.6
Fields	235	4	429	2.1	7.5
Health Facilities	25	6	72	-	-
Internal Crop Marketing	11	-	4	0.2	0.3
External Crop Marketing	20	0	55	0.4	4.4
External Markets	91	9	450	-	-
Other External Trips	34	-	(93)*	-	-
Total	1,970		2,345	28.5	83.3

The following data was obtained from the household survey: number of trips, trip duration, mode of transport.

The following assumptions were made: walking speed = 4 km/h, average headload = 20 kg

* Estimate, not included in total time

Tab. 3.2-7 Transport pattern of an average household in the survey villages 1994

During the survey period 1986/87 to 1994 the total transport burden expressed in time and tkm stayed relatively constant. The biggest change was an increase in the number of trips by 22 %, especially for water and firewood collection. In the same period the average distance decreased, which resulted in a compensating effect thus leaving the time and tkm unchanged. The reduction of distances might be partly a result of the donor activities, which where designed with the target of reducing the transport burden of women. The repair of grinding mills, installation of woodlots and piped water supply, might result in a reduction of the walking distance. The changes in the number of trips can be partly explained by the reduction of the trip distances, which made more short trips possible[28]. Other explanations are the different frame conditions like f. ex. the marketing system, which affected crop marketing; crops are marketed nowadays more on external markets. In general an increase of external trips[29] by 14 % (16 trips/annum) can be observed. The number of trips, the time used and the dis-

---

28 The village Kidope is a good example, where after the installation of piped water supply the distance decreased by 43 % but the number of trips nearly doubled.

29 Trips to markets and other external trips.

tance walked to the locations of health services remain unchanged. Some differences in the transport patterns might occur because the evaluation methods in both surveys were slightly different[30]. This holds true for the trips to the village centre and to the fields which were evaluated differently.

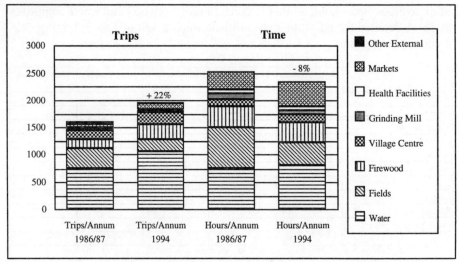

Fig. 3.2-4   Transport activities per household in Makete 1986/87 and 1994

Almost every village has some kind of road access but the poor conditions of the roads, especially during the rainy season and the lack of motorised vehicles makes motorised transport a seldom event. On average one motorised trip is annually undertaken per household. 65 % of the households did not travel at all with motor vehicles; 3 % travelled once per month or more. The relatively high transport costs compared to the low income is the main reason; households undertaking motorised trips spend 13 % of their total expenditure on transport. In addition they have a 60 % higher total expenditure than households which are not undertaking motorised trips.

About half of the villages in Makete have their main access via footpaths and another quarter can hardly be reached during the rains. A network of footpaths and tracks that cross the district is the main transport infrastructure. It provides the most direct routes between places, often over difficult terrain but offering shorter walking distances than following the roads. Sometimes shortcuts are so efficient, that driving is only $^1/_3$ faster than walking. Paths down the escarpment

---

30 Indeed three surveys (1986, 1987 and 1994) have to be compared, which were conducted and analysed by different persons. For each survey a (slightly) different questionnaire was used and sometimes different statistical methods (definition and extinction of extreme values) were used.

are the only possibility to reach the lowlands in the western direction. The road network consists of 850 km of motorable roads, with 160 km of regional roads, 190 km of district roads and about 500 km of feeder roads. While the first two road categories are under the supervision of the regional and the district engineer, the feeder roads are maintained through the villages. In 1994 the regional and district budgets received central government allocations from the road fund. The money was often used for emergency repairs. In general the condition of the regional and district roads was worse than that of many feeder roads, which were maintained with Self Help labour. It seems obvious, that the population is willing to invest working time to improve the access of their village. In Matamba Ward the villagers preferred to pay a local tax to pay labourers to improve the feeder road instead of working themselves[31].

	Motor vehicles		Donkeys		Bicycles		Wheelbarrows	
	1994	1986/87	1994	1986/87	1994	1986/87	1994	1986/87
Bulongwa	4	2	0	0	16	7	10	1
Matamba	0	2	56	12	47	57	3	1
Survey Area*	4	4	56	12	73	61	16	3
In Working Order	2		-	-	59			
* Including Ihela								

Tab. 3.2-8 Means of transport in survey villages

In 1987 only 65 motor-vehicles in working order were counted in Makete, which implies a ratio of 0.6 vehicles/1000 inhabitants. 85 % belonged to missions, to development projects, to the government or to the District Council. The number of motorised vehicles in working order in the surveyed villages decreased. In 1987 two buses were each operating three times a week carrying 25,000 passengers per year. The improvement of the Njombe-Makete-Bulongwa road had effects on public transport in Makete. In 1993 buses were also operating during the rainy season and the service was extended to Bulongwa. During the next rainy season the condition of the improved road deteriorated fast after preceding unprofessional upgrading. In 1994 the road was in such bad repair that the bus stopped the service to Bulongwa.

In 1994 only 3 % of the survey households owned a bicycle in working order and 2 % a donkey. The number of IMT increased significantly: in 1981, when the first surveys were conducted no bicycles or donkeys were found in the district. Since 1987 the number of bicycles has increased by 20 %, but in

	Bulongwa	Matamba	Survey Area
Donkeys	0.0%	3.5%	2.0%
Wheelbarrows	0.1%	0.4%	0.3%
Bicycles	1.3%	4.2%	3.3%

Tab. 3.2-9 Households possessing IMT in working order

31 A detailed description of the Self Help activities in Matamba is given in Box 5-1.

1994 many of the bicycles were not in working order. A reason for this growth might be the reduction in import taxes. Most of the bicycles are used in Matamba, where the terrain is flat. The MIRT Project enhanced the ownership of donkeys, which more than tripled during the observed period. All of the donkeys can be found in two survey villages of Matamba. The number of wheelbarrows in the survey area increased by a factor of five. However, very few households actually possess a wheelbarrow, as most of them are in the ownership of NGOs or other institutions.

3.3 Transport Interventions in the Makete District

The Makete Integrated Rural Transport Project (MIRTP) was conducted by the International Labour Office (ILO) from 1986 to 1995. The MIRTP was a pilot-project in the field of rural transport and had the following objectives:
• the introduction/development of low cost means of transport,
• the improvement of feeder roads and tracks by self-help labour,
• the development of existing tracks and trails,
• the improvement of existing bus and truck services,
• transport avoiding measures such as the repair of grinding mills and the planting of woodlots and
• the establishment of capacity within the District Council to plan, organise and implement rural transport interventions.
Numerous activities were conducted in the district and the follow up phase was still going on in 1994. In 1992 a Tripartite Evaluation (CHIWANGA et al 1992) assessed the output from the Project as listed in Tab. 3.3-1. A more detailed synopsis of the MIRTP Activities is given in the appendix.

Objective	Main results
Technical support for improvement of paths on a self-help basis	27.3 km of local paths improved
Capability established in District to improve and maintain feeder roads	40.5 km of feeder roads and tracks improved
Donkeys and donkey panniers made available	144 donkeys and 120 panniers sold
Capacity to produce wheelbarrows established	181 wheelbarrows in use
Hand operated grinding mills made available and motorised grinding mills repaired	25 motorised grinding mills repaired, 3 hand operated Grinding Mills made available
Road Maintenance Unit of District established	Capacity partly established
District Mechanical Workshop improved	Performance not improved
Capacity established in district to provide managerial support to District Council Bus and Village Truck Service	Objective not fulfilled
Capacity developed within the district Council to analyse, plan, promote and support rural transport improvements.	Training of Counterpart conducted

Tab. 3.3-1 Objectives and Main Results of the MIRT Project

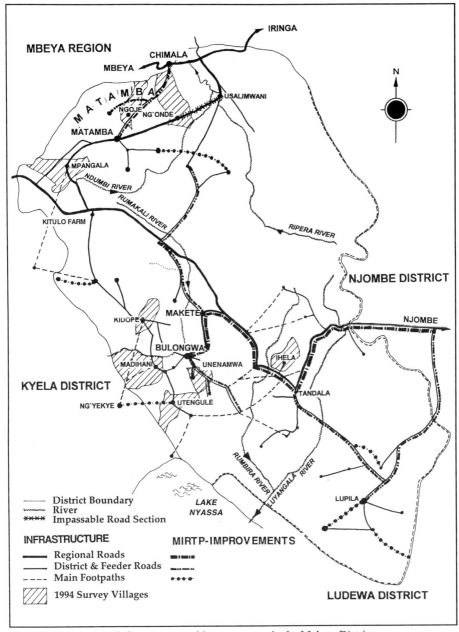

Fig. 3.3-1 Transport infrastructure and improvements in the Makete District

3.4   Methodology of the Field Study

Several pre-evaluation-studies[32] had been undertaken in the region before the MIRT Project started. "While projects are usually criticised in evaluations for gathering insufficient planning data, the MIRTP is one of the few cases where the opposite holds true." (CHIWANGA et al 1992, p.35). In 1986 and 1987 a survey conducted by BARWELL and MALMBERG questioned 431 rural households in 19 villages in the Makete District about their household endowment, expenditure, transport behaviour, agricultural production and marketing. In 1994 this survey was conducted in a similar way in order to appraise the socio-economic changes by comparing the evaluated data with the previous studies. This time 248 households in 8 villages were interviewed: 171 households belonged to a 10 % random choice of households in the villages and 77 households were interviewed, because they possessed a donkey, bicycle or wheelbarrow.

Interviews with the village leaderships were conducted to obtain qualitative assessments of the changes due to the MIRT Project. In addition, the traffic was counted on improved and not improved footpaths and on an improved road.

Village	Area	Households Interviewed		Changes in Transportation
		Random	IMT-HH	
Unenamwa		21	2	Improvement of internal access Improvement of footpath
Utengule	Bulongwa	15	4	Improvement of footpath Breakdown of grinding mill
Madihani		15	2	
Kidope		22	1	Installation of piped water supply Installation of grinding mill
Ihela	Central Region	21	6	Improved of external access Installation of woodlots Installation of dispensary
Mpangala		30	29	Improvement of external access
Ngoje	Matamba	16	22	Improvement of external access Installation of grinding mill
Ng'onde		31	11	Installation of grinding mill deterioration of external access
Total		**171**	**77**	**Total: 248**

Tab. 3.4-1 Survey villages 1994

The map overleaf shows the survey villages and the main MIRTP improvements. The study area Bulongwa is located in a peripheral part of Makete; the villages of Utengule and Madihani are situated close to the escarpment, which forms the western border of the district and which can only be crossed by foot.

---

32 BARWELL / MALMBERG CALVO (1989), DIXON-FYLE / FRIELING (1990), JENNINGS (1992) and many others more.

Motorised external access is possible via the regional road from Makete to Bulongwa, which had been partly improved, but had deteriorated at that time to a very bad condition. The track to Unenamwa and the footpath to Utengule were improved. The terrain is often very steep so bicycles are rarely used.

The second study area Matamba is located in the north western part of the district. It is the region with the best external access, because a 24 km long road drives down the northern escarpment, where a tarmac road leads to the capital Dar Es Salaam and to the next big town Mbeya which counts 100,000 inhabitants. The villages of Mpangala and Ngoje are directly adjacent to this improved road. Ng'onde is located besides the regional road, which is no longer passable. The terrain is relatively flat and the use of bicycles is much more common than in Bulongwa. The whole area is very active in agricultural production, because of its favourable agroecological conditions and its good external access.

The Village of Ihela is located beside the regional road Njombe-Makete and also has a good external access. During the dry season a regular bus passes through every day. The agricultural potential is mediocre.

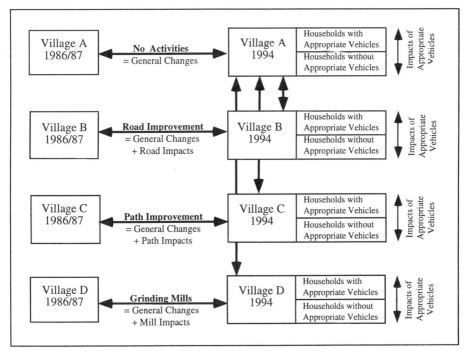

Fig. 3.4-1 General methodology of impact assessment

Only the objectives 1 to 5 on Tab. 3.3-1 will show measurable effects upon the household level and are therefore part of this study. Furthermore the Danish development aid organisation DANIDA installed a piped water supply in one village.

In general, a distinction has to be made between short term effects and long term impacts. The effects comprise the immediate benefits after or during the improvement such as revenues generated by the construction and maintenance activities, reductions of transport time and Vehicle Operating Costs. The impacts try to assess the long term benefits like increased production- and marketing activities induced by the transport improvements. Impacts presume that the maintenance will henceforth be carried out properly in order to guarantee a long duration of the benefits. Due to the short observation period of seven years and to the fact that the last phase of the MIRTP was still going on no clear judgement of the sustainability can be given.

In general, three methodologies for the assessment of the impacts are used in this study: Methodology I can be applied for the assessment of road and footpath improvements. The changes occurring between 1986/87 and 1994 in a village with improvements are compared with the changes of a control group i.e. villages without improvements of the transport system. It can be assumed that the difference of the changes represent the impacts of the transport intervention.

	Village A	Village B
1986/87	$\overline{X}_{A86}$	$\overline{X}_{B86}$
1994	$\overline{X}_{A94}$	$\overline{X}_{B94}$
Change	$\Delta\overline{X}_A = \overline{X}_{A94} - \overline{X}_{A86}$	$\Delta\overline{X}_B = \overline{X}_{B94} - \overline{X}_{B86}$
Impact	$I = \Delta\overline{X}_B - \Delta\overline{X}_A$	

Tab. 3.4-2 Methodology I for impact assessment

Methodology II can be applied for the assessment of grinding mills and piped water supply; a simple comparison of 1994 villages (B, C, D, ...) with improvement and 1994 villages A without improvements gives an indication of the impacts. The results can be compared with the outcomes of the application of Methodology I, which can also be sensibly applied in this case. In many cases only the mean values of the 1986/87 survey were available. Therefore a comparison of median and standard deviation was not always possible.

Methodology III tries to assess the impacts of the purchase of IMT. Because the household survey 1986/87 was conducted anonymously no data exist about the performance of households before the purchase of an IMT. Therefore the impacts have to be assessed by comparing households of the same villages with a similar household structure; i.e. size of household, profession, source of cash income etc.

Often assumptions have to be made for the estimation of the impacts. In order to reduce misjudgements due to wrong assumptions two approaches were chosen: the 'optimistic approach' chooses those assumptions, which are most

66

favourable for the impacts of the concerning transport intervention, while the 'pessimistic approach' takes into account the unfavourable assumptions. The comparison of mean values (for the estimation of impacts on marketing) might give a too optimistic picture of the changes, because extreme values may influence the average. Therefore a more pessimistic approach is also calculated by comparing the median values, which give a clearer impression for the majority of households.

A couple of methodological problems occur due to missing or non comparable data. The revenues from marketing activities is one of the salient features of the impact assessment. As mentioned above the agricultural producer prices changed during the observation period. Because a rural price index has not yet been calculated for Tanzania, the estimation of the real price changes is problematic. Furthermore the nominal prices only of the next big towns Mbeya and Njombe can be obtained but not the prices in Makete. Therefore all the revenue changes where calculated by multiplying the amounts (in tons) marketed in 1986/87 with the 1994 producer prices. This methodology does not reflect the actual income situation in 1987, but rather gives an indication of the comparable changes in marketing.

All values are transformed into Dollars using the June 1994 exchange rate of 518 Tsh per US $. Monetary values of previous years are first adjusted to the local 1994 price level before the exchange rate is applied.

4 Impact Assessment of Transport Interventions

4.1 Rehabilitation of the Feeder Road: Matamba-Chimala

The Matamba Region is situated on a plateau of 2000 m altitude in the northern part of the Makete District. Three villages were observed during the survey, which are mainly trading their products to the lowland market Chimala, where a tarmac road provides excellent connections to the capital Dar Es Salaam and to the regional centre Mbeya. Two roads lead down the escarpment. In 1987 the old regional road passing through Ng'onde was the only access to the Matamba Region. In order to improve the transport situation the local authorities decided to rehabilitate an old feeder road leading from Matamba down the escarpment to Chimala. The road was upgraded to all weather standard as a part of the MIRT Project from 1989 to 1992 by paid labour and self-help. The project trained foremen and gang leaders, produced a manual, paid salaries and provided hand tools, machinery and transport. In 1994 the regional road through Ng'onde was no longer passable due to lack of maintenance by the regional administration. The only motorable connection from Ng'onde to the rest of the world is a track to Matamba, which is rarely used by vehicles. The village leadership stated, that the transport situation of Ng'onde has deteriorated over the last few years.

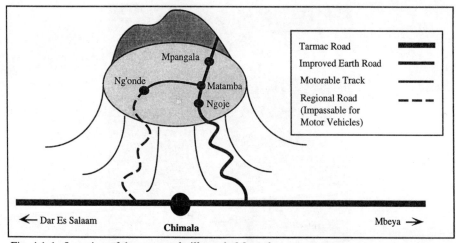

Fig. 4.1-1 Location of the surveyed villages in Matamba.

The maintenance work was initially done with unpaid self-help labour. Because no motorised transport was available the labourers had to walk long distances before starting work[1]. Inefficient work and high opportunity costs of labour were the reasons why it was decided to conduct the maintenance with paid labour. The funds will be raised by a local tax of 40 ¢ per able person and year.

4.1.1 Transport Volume

A traffic count was undertaken from Wednesday, June 15 to Saturday, 18 1994 on the Matamba Chimala Road[2]. On an average day 11 vehicles left Matamba in the direction of the lowlands, carrying 31 passengers, 2.4 t of potatoes and 8.8 t of bamboo juice "ulanzi". A comparison of the village leadership discussions indicates that the number of vehicles stayed constant in Mpangala, while it decreased in Ng'onde, where the road has deteriorated. It seems that during the harvesting period from July to October most of the incoming vehicles visit the Matamba highlands. Traffic estimates for the whole year can only be done approximately. The number of motor vehicles driving down the escarpment will be to the order of 3-4,000, carrying about 10,000 passengers and roughly 3-4,000 tons of goods.

Village	1987	1994
Mpangala	5/day (May/June)	5/day (May/June)
Ngoje	no data	5/day (May/June) 2/day (rainy season) 8/day (harvesting season)
Ng'onde	7/week	1/week

Tab. 4.1-1 Number of vehicles visiting Matamba villages

An indication of the effects of the road can be given by the example of the export of bamboo juice "ulanzi" from Matamba. In the early morning many of the farmers are busy collecting "ulanzi" from the bamboo bushes. In May and June every day 8 Four-Wheel-Drive Pick-Ups enter Matamba to collect 8,200 l of ulanzi and sell it in Mbeya, which is the biggest town, 90 km away. The price difference of $ 140 per load allows a profitable operation of the vehicles and gives income to the personnel and the farmers. The average household in Matamba sells 450 l of ulanzi annually, which gives them an income of $ 10.

---

1 A road camp was not constructed on the escarpment, because the villagers were afraid of witchcraft during the night.
2 The counting was undertaken during daytime at the Matamba road toll station. The traffic during the night time was estimated.

4.1.2   Marketing of Agricultural Products

The villages in the Matamba Region have to be observed very carefully because their individual situation explains the transport patterns. Ng'onde and Ngoje villagers can reach the market in Chimala within 2 ½ - 3 hours, while the people from Mpangala have to walk for four hours. Even though Ng'onde has a bad road access the village earns the highest revenues from marketing activities, followed by Mpangala and Ngoje. All of the households in Ng'onde use fertiliser and the amount per household is higher than in the other villages. The farmers produce mostly high value crops like cereals, beans, peas and onions, which can be more easily transported to the market than e.g. potatoes. Mpangala gives a completely different picture: the more humid and cold climate and the good road access favours the production of potatoes causing big marketing weights of more than two tons per household, which are mainly transported by trucks to the markets. The revenues per ton are much lower than in the other villages. Ngoje represents an intermediate situation: the agro-ecological conditions, which are comparable with Ng'onde do not favour the production of potatoes, but good access to motorised transport enables the production of relatively heavy crops. Ngoje and Mpangala, which have good road access, are marketing a comparable amount of the alcoholic bamboo juice „ulanzi", in contrast to Ng'onde, where the ulanzi has to be transported by headload to the lowland markets.

1994	Unit	Mpangala	Ngoje	Ng'onde
Distance to Chimala	min walk	235	150	190
Fertiliser used per household	kg/HH	54	130	147
Amount of crops marketed	kg/HH	2,080	623	749
Average revenue per t crop marketed	$/t	46	127	172
Amount of ulanzi marketed	l/HH	590	577	220
Total revenues from marketing activities	$/HH	113	100	140

Tab. 4.1-2 Salient features of the Matamba survey villages

In Fig. 4.1-2 the changes in marketing since 1987 are visualised; obviously the weight of crops marketed increased tremendously. The major reason might be the breakdown of the Pyrethrum Marketing Board in Matamba, which was mentioned earlier. In 1987 half of the revenue was earned by the marketing of pyrethrum; in 1994 no farmer was producing pyrethrum after the 1993 harvest was collected, but not paid for by the board. In 1994 private traders took over the role of the pyrethrum marketing board; the light product pyrethrum was replaced by a number of heavy food crops like Irish potatoes, maize, beans, peas and onions. In 1987 most of the products were collected in the villages as shown in Fig. 4.1-2. After the breakdown of the marketing board the farmers had to transport a bigger share of their products to external markets. Nevertheless, many farmers increased their marketing weights by transporting bigger loads by walking.

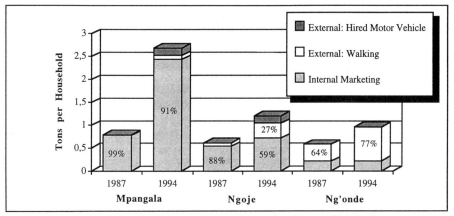

Fig. 4.1-2   Marketing of agricultural products in the survey villages of Matamba

Mpangala sells 91 % of the weight of its products within in the boundaries of the village. The heavy potatoes (67 % of weight), are only transported from the field to the nearby road, where they are loaded onto trucks. Most of the trucks belong to private traders, who collect the potatoes and sell them in lowland markets[3]. Some farmers decided to hire a vehicle in order to transport products (6 %) by themselves to the lowland markets, where the producer prices are higher. Only 3 % is carried by headload to a nearby highland market. Ulanzi is collected in and around Mpangala, transported to the street and sold directly to private traders with motor vehicles. The ulanzi and potato marketing were only possible because the conditions of the rehabilitated road allowed the transport of the heavy crops to markets outside the district.

In **Ngoje** 59 % of the products are sold internally in the same way as described for Mpangala, but 27 % are carried by headload to lowland markets. This means that farmers prefer to carry annually 300 kg of their crops by headload for two to three hours and walk back even longer up the escarpment, rather than selling these products in the village directly to traders and receiving smaller revenues[4]. Such an arbitrage is not possible for the farmers in Mpangala, because their potatoes are too heavy and the distance to the lowland market is much longer. In Ngoje good access to the road makes the transport of crops with

---

3 The potatoes are quite often transported to the markets in Dar Es Salaam
4 There are of course a lot of other reasons for travelling to the lowland markets: Social contacts can be made, goods are cheaper to purchase, the wife/husband cannot control expenditures, etc.

71

hired vehicles possible; 13 % of the products are transported in this way to the lowland markets.

In **Ng'onde** bad motorised access does not offer the same opportunities as in the other villages. Nevertheless the households received the highest revenues compared to all the other villages surveyed! An explanation might be the existence of a 'traditional' barter economy between Ng'onde and Chimala and a strong social cohesion by kinship. 77 % of the products are transported by headload down the escarpment. Part of the products which are marketed internally are probably transported down by other members of the village. The case study about the transport activities of a woman in Ng'onde may elucidate this phenomenon.

Box 4-1: Headload Transport from Ng'onde

A woman from Ng'onde earns a considerable income by transporting products, which she buys in the village, to lowland markets. Four times per week she transports 20 l of bamboo juice „ulanzi" to Chimala to where she has to walk for four hours. She brings back the same amount of kerosene, which she sells in the village. In May traders come to the village of Usalimwani, which she can reach in two hours. Even though the producer prices are lower she prefers to walk the shorter distance and compensates the lower prices by walking every day of the week. If the price differences between highland and lowland markets are regarded as the income generated by the transport, then she values in both cases the transport at 19 ¢ per hour. This is 70 % more than the minimum salary offered to government employees.

Market Place	Distance	Trips/Week	Price Difference	Transport Revenue	Income
	[hours]		[$/20 l]	[$/hour]	[$/week]
Chimala	4	4	0.77	0.19	3.08
Usalimwani	2	7	0.39	0.19	2.73

Another restriction for the production of crops is the transport of the crops from the field. The location of the Mpangala potato-fields beside the road favours marketing directly from the field or on the street. Even though the biggest amount is harvested there, only half of it has to be transported home. Ngoje had to transport the biggest loads home from the fields. Here seems to be a restriction for further expansion, which Ngoje reduced by producing high value crops.

Tons per household	Mpangala	Ngoje	Ng'onde
Products Harvested	4.01	3.13	2.38
Transported Home	2.17	2.61	2.04
Not Transported Home	1.85	0.52	0.34

Tab. 4.1-3 Annual transport of agricultural products from the field 1994

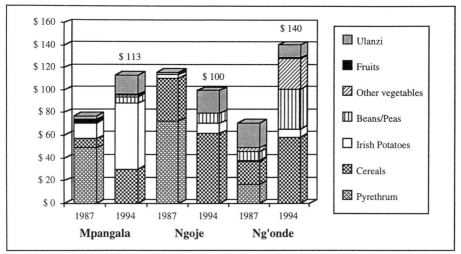

Fig. 4.1-3 Revenues per household from marketing in Matamba villages (1994 prices)

A comparison of the mean revenues[5] before and after the rehabilitation of the road, visualised in Fig. 4.1-3, is an indicator of how farmers were able to react to the changing conditions. **Remarkably the village with the worst road access Ng'onde had the best performance, while the village with the best motorised access Ngoje had to register a decline in income.** One of the reasons is the smaller dependency on pyrethrum in Ng'onde (24 % of the 1987 revenues) compared to the other two villages (63-64 %). Ng'onde reacted to market liberalisation by increasing the output of all its products. Because the road conditions were deteriorating in Ng'onde the marketing concentrated more on high value crops like cereals, beans, peas and other vegetables which were transported by headload to the lowland markets. The marketing of ulanzi, which in 1987 was collected by motor vehicles decreased.

	Mpangala		Ngoje		Ng'onde	
	$/HH	%	$/HH	%	$/HH	%
Mean Values						
Including Pyrethrum	+36	+47%	-17	-14%	+70	+98%
Excluding Pyrethrum	+86	+324%	+53	+113%	+86	+160%
Median Values	+28	+47%	-11	-13%	+82	+279%

Tab. 4.1-4 Change in value marketed in Matamba villages 1987-1994

---

5 In order to eliminate the distortions caused by changes in producer prices, the 1994 producer prices were multiplied by the 1987 weights marketed.

The performance of Ng'onde is remarkable especially if it is compared with Ngoje, which has comparable agroecological conditions. Although Ngoje increased the production of cereals and ulanzi, the revenue losses from pyrethrum could not be compensated for. Even if the marketing of pyrethrum is not taken into account, as shown on table 4.1-4, the marketing increase in Ng'onde is still much stronger than in Ngoje. If instead of the mean values the median values are compared, the marketing of half of Ng'onde's households nearly triples, while the people in Ngoje suffer from decreasing revenues. Even thought Ngoje had an improved motorised access the absolute and relative increases in Ng'onde were by far stronger! This leads to the following conclusion:

If the markets are within walking distance, no measurable benefits[6] of road rehabilitation on the marketing activities can be observed. Missing motorised transport can be compensated for by walking, and even villages close to the road prefer to carry more than a quarter of their goods by headload to the markets.

Mpangala is in a different situation than Ngoje and Ng'onde; the distance to the local market is longer and the agroecological conditions favour the production of heavy potatoes. The village could offset the losses from the breakdown of the pyrethrum market by shifting to intensive potato production, but the marketing of cereals and ulanzi also increased. If pyrethrum is excluded from the analysis Mpangala had even a stronger relative increase in marketing than Ng'onde, while the absolute growth was similar (Tab. 4.1-4). The increase in marketing would not have been possible without the rehabilitation of the road, which allowed the transport of heavy loads to the distant markets. A comparison of Mpangala with another Matamba village with similar agroecological conditions but no motorised access

$ (1994)	Mpangala*	Bulongwa**	Impact
Mean Values			
1994	106.0	52.3	
1986/87	77.0	31.3	
Change	29.0	21.0	8.0
Median Values			
1994	80.5	27.1	
1986/87	59.5	20.4	
Change	21.0	6.7	14.3
Variation Coefficient*			
1994	104%	129%	
1986/87	82%	92%	

*   Impacts by donkey households subtracted
**   Madihani and Kidope
*** Variation Coefficient = Standard Deviation / Mean

Tab. 4.1-5 Revenue per household by marketing

---

6 It could be argued, that without the rehabilitation of the road the situation of Ngoje would have been worse. Households would have lost income by the marketing of ulanzi, which is sold to the private traders. A quantification of this assumption is not possible.

was not possible[7]. Therefore a comparison with the changes in the Bulongwa region has to be undertaken. The villages Madihani and Kidope are chosen because no improvements of the transport system occurred and the marketing patterns[8] changed from predominantly internal to external marketing. The impact assessment is undertaken by comparing the changes in the villages listed in table 4.1–5. If the changes in Bulongwa are regarded as general changes due to non-transport interventions (e.g. market liberalisation, breakdown of marketing boards), the benefits can be derived by comparing the growth of the revenues.

$$\text{Impacts}_{\text{Mpangala}} = \Delta \text{Marketing}_{\text{Mpangala}} - \Delta \text{Marketing}_{\text{Bulongwa}}$$

A comparison of the mean changes estimates the annual impacts of the road improvement in Mpangala at $ 8.00 per household. This value can be regarded as a conservative estimate because a comparison of the median values indicates stronger impacts[9]. A comparison of the median gives a better view how the majority of the population was profiting from the road improvement. An optimistic view would estimate the annual impacts in Mpangala at $ 14.30 per household.

4.1.3 Marketing with Hired Vehicles

Farmers can increase their income by transporting their crops with hired motor vehicles to the lowland markets. 6 % of the weight of crops in Mpangala and 13 % in Ngoje are transported by hired vehicles to the lowland market Chimala. Even though the distances are different, the costs per ton transported[10] range between $ 8.50 and $ 10.90. These costs can be covered by higher producer prices on the lowland market. The profit, which farmers make by hiring vehicles ranges between 25 $/t for maize and 29 $/t for potatoes. Unfortunately only a few farmers are able to take advantage of this possibility, probably because of the lack of financial resources. Therefore the annual profit per household is, with $ 4.36 in Mpangala and $ 3.90 in Ngoje, relatively low.

---

7 No other suitable village had been researched in 1987.
8 In 1986/87 in Kidope 87 % of the crops, in Madihani 46 % and in Mpangala 99 % were marketed internally. Until 1994 no significant changes in crop marketing occurred in Mpangala, while the share decreased to 18 % in Kidope and to 9 % in Madihani. Kidope and Madihani transport all their crops by headload to the external markets. The distances from the three villages to the lowland markets are comparable.
9 The differing results can be explained by an analysis of the variation in the household data. Since 1986/87 the variation was growing much stronger in Bulongwa than in Mpangala, which had a strong influence on the mean value.
10 The costs for hired vehicles from Matamba to Chimala range between 33 ¢/tkm and 68 ¢/tkm. This seems to indicate high profit margins for the vehicle owner, when the vehicle operating costs for a four-wheel-drive of 25 ¢/tkm is taken into consideration.

4.1.4 Reduced Vehicle Operating Costs

The rehabilitation of the road could reduce the Vehicle Operating Costs (VOC). A 17 km stretch of road was improved and it is assumed that 3,600 vehicles pass up and down this segment of the escarpment. The reduction of VOC[11] can be estimated at annually $ 10,000 or $ 2.24 per household. An optimistic approach would assume, that the total benefits will be passed on to the local population by way of reduced passenger fares, higher producer prices or will be directly earned by the local vehicle owners. A pessimistic approach would assume that the region profits from only half of these benefits because many vehicles entering the district do not belong to Matamba owners. On top of this reduced transport costs will probably cause a reduction of consumer prices for agricultural produce rather than an increase in producer prices. The benefits per household would thus amount to only $ 1.12.

4.1.5 Time Savings

Ngoje and Mpangala farmers save time by selling their products to traders, who transport them to the markets or by hiring vehicles. These time savings can be regarded as the benefits stemming from the road rehabilitation. It can be postulated that the Mpangala farmers would not be able to transport all their potatoes down the escarpment by headload; they would therefore grow a different set of crops, which are assumed to be similar to those grown in Ng'onde. Tab. 4.1-6 lists the additional transport burden, which would have to be carried, if the same revenues received in 1994 should be earned. In Mpangala annually more than 8 tkm would have to be transported per household and additional 200 hours of time used. If the time savings are valued with the opportunity costs of time[12], then the benefits can be estimated at $ 15 per household. The smaller volumes and the shorter distance to the lowland market causes lower benefits in Ngoje. 63 % of the time benefits can be attributed to women.

		Mpangala	Ngoje
Additional Weight	tons	0.5	0.2
Trips		26	10
Distance Market	km	15.7	10.0
Tkm	tkm	8.1	2.1
Time	hrs	203	52
Value Time	$	14.9	3.8

Tab. 4.1-6 Time savings by road transport

---

11 The cost savings range between 7 ¢ and 10 ¢ according to the vehicle used and the terrain.
12 The economic effects of time savings are discussed in the Chapters 2.4.2 and 6.3. The opportunity costs of time equal the marginal productivity of labour which is calculated with the production function estimated in chapter 5.2.3. The marginal value of labour amounts to ¢ 7 in Makete.

4.1.6   Other Benefits

The two surveys give no indication of the effects of the road rehabilitation on external travel activities outside the district. Neither were the villages with good access undertaking more external trips, nor was the increase since 1987 any stronger than in the remote villages. In the most accessible village, Ngoje, the worsening income situation even caused a reduction in the number of external trips. No measurable effects on out-migration from Matamba could be observed. Better motorised access to the lowlands also might account for negative effects on the health situation as described in Chapter 4.3.5 for the footpaths. Furthermore vehicles are more likely to carry flies and mosquitoes which spread lowland diseases like Malaria, Sleeping Sickness and Onchozercosis. Agricultural experts state that lowland pests are increasingly appearing on the Matamba highlands.

The economic performance also had its impacts on the use of fertiliser. In Ng'onde the number of households using fertiliser is higher and it increased strongly, while in the easily accessible villages this amount has decreased since 1987. Thus in the Matamba Region the price has a stronger impact on the use of fertiliser than the motorised accessibility.

4.1.7   Total Benefits

Until now only the benefits for the three Matamba villages Mpangala, Ngoje and Ng'onde could be assessed. The impact of road rehabilitation in the whole Matamba Region, which is considered as the catchment area can be estimated by taking the number of households, the distance to the markets, the accessibility, the transport volume registered in the traffic countings and the agroecological conditions of the villages into account. The traffic counting showed that more than half of the ulanzi collected in Matamba stemmed from the village Mpangala, where the strongest benefits can be expected. Salaries from the road works have to be added to the local benefits, while VOC are not included, because it is assumed they are included in the benefits by increased market production. The total annual benefits per household are estimated at $ 17 according to the pessimistic view and at $ 20 for the optimistic approach.

$/Household	Marketing Activities		Hiring Vehicles	Time Savings	Wages
	optimistic	pessimistic			
Mpangala	14.30	8.00	4.36	14.89	-
Ngoje	0.00	0.00	3.93	3.83	-
Ng'onde	0.00	0.00	0.00	0.00	-
Matamba	6.27	3.51	3.81	8.38	1.09

Tab. 4.1-7 Benefits from the Chimala-Matamba Road

4.2 Track Construction: Unenamwa-Bulongwa

In the Bulongwa Region, a trail leading from the village Unenamwa to the ward centre Bulongwa was upgraded to a dry weather motorable track. The work was done with the "self-help" labour of the inhabitants. The village leadership was very enthusiastic[13] about the effects of this local track. In emergency cases the ambulance is nowadays able to reach the village and transport sick persons, especially pregnant women to the hospital in Bulongwa. Before the improvement it was reported that several people died while being carried to the hospital[14]. In 1994 a mobile Mother and Child Health service was operating in the village. Nowadays traders enter the village to buy crops from the farmers, which they had to transport on headload to the local markets before the improvement was undertaken. In addition traders using bicycles are now visiting the village. According to the village leadership the track made the village so attractive that 20 new households moved to Unenamwa. The number of households in Unenamwa increased from 170 in 1986 to 220 in 1994. This implies an annual growth rate of 3.2 %, which is well above the regional average.

		Unenamwa	Other Bulongwa Villages	Impact**
Marketing (Mean)*	1994	45.1	46.9	
[$]	1986	25.3	29.3	
	Change	19.8	17.6	2.2
Marketing (Median)*	1994	22.8	26.6	
[$]	1986	14.9	16.2	
	Change	7.6	10.4	-2.8
External marketing	1994	46%	64%	
[kg]	1986	92%	28%	
	Change	-46%	36%	
Vehicles/month	1994	15	7	
	1986	2	6	
	Change	13	1	12

* The impacts on marketing from the footpath improvement are subtracted
** Methodology I described in Tab. 3.4-1

Tab. 4.2-1 Impacts of the Unenamwa-Bulongwa track

The frequency of vehicles visiting the villages increased from 2 per month in 1986 to 15 per month in 1994, while in the other villages the increase was nearly zero (see table 4.2-1). The vehicles were collecting the products from the farmers in Unenamwa, which gave incentives for higher market production. The mean increase of the revenues from marketing in Unenamwa was slightly stronger than in the other observed Bulongwa villages. An optimistic impact

---

13 The group of enumerators was welcomed very warmly and accompanied half their way home. The village presented a chicken as a gift for the research group.

14 JENNINGS (1992, p. 33) reports, that sick people are carried long distances on stretchers made from bamboo poles to reach health services. "In such instance the bearers slipped in the mud, the woman delivered her baby on the track in the rain, the child died shortly afterwards. This is not an unusual occurrence."

assessment estimates the benefits by increased market production at $ 2.20 per household. The pessimistic approach would result in negative impacts, which makes no sense and therefore it is assumed, that the benefits are zero.

Internal marketing 1986	tons	0.01
Internal marketing 1994	tons	0.22
Reduced weight	tons	0.20
Saved trips per annum		10
Distance external market	km	8.2
Saved pkm per annum	pkm	167
Saved tkm per annum	tkm	1.7
Saved time per annum	hrs	42
Value Time Saving	**$**	**3.06**

Tab. 4.2-2 Time savings by internal marketing

Tab. 4.2-1 shows also that the amount of external marketing decreased during the observed period from 92 % to 46 %, while in the other villages an increase of external marketing could be noticed. When mobile traders are collecting agricultural products in the village, the total transport burden of the farmers and the time dedicated to crop marketing is reduced. These benefits can be quantified by the reduction of the time which it would take to carry the same load to the external markets. Every household would need 42 hours annually more to carry the additional weight of 200 kg of products to the markets. The annual benefits from time savings amount to $ 3 per household.

The village leadership stated that about 15 vehicles per month visit the village, which are profiting from the better standard of the track. Annually, 1980 vehicle-km are driven on the improved track, causing reduced vehicle operating costs[15] of $ 153. If a pessimistic approach is chosen, which assumes that only half of the benefits have a regional effect, in the form of reduced passenger fares, increased producer prices or savings by local vehicle owners, the annual benefits can be estimated at 15 ¢ per household in the catchment area. An optimistic approach would double the benefits.

No effects could be observed concerning the use of agricultural inputs, outmigration, the total quantity of products harvested, or the number of trips outside the district. No household was hiring a vehicle to transport crops to the markets. The total benefits per household of the track construction amount to $ 3 according to the pessimistic view and to $ 5 according to the optimistic approach.

---

15 The vehicle operating costs are calculated according to data given by the Tanzanian Ministry of Transport: 7 ¢/vehicle-km for a four wheel drive and 9 ¢/vehicle-km for a medium truck.

Box 4-2: The Effects of the Road Improvement in Ihela

The village of Ihela is located 1-2 km away from the main regional road from Njombe to Makete. During the MIRT Project spot improvements were undertaken on this road, with the result that a regular bus service was operating the whole year on this route. During the rainy season of 1993 the condition of the earth road deteriorated due to unprofessional maintenance.

Although the village has the best external access compared with the other Bulongwa villages it could not benefit from the road improvements. The increase in agricultural production and marketing noticed in all the other villages of the survey could not be observed in Ihela. Farmers were harvesting less agricultural crops and the revenues derived from crop marketing had been stagnating since 1986. The number of households stating agriculture as the main source of cash income declined from 61 % to only 38 %, while households living from transfers from relatives increased from 6 % to 14 % in 1994. This suggests a high out-migration of males, which can be verified by the highest male-to-female ratio observed in Makete; every fourth woman is living without her husband. Ihela was traditionally living from the transfers of migrant labourers on tea plantations or from pit sawing. The improving market conditions in Tanzania, entailing an increasing demand for labour, might be the reason for the growing out-migration in Ihela. **It can be concluded that the exceptional good motorised access to Ihela could not prevent the stagnation of the agricultural market production and the increase of migration.**

4.3   Footpath Improvement: Utengule-Ng'yekye

In Chapter 2.3 the importance of footpaths for the transport in rural Africa was emphasised. In Makete especially during rainy season the paths become slippery like soft soap due to the very fine grain size of the soils derived from lava ashes. Therefore travelling on steep paths during rains is a dangerous undertaking and more often than not these paths are avoided (DIXON-FYLE/FRIELING 1990). Obstacles like rivers, marshes and invading vegetation force the travellers to walk big detours. Often paths have a drainage function during rains and at steep slopes severe erosion problems might occur, sometimes causing deep gullies. The narrowness of many paths makes the use of IMT impossible and creates difficulties when passing travellers in the opposite direction. These restrictions were the reason for the improvement of 27 km of footpaths in Makete. The MIRTP trained gang leaders and foremen to conduct simple improvements on these paths, such as building wooden bridges and stairs, digging small ditches for drainage and constructing timber guard barriers.

Eight footpaths lead down from the western highlands to the lowland north of Lake Nyassa. The people from the Bulongwa Region use these footpaths to visit the weekly market in Ng'yekye or to catch the bus to Mbeya. Therefore the Utengule-Ng'yekye footpath (Fig. 4.2-1) was classified as a district footpath and integrated into the district roads and path system. The footpath was improved by paid labour during the MIRT Project.

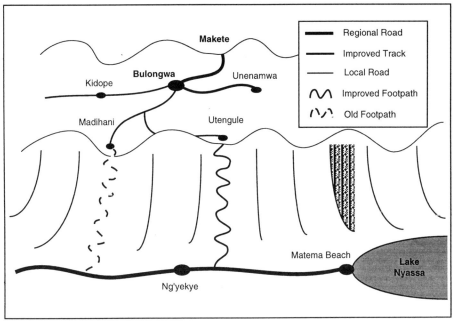

Fig. 4.2-1   Location of the surveyed villages in the Bulongwa Region

The improvement of the path received a very positive reception from the inhabitants of the concerned villages. The village council in Utengule describes the main effects of the path as follows:

• The number of people using the path increased.
• The number of accidents on the footpath decreased.
• The travel time declined significantly.
• More traders travel up the footpath to purchase agricultural produce in the highlands.

Tab. 4.3-1 gives an overview of the statements of footpath users in these two villages interviewed during the household survey. 87 % of the households in Utengule and 52 % in Unenamwa use the path. Over 90 % of the users proclaim that they are travelling much faster, more than two thirds declare that the security increased and one third of the users are able to reach new places. The effects of the latter statement should not be underestimated: 19 % of the households in Unenamwa and 27 % of Utengule are travelling to places in the lowlands, which they could not reach before and where they can get in contact with other people, exchange goods and opinions and receive wares and information. **Isolation, which is regarded as one of the salient features of poverty can definitely be reduced by the improvement of a footpath!**

Households answering "yes" to the following questions :	Unenamwa	Utengule
There has never been a real advantage	0 %	0 %
The improvements have already disappeared	9 %	0 %
No advantages in the rainy season	18 %	0 %
We can reach places we could not reach before	36 %	31 %
Safety is better	64 %	100 %
Faster travelling	91 %	100 %

Tab. 4.3-1 Improvements in the eyes of footpath users

4.3.1   Transport Volume

Next to the improved Utengule path another unimproved footpath leads from Madihani down to Ng'yekye. On both footpaths the traffic was counted before the improvement in October 1988 (BARWELL/HARRISON 1989) and in May 1994. A comparison of the data makes the appraisal of the benefits possible; on Thursday May 27 1994 and the following Friday, which is market day in Ng'yekye, 848 persons from Utengule used the footpath to and from Ng'yekye.

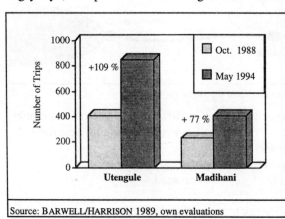

Source: BARWELL/HARRISON 1989, own evaluations

Fig. 4.3-1 Number of trips to and from Ng'yekye on a Thursday and Friday

Between October 1989 and May 1994 the number of one way trips on the improved footpath on a Thursday and Friday increased by 109 %, while the transport volume on the unimproved path rose by 77 %. If it is assumed, that the increase on the unimproved path accounts for the regular increase of transport volume to Ng'yekye between 1988 and 1994 (Methodology I), at least 32 % of the increase is caused by the footpath improvement.

Assuming that the temporal distribution[16] observed in 1988 is also valid in 1994, **the annual number of persons using the Utengule footpath (one direction) can be estimated at least at 58,000. Consequently it can be assumed that a minimum of 9,000 return trips per annum are generated as a result of the improvements.**

Annual trips per household	Footpath Survey	Household Surveys		
	1994	1994	1986	Change
Utengule	28	46	17	165 %
Unenamwa	10	15	0-1	-
Madihani	15	36	10	131 %

Tab. 4.3-2 Comparison of footpath and household surveys

This estimation is a minimum approach and does not include the seasonal variations of transport activities. BARWELL/HARRISON (1989) made it clear that they conducted their survey in October during the peak period of the year, which is not true for the 1994 survey, which was conducted in May[17]. The household survey of 1994 gives comparable data for the annual transport activities of three villages in the catchment area. Tab. 4.3-2 shows that the footpath survey tends to underestimate the annual number of trips.

May/June 1994	Utengule-Ng'yekye Footpath	Matamba-Chimala Road
Households in the catchment area	1,500	4,500
Passengers/day	80	31
Tons/day	1.1	11.2

Tab. 4.3-3   Transport down the escarpment

An optimistic estimation of the trips on the Utengule path is not possible due to the uncertainty of the data. Thus the pessimistic approach shall henceforth be the basis of the assessment. However, the household survey confirms the generation of trips: using the same argument as above, 34 % of the increase in trips was generated by the improvement of the footpath[18].

A comparison of the footpath evaluation and the traffic counting on the feeder road Matamba-Chimala shows that the transport volume reaches the same magnitude, if the population in the catchment area is taken into account; on the road more freight is moved, but less passengers are transported.

---

16 The following assumptions had to be made: (1) The weekly distribution of transport activities stated in BARWELL/HARRISON (1989) did not change. (2) The transport volume measured in May represents the annual average.
17 BARWELL/HARRISON state, that 18 % of the households undertake most trips in May, but 72 % in October. Thus the average probably will be higher than assumed.
18 Assuming that the increase of 131 % in Madihani is the regular change, the difference of 34 % between Utengule and Madihani would be due to the path improvement. Compare Methodology I in Tab.3.4-2.

Footpath	1988	1994
Utengule	61 %	65 %
Madihani	64 %	58 %

Tab. 4.3-4 Share of female footpath users

The main beneficiaries from the improved footpath are women and girls, who make up 65 % of travellers. Tab. 4.3-4 shows that since the improvement the percentage of women using the path has increased by 4 %, while on the unimproved path the percentage has decreased by 6 %.

4.3.2 Walking Time

People travelling down the escarpment on the Utengule path need on average 5h 50 min for the distance of 21 km between their home village and Ng'yekye. Fig. 4.3-2 shows that the distances did not change significantly due to the improvement. This means that even though more people are using the path, they are not coming from more remote locations, but rather that there are more people travelling from the same villages. An analysis of the catchment area of the path shows, that 91 % of the travellers stem from eight villages.

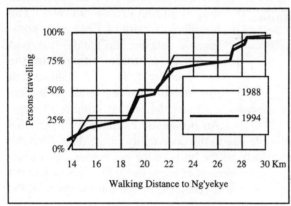

Fig. 4.3-2 Walking distances on the Utengule footpath

In 1994 the average return trip from Utengule to Ng'yekye on the improved path took 7 3/4 h. Compared with 1988 the journey was 1 1/4h faster. The walk from Madihani to the market and back took eleven hours on the same days as compared with 1988 when people walked 3/4 h longer. The delay can be explained by the strong rainfalls in the early morning of May 27, 1994, which made the path slippery and reduced the walking speed on the unimproved path, while the speed on the improved path was still faster than during the dry season in October 1988. The delay caused by the rain can be corrected by comparing the absolute changes in travel time on the improved and unimproved path. In dry weather a return trip on the improved path would be 1 3/4 hours faster than before the improvement.

Footpath Section	1988	1994	Absolute Change
Utengule-Ng'yekye	535	466	-69
Madihani-Ng'yekye	620	657	+37
Effect without rain on improved path			+106

Tab. 4.3-5 Average walking time (minutes) for a return trip Utengule-Ng'yekye

A comparison with the 1994 household survey gives similar results: over 90 % of the interviewees in Utengule and Unenamwa stated that the improvement of the path has reduced their travel time. The average time reduction for a one way trip down the escarpment was 83 minutes in Utengule and 68 minutes in Unenamwa. Assuming that on the way back up the escarpment, only half of the time is gained by the improvement, the average time saving for a return journey would be 1h 50 min.

If only half of the benefits to generated traffic are valued[19], then annually nearly 48,000 hours are saved by faster travelling after the improvement of the path. Every household in the catchment area saves annually 31 hours. If the time savings are valued with the opportunity costs of time the monetarised benefits comprise $ 2.28 per household.

4.3.3 Weight Transported

Many of the trips are undertaken to sell agricultural produce from the highlands on the market and to buy tropical products from the hot lowlands. The different seasonal harvesting periods in the low- and highlands also contribute to the exchange of products which grow on the different altitudes. On top of the agricultural products a number of consumer goods are transported up the escarpment, most notably smuggled beer and sugar from Malawi. The amount of goods transported annually up and down the improved path can be estimated at 830 tons or 540 kg per household.

The improvement did not only give rise to new trips on the path but also made the transportation of bigger loads possible. In 1988 on the said market days 4.7 t of goods were transported up and down the escarpment below Utengule. Until 1994 the weight increased by 156 % to 12 t. During this period the weight transported from Madihani on the unimproved path increased by only 111 %. Using the same reasoning as above, 45 % of the increase on the improved path can be attributed to the improvements. This means that annually,

---

19 It is assumed that the demand curve D for transport is linear. If the transport costs are reduced from C_1 to C_2 then the transport volume increases from T_1 to T_2. The graph shows that the benefits of the generated traffic can be calculated as $B_G = (C_1 - C_2) * (T_2 - T_1) / 2$, while the benefits of the already existing traffic before the improvement amount to $B_E = (C_1 - C_2) * T_1$. Thus the total benefits can be calculated as follows:
$$B = B_G + B_E = (C_1 - C_2) * (T_2 + T_1) / 2$$

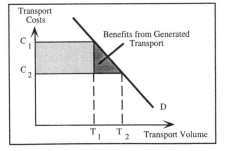

according to the pessimistic view, 133 tons (90 kg/household) would not be transported without the improvement of the path.

kg/person	1988	1994	Change
Downhill Men	6.3	10.7	+70%
Downhill Women	12,5	15.9	+27%
Uphill Men	11.6	12.7	+10%
Uphill Women	15.5	15.1	-2%
Up and down	10.6	14.2	+22%

Tab. 4.3-6 Weight per person on the
Utengule footpath

The bigger transport volumes were only partly due to the increased number of travellers, but also caused by the rising loads per person. The improvement of the path made the transport of heavy loads more secure: Tab. 4.3-6 shows that the average loads increased by 22 %. The increase of loads carried downhill can be attributed to the improvement of the path, which made transport more secure. Only men were carrying heavier goods up the escarpment. It seems that men increased their share of the loads, but they are still carrying less weight than women: 30 % of the men are using the footpath without carrying anything, while most women (89 %) carry loads. Many of the men are probably using the path for other purposes than selling or buying[20].

4.3.4 Marketing

The increased weight transported is a strong indicator that the marketing of agricultural produce increased due to the footpath improvement. The weight of the products transported down the escarpment, which had been generated by the improvement of the path can be estimated at 43 kg/household. The goods are transported to the lowland markets where the producer prices are higher than in Makete. The difference of the prices multiplied by the generated weight is an indicator for the revenue generated by the improvement of the path. On the lowland markets crops which obtain high revenues per kg, mainly wheat and beans, are sold. The generated revenues in Utengule amount to annually $ 1.87 per household. More distant villages will register lower effects, because their share of lowland marketing is lower.

	Share of	Price			Annual Benefits	
	Weight	Lowland	Highland	Difference		
	%	[$/ton]			$	$/HH
Wheat	63%	212	157	56	1,513	0.98
Beans	34%	434	350	84	1,243	0.81
Other	3%	-	-	50	130	0.08
Total					2,886	1.87

Tab. 4.3-7 Benefits from food crop marketing in Utengule

20 In 1988 about 30-40 % of the travellers used the path for social purposes or to visit health services. In 1994 no purposes were recorded.

The above mentioned approach is a minimum approach, because it only includes the immediate effects of price arbitrage and does not observe the impacts of the increase of the market production. The latter can be achieved by comparing the marketing activities of Utengule and Madihani. Fig 4.3-3 represents the mean changes in revenue which occurred after the path improvement. The average revenue from marketing in Utengule increased since 1986 by $ 13. Marketing in the lowlands nearly tripled and in 1994 more than half of the revenues (56 %) stemmed from lowland markets. In Madihani the mean revenues increased only by $ 8.20. No absolute changes of the lowland marketing occurred and the share of the revenues from lowland markets decreased to less than two percent. Assuming that the difference of the changes in Utengule and Madihani represents the benefits from the improvement, $ 5.20 per household can be attributed to the footpath improvement.

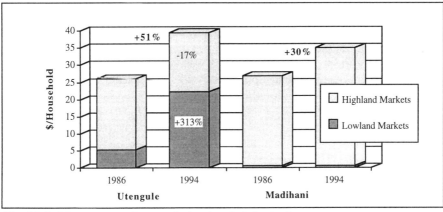

Fig. 4.3-3   Mean revenues from marketing (pessimistic view)

The latter estimation represents a pessimistic approach because the comparison of the mean values might underestimate the changes. The reason is a big change in the variation of the revenues in Utengule. While in 1986 one household was very active which increased the mean revenues significantly, the variation in 1994 is much lower[21]. The median value can give a better assessment of how much the majority of the population was benefiting from the improvements. An optimistic view estimates the changes in revenue generated by the footpath improvement in Utengule at $ 9.50 per household. Because the expenditure for

---

21 Two explanations can be given: (1) the changes in Makete were directed towards an equal income distribution or (2) the low number of sample households does not give a sufficient statistical evidence of the distribution.

87

agricultural inputs is negligible in the Bulongwa region, the increased revenue can be calculated as direct growth of income.

US $		Pessimistic View: Mean Values	Optimistic View: Median Values	Variation Coefficient*
Utengule	1986	26.10	9.10	221%
	1994	39.50	31.70	86%
	Change	13.40	22.60	
Madihani	1986	26.90	6.80	125%
	1994	35.10	19.90	111%
	Change	8.20	13.10	
Benefits	Δ Changes**	5.20	9.50	
* Variation Coefficient = Standard Variation / Mean				
** Methodology I, Tab. 3.4-2				

Tab. 4.3-8 Impact of footpath improvement on marketing in Utengule

The above calculated optimistic and pessimistic benefit assessments only concern the village of Utengule. The values indicate the upper boundary, because the generated benefits decrease with growing distance to the market. The impact assessment for the whole catchment area was achieved by taking into account the number of travellers counted on the footpath. The pessimistic view estimates the annual benefits per household in the catchment area at $ 3.31, while the optimistic view calculates increased revenues of $ 6.04. These amounts seem to be very small, but they have to be calculated for the whole catchment area, where more than 1,500 households are living. Here the annual revenues from marketing increased between $ 5,000 and $ 9,000. It has to be taken into account that the annual marketing revenues in the Bulongwa region amount to less than $ 50 per household. Thus the footpath improvement could generate a considerable increase of local income and contribute to a market integration.

Village leaders from Utengule stated that more traders are travelling up the escarpment after the improvement of the footpath. The higher demand for agricultural produce would be the reason for an increase of producer prices, especially for beans and wheat in the village. Due to lack of comparable data it could not be observed whether the price increases in Utengule were higher than elsewhere in Bulongwa. The share of internal marketing is an indicator for stronger activities of traders in Utengule, where 31 % of the crops are marketed in the village, while in Madihani this share amounts to only 9 %.

4.3.5 Effects on Security and Health

The village leaders reported, that before the improvement of the Utengule-Ng'yekye path four people died while walking to Ng'yekye. Since the improvement no fatality has occurred. It was reported that the footpath was now so sec-

Box 4-3: Transport Costs

In Makete most of the households transport tasks are undertaken by walking. A small share of the transport from the field or to the market is done by hired porters, hired donkeys or hired vehicles. Here the costs for the transport service can be calculated:

Hired Vehicle	Transport to Market	15-26 km	0.3 - 0.7 $/tkm
Hired Porters	Transport to Market	20-24 km	0.8 - 1.0 $/tkm
Hired Porters	Transport from Fields	1-12 km	0.1 - 1.7 $/tkm
Hired Donkey	Transport from Fields	1- 7 km	0.0 - 2.1 $/tkm

Hired motor vehicles are only relevant in Matamba, where the weights marketed are bigger, the revenues per ton lower and the road conditions better. Here 8 % of the weights marketed on external markets are transported by hired vehicles to the lowlands. In Makete hired Porters are either used to transport crops from the fields (14 % of tkm) or to carry the products to the external markets (10 % of tkm). The strong variation in prices indicates that the pure ton-kilometres milcage is not a sufficient measure. Other factors like steepness of the terrain, family relations or combination of trip purposes are relevant as well. The same holds true for hired or loaned donkeys, which are used for a small share of the transport burden (Fields: 2 %, Markets: 4 %) in Matamba only. Most of the donkeys are loaned without direct compensation to the donkey-owner. Only two cases could be registered where donkeys were hired.

In general the lowland prices for agricultural products are higher than on the highlands. Many farmers increase their revenues by transporting their products down the escarpment instead of selling them on the highlands. The value of headload transport can be estimated by calculating the differences of the lowland- and the highland prices and set them into relation with the tkm or the hours of transport time. The transport to lowland markets can be valued as follows:

Porterage	Bulongwa	Matamba	Makete[22]
$/tkm	2.88	4.51	4.23
$/hour	0.12	0.18	0.17

The generated income per tkm is higher than the costs for the above mentioned modes of transport. It has to be mentioned, that the transport of one tonne is associated with 50 return-trips, which are time consuming. The income per hour is above the Tanzanian Minimum Salary of 11 ¢/hour.

---

[22] Weighted average

ure that it is even used in the night. During the 1988 survey not one journey was observed before sunrise on the Utengule footpath!

The positive role of the footpath improvement in reducing the isolation of the district has been emphasised above. But increasing contacts with the external world also involve negative effects. Especially diseases like Malaria and Aids, which are more common in the lowlands, are spreading nowadays into the district. A survey of pregnant women in Mbeya Hospital (lowland) estimated the share of HIV infections at one third. Medical staff of the Bulongwa hospital reported an increasing spread of the disease on the highlands as well[23]. Out-migration and the increasing external contacts of men in particular contribute to the spread of this disease. JENNINGS (1992, p.20) states, that 22 % of all women interviewed in Makete were widowed, more than half of them in their 20's or 30's. It has to be mentioned that comparative effects occur if roads are improved.

The total benefits per household from the footpath improvement comprise $ 5 according to the pessimistic view and $ 9 according to the optimistic approach.

4.4   Intermediate Means of Transport

The MIRT Project promoted the purchase of donkeys and developed a new wheelbarrow. Bicycles were not part of the project, but their impacts shall nevertheless be assessed. Households were asked which IMT would be most useful for their transports tasks. 58 % named a bicycle, 30 % a donkey, 6 % a wheelbarrow, 3 % an animal drawn cart and 4 % did not believe that an IMT would be of any use.

4.4.1   Donkeys

The MIRT Project constructed a donkey centre in Bulongwa and one in Matamba where donkeys could be purchased and their use demonstrated. The main reason for the purchase of the animals was the high burden stemming from the transportation of heavy crops, especially potatoes from the field. As explained later on they are never used for water and firewood collection! Donkeys were only bought if their use generated an increase in revenues, which could quickly compensate the high investment costs. Only in regions with a strong market orientation like in Matamba is the purchase of a donkey rational behaviour[24]. The Bulongwa Region is more subsistance oriented, the weight harvested and marketed is much smaller and a donkey is not needed for the trans-

---

23 During the survey an astonishing high number of funerals was observed . Mainly people in the 30 - 40 age bracket were buried, after suffering from a short disease.
24 One farmer in Bulongwa Region was reported to own a donkey, but he is regarded as crazy by other inhabitants.

port of crops. Therefore the donkey centre in Bulongwa did not sell the animals which are nowadays used in the region.

In the survey villages of the Bulongwa Region not one household was in possession of a donkey, while in Matamba 33 households could be interviewed, which owned 50 donkeys. These donkeys were found only in the two villages of Mpangala and Ngoje. In 1984 one donkey was counted in Mpangala and two in Ngoje. This number increased over the following ten years to 37 and 19. In the beginning few animals were bought from the MIRTP donkey centre, later breeding activity and barter with the lowland was the main factor of growth. Today 62 % of the donkeys in the two villages are female and often used for breeding. The growth would have been much stronger, if the mortality rate of the donkeys was not so high. It can be estimated, that 15 % of the animals died during this period, probably mainly because of diseases. The climatic conditions could be one of the reasons for the high mortality; in Tanzania donkeys are mainly used in hot and dry areas, while the climatic conditions in the mountainous region of Makete District are wet and cold. Mules, would have been more appropriate animals to introduce. The high mortality rates were compensated by breeding activities, which increased the number of donkeys in Matamba region probably more, than the purchase of new donkeys from abroad.

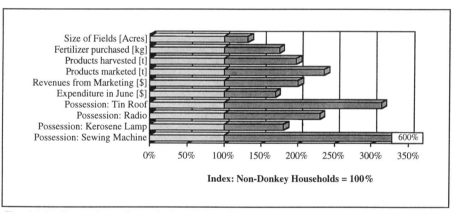

Fig. 4.4-1   Comparison of non-donkey and donkey households

A comparison in the Mpangala and Ngoje villages between donkey and non-donkey households with comparable socio-economic structures[25] shows that donkeys have strong impacts on the welfare of their owners. The donkey enables the household to cultivate bigger plots, because the transport from the field can be managed more easily. The farmers use more fertiliser, because it can be

---

25 The following features are comparable: number of household members, number of children, number of members over 45 years, male to female ratio, number of female headed households, profession of head of household and main source of cash income.

effortlessly carried home and to the fields. The bigger size of the fields and the higher inputs enable the farmer to double the amount harvested as well as the tons marketed. The revenue received from marketing activities increases from $ 120 annually for non-donkey-households to $ 241. The higher income gave rise to bigger expenditures and a better endowment of the household with kerosene lamps, radios, sewing machines and tin roofs.

Box 4-4: Case Study - Donkey Owner in Mpangala

The farmer bought a donkey in 1990 from the MIRTP Donkey centre, which in the mean time died. But he could breed three other donkeys, which he uses today for his transport purposes. They carry 4.2 t of crops home and another 4 t from the field to the street, where the products are sold to traders. The owner does not use the donkeys for transport to the grinding mill and to fetch water, because both are located close to the house. He also uses the donkey to transport products to the nearby market in Matamba, which he visits weekly. The donkeys transport 18 tkm annually and save 285 hours of arduous work and drudgery. This fact enabled the farmer to put more plots under cultivation, which were more distant from the homestead. He doubled his cultivation area and increased his income, which nowadays amounts to $ 168 annually. The higher income enables him to send his children to the secondary school.

Impacts on marketing

Non-donkey households market 2.1 t of agricultural products, while the donkey households sell 5.1 t every year. The revenue from marketing activities differs between $ 120 for non-donkey households and $ 241. The increased production is only possible with the growing use of agricultural inputs. 91 % of the donkey-households use fertiliser compared with 67 % of non-donkey households. The donkeys carry 87 % of the fertiliser purchased. In order to assess the increased income, the expenses for the additional fertiliser have to be deducted from the revenues. The purchase of a donkey generates a net income of annual $ 112 per household.

The latter assessment can be regarded as an optimistic view, because the possession of donkeys is limited to the wealthy households. FRIELING and MCHOAVU (1991, p. 20) safely state that donkey owners were relatively rich when they purchased the animals. Therefore the above mentioned assessment might overestimate the revenues generated by the donkeys. Unfortunately no study of the market production of households before and after the purchase of a donkey could be undertaken[26]. Therefore a rough assumption has to be taken in

---

26 The names of the 1986/87 survey households were deleted due to data protection.

order to assess the revenue generation according to the pessimistic view. Fig. 4.4-2 shows that the income gap between donkey and non-donkey households is smaller for the poorer households than for the wealthy ones: about half of the non-donkey households register bigger revenues than about a quarter of the donkey households. Thus they would be in the same position to purchase an animal. The large revenue gap occurs between the richer half of the households. It can be argued that a comparison of the median would be a more appropriate methodology. A pessimistic view, which is using a median assessment estimates the income generation of donkeys at annually $ 43.

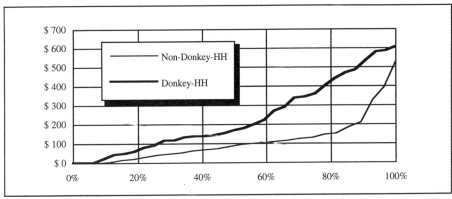

Fig. 4.4-2   Revenue of donkey- and comparable non-donkey households

Time savings

Donkeys are used to carry 15 % of the households transport burden measured in tkm. They reduce the effort and drudgery mainly of women. Not a single household was using the animal for water and firewood collection. In the first case there are no containers for the transport of water and in the second case firewood is transported in long pieces, which cannot be loaded on a donkey. The animals are mainly used for the transport of crops from the field (64 % of tkm from the field). 65 % of the tkm to grinding mills, 87 % to purchase fertiliser, but only 7 % of the tkm for marketing are transported by donkeys. Assuming that the average load of a donkey is three times that of a human being, a donkey saves annually 93 trips, 531 pkm and 133 hours (Tab. 4.4-2). If this time is valued with the opportunity costs of time

	t	tkm	Share total
Field	2.17	6.77	64 %
Market	0.39	0.47	7 %
Fertiliser Purchase	0.13	0.52	87 %
Grinding Mill	0.10	0.41	65 %
Total Donkey	**2.78**	**8.17**	**15 %**
Total Household	**30.82**	**56.10**	

Tab. 4.4-1 Total transport with donkey

the annual monetary benefits amount to $ 9.74 per household. Women benefit with 54 % of the time savings. More time could be saved if donkeys would be used for household tasks like water and firewood collection.

	With Donkey	Without Donkey	Effect
Trips	46	139	-93
Pkm	266	797	-531
Time [Hrs]	66	199	-133
Value Time [$]			9.74

Tab. 4.4-2 Time savings by donkey transport

Generation of Other Income

15 % of the trips undertaken by donkeys can be classified as transport services for other households in the village. In Mpangala 0.9 tkm per household are transported by hired donkeys. Sometimes the service is given for free, but in many cases a fee has to be paid which varies markedly. The total income generated by hiring donkeys can be estimated at $ 1.97 per year. Benefits from breeding activities and reduced spoilage of the harvest due to better transport conditions cannot be estimated in this survey.

The total annual benefits per donkey range between $ 55 and $ 124.

Demand for Donkeys

If households were asked which means of transport would be most useful for their transport tasks 30 % would choose to buy a donkey. At the beginning of the project the price for the animals was highly subsidised in order to accelerate the dissemination of the animal. After the cessation of the subsidies the purchase of donkeys nearly stopped and the remaining animals had to be sold

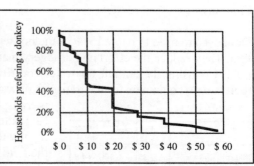

Fig. 4.4-3 Willingness to pay for donkeys

at a lower price. The average price[27] for a donkey was calculated at $ 88. The Fig. 4.4-3 shows the willingness to pay[28] of the households preferring to

27 The nominal prices were multiplied with the inflation index of the year of the purchase. Project documents give a price of $ 50-58.
28 The non-IMT households were asked which IMT would be most useful for their transport purposes and which price they would be willing to pay for it.

94

purchase a donkey, which can be estimated at $ 15 on average. 50 % of the households would be willing to pay $ 10 or less, 20 % $ 29 or less and 10 % $ 39 or less. Without any access to credit none of the non-IMT-households would be able to buy a donkey. A credit scheme could increase the purchase of donkeys. If $^4/_5$ of the price for a donkey was financed by a credit scheme then more than 40 % of the households preferring a donkey (13 % of all the households not owning an IMT) would be able to purchase an animal.

4.4.2 Bicycles

In the eight surveyed villages 54 households were in possession of a bicycle in working order, a total of only 3 % of all households. The same number of bicycles was counted, which were not in working order. In Bulongwa, where the terrain is steeper and the farmers have lower income the number of bicycles was very low. In Makete the household structure of bicycle owning households is very different from non-bicycle households. The number of household members is higher, the percentage of female headed households lower and the main source of cash income is different: only 60 % indicate agricultural marketing (non-bicycle households 78 %), 11 % receive regular salaries (4 %), 7 % are trading (1 %) and 11 % are artisans (8 %).

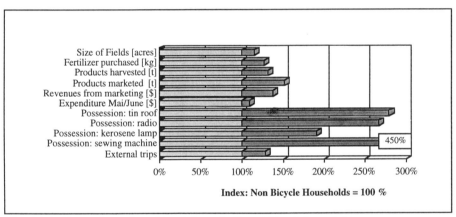

Fig. 4.4-4 Comparison of non-bicycle households and bicycle households

The bicycle households were compared with non-bicycle households with similar household structure, main source of income and geographic location. Generally it can be stated that bicycle possessing households are better off but the difference is not as big as that observed between donkey and non-donkey households. The size of the fields is bigger, they purchase more fertiliser and larger quantities of agricultural produce are harvested and marketed. The bicycle households have higher revenues, they spend more money and they have a better endowment with tin roofs, radios, kerosene lamps and sewing machines. In general, the effects for farmers in Bulongwa are stronger than for farmers in Matamba. Non-farm households register smaller effects than households with agriculture as the main cash income. It is remarkable that bicycle households undertake 28 % more external trips outside the villages. Bicycles seem to reduce isolation, especially in the Bulongwa region were motorised access is worse than in Matamba.

Impacts on Marketing

Bicycle households are marketing 1.8 t of agricultural products, while non-bicycle households only sell 1.2 t. The revenues from these marketing activities amount to $ 121 and $ 88, respectively. Higher production is possible because bicycle households purchase 27 % more fertiliser, which is quite often transported with the bicycle. These additional inputs have to be deducted from the increased revenues in order to obtain the net revenues, which can be estimated at $ 32. Farmers in the Bulongwa region register much higher benefits followed by the group of non-farmers, while the impacts for farmers in the Matamba region are much smaller. They only register 4 % higher revenues than non-bicycle farmers.

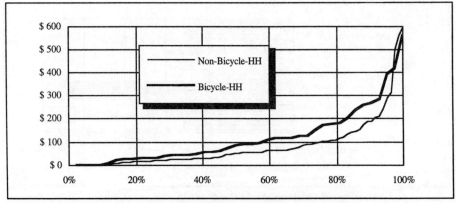

Fig. 4.4-5   Revenue of bicycle- and comparable non-bicycle households

The same argumentation as in the previous chapter could also hold true for bicycles: the vehicles are often regarded as luxury goods and the price limits the purchase to richer farmers. From a pessimistic standpoint the revenues might be overestimated. However, Fig. 4.4-5 shows, that half of the non-bicycle households have bigger revenues than 40 % of the bicycle households. The gap is much smaller than the difference in revenues between donkey and non-donkey households. A pessimistic approach comparing the median values estimates the impacts on the marketing activities at $ 28.

Time Savings

Bicycles are used to carry persons and goods. Households use the bicycle to travel annually 1,312 pkm, which is 18 % of the total pkm travelled by the household. Because the bicycles are exclusively used by men, the transport patterns reflect the typical male transport purposes: three quarters of the km are rode to external places and markets, 7 % to health facilities and 3 % to the village centre.

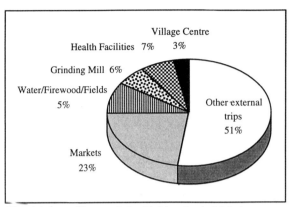

Fig. 4.4-6   Pkm carried with bicycles in Makete

Only 11 % of the transport volume is undertaken for the female task of water and firewood collection and grinding. Therefore social purposes dominate with 69 % of the trips undertaken.

Bicycles can carry considerable weights, which exceed the average headload capacity of 20 kg. Special carriers can be fitted, which allow loads of 30 kg for water, firewood and flour, 40 kg for transport of the harvested crops from the field and even over 50 kg for various transport services[29]. Annually 5.2 tkm are transported with the bicycle, of which 42 % for the female transport task to the grinding mills, 31 % for water collection, 16 % for evacuation of crops from the field, 6 % for the marketing of crops and 4 % for the purchase of fertiliser.

The bicycle saves time, because its speed is faster than walking and the bigger loads cause a reduction in the number of trips. Annually 203 hours per household can be saved by using a bicycle, 90 % due to faster travelling. Because exclusively men use the bicycle, only 59 hours can be attributed to the women, who profit from the reduction of typical female trips, that are now undertaken by men. The monetarised annual benefits from time savings amount to $ 14.89 per household.

---

29 This item was not specified in the questionnaire; it contains a variety of services for goods and persons.

Other Benefits

Because bicycle-households are not undertaking more trips to the public health services, health benefits are only generated by the reduced human porterage. 2 % of the trips with a bicycle can be classified as transport services for other households and 1 % were undertaken for commercial purposes other than marketing. The benefits generated by these trips cannot be estimated. Owners of bicycles undertake twice as many external trips as non-bicycle households, which allow them to reduce social isolation. 62 % of these trips are undertaken by bicycles. The benefits cannot be monetarised. Because generally bicycles are not loaned or hired, no income is generated.

The total annual benefits per bicycle range between $ 43 and $ 47.

Demand for Bicycles

The cheapest bicycle on the market, which is assembled in Tanzania, costs $ 68, imported bikes from China are more expensive. 80 % of the bicycles in Makete were new when they were purchased; the average price for a new bicycle was $ 74. Every bicycle was repaired 2.8 times per year and $ 3.74 had to be spent annually for spare parts. 58 % of the households not owning an IMT prefer to purchase a bicycle and would be able to pay $ 19 on average. Fig. 4.4-7 shows the willingness to pay of the non-IMT households preferring a bicycle. 60 % would pay $ 19 or less and 20 % could afford $ 39 or less. The lack of funds is the main reason for not buying a bike. If a credit scheme was introduced, covering ³/₄ of the price, more than 60 % of the households desiring a bicycle (36 % of all households) would purchase a vehicle.

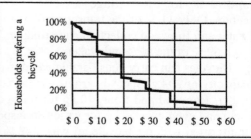

Fig. 4.4-7   Willingness to pay for bicycles

4.4.3   Wheelbarrows

The MIRT Project developed a wheelbarrow, which had the main purpose of providing a cheap means of transport and which could be produced by local craftsmen using few imported materials. About 200 wheelbarrows were produced in Makete, of which 58 were sold, 76 used by the MIRTP and 47 given as gifts during promotional activities until December 1992. Most of the vehicles were used for road works and many are possessed by NGOs or the communities.

In the eight surveyed villages, where more than 1,700 households are living, only five households possessed a functioning wheelbarrow, two more vehicles were not in working order. Two of the heads of these households were regularly employed and not farmers.

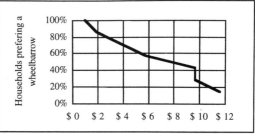

Fig. 4.4-8   Willingness to pay for wheelbarrows

In 1994 no carpenter was found, in the surveyed area who continues the production of wheelbarrows. The main reason is the lack of demand: only 6 % of the households not possessing an IMT would purchase a wheelbarrow if they had sufficient funds. In 1994 they were able to pay $ 4.83 on average. The actual price ranges between $ 9 and $ 19 depending on the quality of the timber and type of wheel used. An imported

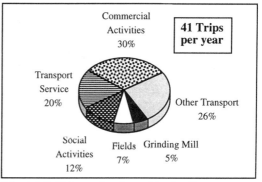

Fig. 4.4-9   Trips undertaken with wheelbarrows

wheelbarrow made of metal is at $ 40-60 much more expensive. The lack of funds seems to be one of the major restrictions for the purchase.

It is not only the price but also the utility of the vehicles which seems to set strong restrictions. Because the construction is completely of wood[30], the weight of the wheelbarrow is too heavy to make transport of goods an easy undertaking in the hilly landscape of Makete. Therefore households possessing a wheelbarrow use the vehicle only for 41 trips per year. Only 12 % of the trips were undertaken to fulfil subsistence tasks. The main purpose is for all types of commercial activities, e.g. transport of bricks, soil, dung and meat from the slaughter place to the local market. Social activities and transport services, which were undertaken for other households play an important role as well. No statement can be given about their benefits.The experience with labour-based road construction and maintenance works showed, that the wheelbarrows are useful for these tasks. Because the effects on the household level are low, the benefits cannot be assessed.

---

30 Project documents were even emphasising the advantages of wooden bearings compared with metal bearings.

4.5 Piped Water Supply

The procurement of water is an arduous and time consuming task: every household transports 33 tkm and spends 800 hours per year only on water collection. 94 % of the trips in Makete are undertaken by women and their children (BARWELL/MALMBERG-CALVO 1989). The installation of a piped water supply can have two main effects: it can reduce the transport burden of women and it can improve the health standard of households by making clean water available.

1994	Number of trips	Distance	Travel Time	Person Kilometres	Tonne Kilometres
	[Trips/a]	[km]	[hrs/a]	[pkm/a]	[tkm/a]
Bulongwa Region					
With piped water supply*	1244	0.9	576	2305	17
Without piped water supply**	1193	1.6	919	3674	31
Effect Bulongwa	52	-0.7	-342	-1369	-14
Matamba Region					
With piped water supply***	840	1.5	541	2162	20
Without piped water supply****	967	2.0	936	3746	34
Effect Matamba	-128	-0.5	-396	-1584	-14
* Kidope					
** Unenamwa, Madihani, Utengule					
*** Mpangala					
**** Ngoje, Ng'onde					

Tab. 4.5-1 Villages with and without piped water supply (Optimistic view)

A comparison between villages with and without piped water supply gives an estimation of the benefits according to the optimistic view. The distribution of the rainfalls, causing different transport patterns for water collection, necessitates a distinction between the dryer area of Matamba and the wetter highlands of Bulongwa. In Kidope one domestic point supplies 20 households, while in Mpangala 100 households are supplied. The Tab. 4.5-1 observes the villages in 1994 which have piped water supply and compares them with villages where people have to fetch their drinking water from the rivers.

In villages with piped water supply the average distance to the water is 0.5-0.7 km shorter than in villages without pipes, resulting in an annual reduction of transport of 1,370-1,570 pkm or 14 tkm. Annually 340-400 hours per household are saved by the water pipes, which is 14-16 % of the total time used for transportation in 1994. Especially women benefit from these time reductions with on average more than 300 hours. This optimistic view attributes a monetary value of $ 27.08 to the total time savings.

A pessimistic approach can be assessed in Kidope where during the observed period a piped water supply was installed by DANIDA. This methodology observes the changes between 1986 and 1994 in Kidope and compares them with the changes in the other villages of the Bulongwa region. The assessment

100

shows that the number of trips and the time spent for water collection increased in all the survey villages. The inhabitants of Kidope reacted to the installation of piped water supply by increasing the number of trips to an even greater extent than people from other Bulongwa villages. This was more than compensated by the reduction of the trip length. Compared with the other villages an average Kidope household saves annually 118 hours of walking time, which is 5 % of the total time devoted to transport. According to the pessimistic view the annual monetary value for the time savings comprises $ 8.65.The employment generated by the construction activities is added to the total benefits which range between $ 12 and $ 31 per household.

	Number of trips	Distance	Travel Time	Person Kilometres	Tonne Kilometres
Installed water supply	[Trips/a]	[km]	[hrs/a]	[pkm/a]	[tkm/a]
Kidope 1994	1244	0.9	576	2305	17
Kidope 1986	655	1.6	537	2148	25
Changes	+589	-0.7	+39	+157	-8
Villages without piped water					
Bulongwa without pipes 1994	1193	1.6	919	3674	31
Bulongwa without pipes 1986	805	2.1	762	3047	36
Changes	+388	-0.5	+157	+627	-4
Effects	+201	-0.2	-118	-470	-4

Tab. 4.5-2 Changes in Kidope after the installation of piped water (Pessimistic view)

4.6   Grinding Mills

During the surveyed period 25 grinding mills were repaired in the Makete District. Mainly women use motorised grinding mills to avoid arduous grinding by hand. The traditional division of labour reserves the task of grinding exclusively for women. 70 % of the trips to grinding mills in Makete are undertaken by women and another 20 % by women accompanied by their children. (BARWELL /MALMBERG 1989, p.77). Often the mills are not in working order, causing long walks to the next village, where the mill is still working. The repair or new installation of grinding mills has effects on the transport activities of women and their time budget.

The effects of grinding mills can be estimated by using similar methodologies as in the previous chapter. Tab. 4.6-1 compares the changes in the transport patterns of villages, where a mill was repaired with the changes that occurred without an intervention. Tab. 4.6-2 compares the differences between villages where a grinding mill is working and villages without grinding mills[31]. The ben-

---

31 If the same comparison is done for the 1986/87 survey the results are remarkably similar.

efits calculated with both methodologies show remarkably small differences. Tab. 4.6-3 lists the ranges of the benefits. The installation or repair of grinding mills shortens the walking distance by two thirds. The number of trips does not increase with shorter distances as in the case of piped water supply, because of the constant consumption of flour. A functioning grinding mill reduces the person-km by more than three quarters, the tkm by more than 90 % and the time by nearly 80 %. A motorised grinding mill saves annually over 100 hours per household, which is equivalent to 4.5 % of the total time spent on transportation. Most notably women profit with 88 hours annually. The monetary values for the total time savings range between $ 7.55 and $ 7.92.

	Number of trips	Distance	Travel Time	Person Kilometres	Tonne Kilometres
Repaired grinding mills	[Trips/a]	[km]	[hrs/a]	[pkm/a]	[tkm/a]
1994	43	1.6	35	140	2.7
1986/87	47	6.2	130	519	15.4
Changes	-3	-4,6	-95	-379	-12.7
No interventions					
1994	32	4.3	88	350	7.0
1986/87	37	4.8	79	316	7.9
Changes	-5	-0.6	9	35	-0.9
Effects (Difference in Changes)	+2	-4.0	-103	-414	-11.8

Tab. 4.6-1 Villages before and after the improvement of grinding mills (Methodology I)

1994	Number of trips	Distance	Travel Time	Person Kilometres	Tonne Kilometres
	[Trips/a]	[km]	[hrs/a]	[pkm/a]	[tkm/a]
Grinding mill working*	37	1.4	27	108	2.1
Grinding mill not working**	36	7.7	135	540	10.9
Effect	1	-6.3	-108	-432	-8.8
* Kidope, Mpangala, Ngoje, Ng'onde ** Unenamwa, Madihani, Utengule, Ihela					

Tab. 4.6-2 Villages with and without grinding mill (Methodology II)

	Number of Trips	Distance	Travel Time	Person Kilometres	Tonne Kilometres
	[Trips/a]	[km]	[hrs/a]	[pkm/a]	[tkm/a]
Methodology I	+2	-4.0	-103	-414	-11.8
Methodology II	+1	-6.3	-108	-432	-8.8
Mean	+1.5	-5.2	-106	-423	-10.3

Tab. 4.6-3 Impact assessment of grinding mills

The question arises as to whether hand grinding mills could be an alternative to motorised grinding mills. In the Bulongwa Region, where the Diocese distributed hand grinding mills, they are used by 37 % of the households mainly at home or by 16 % at the neighbours[32]. They are mostly used to grind wheat, while maize is preferably ground by motorised mills[33]. This might be the explanation why in the Matamba Region no hand grinding mills are used. The reason for the use of hand grinding mills is different: in the Bulongwa villages where the motor mill is out of order, 86 % of the hand mill users state that the next motorised mill is too far away. In Kidope, which has a working motor mill, 93 % of the hand mill users state that motorised grinding is too expensive. But the hand mill users still carry a large amount of their crops to the motor mills. JENNINGS (1992, p.29) states that in general women prefer the motorised mills especially if they need bigger quantities of flour e.g. to brew beer. They are willing to spend money and time in order to avoid the laborious task of grinding by hand. The households mainly using hand grinding mills at home are living further away from the motor mill and they walk longer to grind flour than non-owners. Even if the local motorised mill is not working, households owning hand grinding mills prefer to walk long distances to grind their flour. Therefore hand grinding mills will not be accepted as alternative to motorised mills. They will only be used to complement motor mills for people living far away from the motorised mill. An impact assessment for hand grinding mills cannot be given.

4.7   Comparison of Costs and Benefits

Intervention	Location	Standard	Main Features
Feeder Road	Matamba-Chimala	All Weather Standard	Impacts only observed in two villages, effects on agricultural marketing only in one measurable village.
Local track	Bulongwa Unenamwa	Dry Weather Standard	Low impacts measurable, but high non-monetary impacts observed.
Footpath	Utengule Ng'yekye	All weather standard	Regional importance for transport from Bulongwa Region to lowland markets
Donkeys	Mpangala, Ngoje		Donkeys only purchased in two villages in Matamba. Main use for transport from the fields
Bicycles	All villages	Not a MIRTP Intervention.	Mainly used by men for external trips, small reduction of female transport burden.
Grinding Mills	Utengule, Kidope, Ngoje, Ng'onde		Comparison of transport before and after repair or breakdown of grinding mill.
Piped Water Supply	Kidope	DANIDA Project	Reduced trip length partly compensated by higher consumption of water.
Wells	-	Not a MIRTP Intervention.	Not observed in Makete, but effects assumed to be similar as piped water supply

Tab. 4.7-1 Main features of the transport interventions

---

32 The question was: How do you mainly grind your flour? The answers are given to the number of grinding processes and not according to the quantities. Because the hand mills are used for small quantities every day the answers are not an indication of the quantities ground at home

33 Hand grinding of maize is difficult and gives poor quality flour.

4.7.1 Cost Assessment

The first column of Tab. 4.7-2 gives an indication of the total investment costs per unit of the various project components, which comprise the expenditures for purchase, installation or rehabilitation of the item. It is assumed that all of the project components have a durability of ten years. Therefore the investment costs were equally discounted over this period. In addition, the annual expenditure for maintenance and other running costs have to be added. The total annual costs are calculated per household profiting from the project component[34]. The share of wages[35] on the total costs is listed as well in Tab. 4.7-2.

A large share of the project work was fulfilled with self-help labour. It would be wrong to allocate no value to this labour only because it was contributed without any compensation. (1) The self-help labour can be regarded as a sort of tax, which is paid by the community. Often the provision of labour is more or less forced by the village authorities. (2) The opportunity costs of time, especially for women, have to be taken into account. It can be argued that during the construction work income generating activities could be undertaken[36]. Out of these deliberations the self-help and the paid labour was valued at the minimum wage for government employees, which amounted to $ 19 per month in 1994.

US$ 1994	View	Unit	Purchase/ Installation/ Rehabilitation	Annual Maintenance/ Current Costs	Annual Costs per Household	Share wages
			$/Unit	$/Unit	$/Household	%
Feeder Road	optimistic	km	3,242	185	1.94	60-70%
All Weather	pessimistic	km	4,862	277	2.91	40-50%
Local Track	optimistic	km	1,129	64	1.86	60-70%
Dry Weather	pessimistic	km	1,693	96	2.78	40-50%
District	optimistic	km	533	32	0.53	80%
Footpath	pessimistic	km	711	43	0.70	60%
Donkeys		Donkey	89	3	11.37	0%
Bicycles		Vehicle	74	3	10.88	0%
Motorised	Installation	Mill	10,918	3196	19.49	19%
Grinding Mill	Rehabilitation	Mill	157	3196	14.60	25%
Piped Water		System	79,500	795	39.75	11%
Wells		Well	2896	145	7.24	11%

Tab. 4.7-2 Cost assessment of transport interventions in Makete

---

34 For the cost assessment the same number of households is used in the catchment area of roads, footpaths and grinding mills, which had been estimated for the benefit assessment.

35 The share of local wages, which have regional effects is smaller, because salaries for engineers and administration staff have to be deducted.

36 JENNINGS (1992, p. 32) states that women comprise 80 % of the labourers, who were spending three days per week on village activities. This caused a big reduction in the time devoted to agricultural production. „Women indicate, that since they became engaged in MIRTP activities, they spent less time on their shambas and may expect reduced harvests".

Because the MIRTP was designed as a low cost project the road rehabilitation was relatively cheap compared to other road construction projects in Tanzania[37]. This was achieved by the low standard of the construction, the labour extensive works and the low wages. The feeder road was more expensive, because it was constructed to an all weather standard on steep terrain, while the dry weather track leads through an undulating landscape. The annual costs for maintenance comprise 6 % of the construction costs and vary with the road standard and the maintenance methodology[38]. If these costs are divided by the number of households in the catchment area the annual costs range between $ 2 and $ 3. The annual costs for the improvement of the footpath amount to 50 -70 ¢ per household in the catchment area.

The donkeys in Matamba were purchased for 88 $/animal[39] on top of which other investment costs like the construction costs of a stable, fences and the purchase of a donkey pannier have to be added. Annual expenditures are medicine and additional fodder. If the investment costs are discounted over a period of ten years a household pays $ 11 annually for its donkey. The owners of a bicycle paid on average $ 74 to purchase their vehicle and had to allocate $ 3.48 annually for repair. A bicycle household thus also pays $ 11 per annum for the vehicle.

A distinction can be made between installation of a new grinding mill and rehabilitation of a broken down mill. Because of the high running costs, mainly for diesel and personnel, the difference between rehabilitation and installation is not as big as might be assumed in advance. Often churches operate the mills and do not charge the full costs to the users. Instead of full cost coverage social aspects dominate the fixing of the price for the service. Because the price elasticity for grinding is not known, no statement can be given about the effects of the full internalisation of the costs.

The costs for the installation of piped water supply comprise transmission and distribution pipes, a storage tank and 5 domestic points. The investment costs per household, which amount to $ 360, are relatively high mainly due to the low population density and the small number of households served by one system. The costs can be reduced by 10 % if the construction works are done by Self-Help labour. In the mountainous landscape of Makete the construction of

---

37 The costs for the Core Rural Roads Rehabilitation Programme in Tanzania, which comprises 800 km of capital based construction works, range between 8,900 and 22,000 $/km. A commercial road rehabilitation project in Kilimanjaro Region, using 25 % of its expenditure on wages, costs 9,000 $/km. The experience with labour-based construction in Kenya and Botswana shows that the share of wages can be more than twice as high while the costs can be significantly reduced (Compare Chapter 2.4.3).

38 Usually 3 % of the investment costs are calculated for road maintenance. The project documents indicate a higher percentage, because the low standard of the works necessitates more maintenance.

39 The price for an average donkey purchased signifies the upper boundary, because many donkeys are not purchased but result from the breeding activities of the owners.

water pipes was preferred, while in the lowlands wells and hand pumps are used, which would cost only $ 66 per household[40]. Cost/benefit calculations have to take into account that water pipes are five times as expensive as wells. Because it can be assumed that wells would have the same impacts as an equal number of domestic points with piped water, they will be listed in the following tables.

4.7.2 Benefits of Transport Interventions

The following graphs show the average annual benefits per household, which are calculated as the mean value between the optimistic and the pessimistic approach. The important benefits are the time saved by the improved transportation, the monetary benefits and the improvement of the health situation. Time savings serve as an indicator for the reduction of the transport burden measured in pkm. Fig. 4.7-1 shows the changes of the time budget of an average household benefiting from the transport improvement. The biggest effects can be achieved by the installation of water supply systems followed by bicycles and donkeys. While mainly women benefit from the first intervention, the bicycle reduces the time consumption predominantly for men. Women profit more from grinding mills and donkeys. However, the feeder road also causes a significant reduction in the female time used for crop marketing. The local track and the footpath range at the end of the scale. The time savings from IMT could be significantly higher if they were used for the subsistence transport tasks as well.

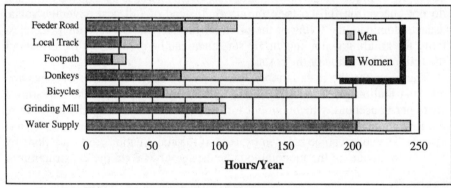

Fig. 4.7-1 Absolute annual time savings per household

European cost/benefit calculations for the assessments of the impacts of road investments include a monetary value for the time savings. In order to compare the monetary benefits of the various interventions, a monetary value for the time has

---

40 WHO estimations quantify the average costs for water supply in Sub-Saharan Africa at $ 200 per household.

to be introduced by calculating the opportunity costs of time. The marginal productivity of labour in Makete can be regarded as the opportunity costs of time. The marginal productivity was estimated with the help of the production function, described in Chapter 5.2.3. In Makete the average revenue per working hour in the field can be estimated at ¢ 16, the marginal value at ¢ 7 while the minimum wage for government employees comprises ¢ 11. Thus the assumed value of time is lower than the minimum wage. As mentioned in Chapter 2.3 and 2.4.2 the tight time budget is a severe restriction for the growth of agricultural production. Most probably the households will use the 'time savings' to expand agricultural production or for other welfare increasing activities. Hence a monetarisation of the time can be justified.

$ 1994	Region	Revenues 1986/87 or comparative household 1994 *	Average generated revenue	Increase in marketing
Feeder road	Matamba	$ 45.90	$ 4.89	11%
Local Track	Bulongwa	$ 28.04	$ 1.10	4%
Footpath	Bulongwa	$ 28.04	$ 4.68	17%
Donkeys	Matamba	$ 120.00	$ 77.50	65%
Bicycles	All villages	$ 88.24	$ 28.60	32%
* Comparison of IMT-households with non-IMT households 1994				

Tab. 4.7-3 Generated revenues from marketing of agricultural products in Makete

Another important feature are the generated revenues by increased marketing of agricultural products. In Tab 4.7-2 the revenue increases observed in the survey villages of Makete are listed. These absolute effects do not give sufficient information, because the Bulongwa and the Matamba Region have different levels of economic activity: while Bulongwa peasants are primarily subsistence oriented, the Matamba farmers are producing predominantly for the market. Therefore the generated percent increase of revenues listed in Tab. 4.7-3 give a better impression of the generated benefits. The major marketing increase is generated by the intermediate means of transport followed by the footpath improvement, while tracks and roads have lower impacts on the marketing activities.

Fig. 4.7-2 lists the total monetary benefits[41], which are made up of the monetarised time values, the increase in marketing, the salaries earned by the project implementation and other sources of income such as the hiring of vehicles, lending of donkeys etc. They are calculated as the mean between the benefits according to the pessimistic and the optimistic approach. The biggest monetary benefits result from donkeys which are mainly influenced by the strong increase

---

41 The benefits from reduced Vehicle Operating Costs are not listed here, because it is assumed they are included in the benefits by increased market production. Compare: Consumer Surplus Theory in chapter 5.2.1 and ADLER (1987, p.34)

in marketing activities. The same holds true for bicycles, which follow the donkeys at a large distance. The benefits from water supply systems, which are in place three and four, stem mainly from time savings. The benefits of the feeder road, following on place five, consist of time savings (46%), marketing increase (27 %), income by hired vehicles (21%) and income by project employment (6 %). The feeder road is performing better than the grinding mills, which benefit mostly from time savings. The footpath and the local track range at the end of the scale. An explanation for their low benefits compared to the feeder road could be also its location in a region which is primarily subsistence oriented (Bulongwa), while the feeder road connects an area (Matamba) which has traditionally a strong market orientation. The benefits generated by the track stem with 72 % from a reduction of transport time and with 26 % from increased marketing. Fig. 4.7-3, which plots the share of effects on the average benefits, shows the importance of the time savings for most of the transport interventions. While the donkeys, the bicycles and the regional footpath have a strong direct impact on market production, the grinding mill and the water supply have the biggest effects on the transport time. Road and track impacts stem from a mixture of various effects.

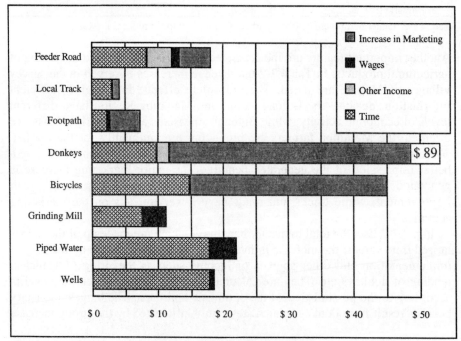

Fig. 4.7-2   Average annual monetary benefits per household

On top of the monetary benefits the non-monetary impacts have to be taken into account as well; most probably a clean water supply reduces infection and mortality rates. The track has strong effects on the health situation because the ambulance can reach the villages, while before the improvement it is reported that people were dying on the way to the hospital. The security measures taken on the improved footpath contributed to the reduction of severe and mortal accidents on the path. A monetarisation of these strong effects was not possible due to missing information.

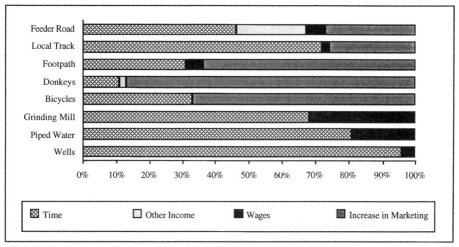

Fig. 4.7-3 Share of effects on average benefits

4.7.3 Comparison of Costs and Benefits

The absolute benefits give no impression about the cost-efficiency of the different transport interventions: Fig. 4.7-4 and Fig. 4.7-5 give an overview of the relative benefits related to the annual costs according to the optimistic and pessimistic view. The alteration between the two views is partly caused by the contrasting assumptions and by the variation of both costs and benefits.

Fig. 4.7-4 plots the relative annual time savings, which a household receives for the annual investment of one Dollar. The footpath and the feeder road have the strongest relative effects, followed by wells, local tracks, bicycles and donkeys. The reduction of time requirements by the installation of grinding mills or piped water supply is more expensive per hour saved.

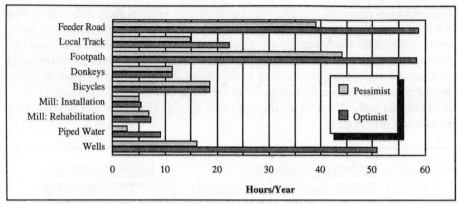

Fig. 4.7-4   Time savings per one $ annual costs

Fig. 4.7-5 plots the ratio between the total benefits (including the monetarised time savings) and the costs. The best ratio was achieved by the footpath improvement, which shows the second lowest absolute effects. This is mainly caused by the very low costs for the improvement of the path. It has to be emphasised that the improved footpath has a regional importance for transportation and no motorised link from Bulongwa Region to the lowland markets is existent. The feeder road shows the second best ratio. The main reason are the low costs of the road rehabilitation with high labour- and low machinery-input. If the costs of commercial capital based road construction projects in Tanzania was applied, the benefit/cost ratio of the feeder road would decrease to 2! Even though the track was constructed with low costs, the smaller benefits could not be compensated. Donkeys can be located on the third place regarding the B/C ratio followed by bicycles and wells. The poor performance of grinding mills can be explained by the high costs for these interventions. The B/C ratio of water supply systems is very much dependent on the costs for the system. While in the case of Makete water pipes were installed, in lowland regions mainly wells are drilled, which have lower investment costs. In this case the ratio ranges between 1.3 and 3.8.

Because some B/C ratios range below one, not all of the investments can be warranted by the above listed transport related benefits. Probably other benefits occur, which are not included in the estimation; the fact that households use their scarce monetary resources to pay the fees for grinding shows that benefits other than transport time savings must be taken into account. The alternative of grinding by hand seems to be so arduous, that the service is valued more highly than the benefits from the saved transport time. If the annual fees, which households pay for the grinding services are regarded as the total benefits, then the B/C ratio for grinding mills exceeds one. The non-monetary benefits from the improved water supply due to enhanced health situation cannot be assessed.

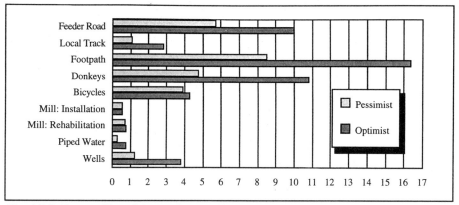

Fig. 4.7-5   Range of benefit/cost ratio according to optimistic and pessimistic view

The B/C ratios are ranked in Tab. 4.7-4 and sorted according to the sum of ranks from the optimistic and pessimistic view. Both views give a similar picture of the cost efficiency of the interventions: the footpath ranges on the first place followed by the feeder road and the donkeys. Bicycles have a higher efficiency than the water supply by wells. The local track follows in the fifth place, while grinding mills and piped water supply come at the end of the scale. All this seems to indicate that non-motorised transport interventions have the same magnitude of impacts as interventions in the motorised sector.

Transport Intervention	Optimistic Approach	Pessimistic approach	Sum of ranks
Regional Footpath	1	1	2
Feeder Road	3	2	5
Donkeys	2	3	5
Bicycles	4	4	8
Wells	5	5	10
Local Track	6	6	12
Mill: Rehabilitation	7	7	14
Mill: Installation	9	8	17
Piped Water	8	9	17

Tab. 4.7-4   Ranking of benefit/cost ratios

4.8   Conclusions

The salient feature of the regional development in the Makete District can be described as a shift from a subsistence economy towards a market orientation. The Bulongwa Region is still in an initial phase due to its peripheral location and the bad transport links, while Matamba is traditionally much more market oriented due to better accessibility. In the latter area the agricultural production is much higher, which implies bigger transport tasks for the production and marketing activities. Therefore intermediate means of transport (IMT) are much more common in Matamba than in Bulongwa. The survey found that donkeys and bicycles have very strong impacts on the market production; donkey-households are marketing twice as much and bicycle-households 40 % more than comparable non-IMT-households. Donkeys are mainly used for the transport of products from the field, while bicycles transport fertiliser and grain to the grinding mills and generate more trips outside the village than in non-bicycle-households. The main restriction for the purchase of IMT are the relative high procurement costs.

The benefit/cost ratio for the donkeys has the same magnitude as the ratio for the rehabilitation of a low cost feeder road, which gives external access to the **Matamba Region**. The biggest share of the monetary benefits from this road is generated by time savings (46 %), followed by marketing increases (27 %). The benefits from road improvements are distributed unequally among the survey villages. Two villages which had the best motorised access were stagnating, while other villages without a good road developed fast. Most remarkable was the development of a village far away from the improved road, which increased its marketing revenues much more than a village directly adjacent to the road, where the revenues even declined. Traditional trading links and walking access to the markets seem to be as important for economic growth as road access. Many inhabitants of villages within walking distance to the market prefer to carry a large portion of their goods by headload to the market in order to profit from price arbitrage. This is even the case when a good road access exists. The biggest road benefits were observed in a village beyond walking distance to the market, where heavy crops are produced and most of them evacuated with lorries. Without the improved road this production would imply long walking trips with heavy loads.

The isolation of the **Bulongwa Region** can serve as an explanation for the lower market orientation compared to Matamba: the travel to the next big external market is long and expensive, the road is in a bad condition and the only access to external markets are footpaths leading down a steep escarpment. The improvement of one of the footpaths generated a large number of new trips, increased security during travel and allowed the transport of bigger loads. The absolute impacts are relatively small mainly because of the low production in the region, but the benefit/cost ratio is favourable because the construction was very cheap. In Bulongwa a local trail connecting a village with the ward centre was widened to a local track. While the village representatives emphasised the large benefits due to increased health care and the appearance of traders in the village, the monetary benefits and the benefit/cost ratio are relatively low. An improved track in Matamba Region would probably generate bigger benefits than in Bulongwa, because the market production is generally higher. Possibly the construction of tracks could be economically warranted if they would be used by bicycle-trailers or animal drawn-carts.

Traffic avoiding measures like the installation of grinding mills and water supply have a significant impact on the time budget of rural households, but the relatively high costs entail a low benefit/cost ratio. Other non-monetary effects like the improvement of the health and environmental situation probably give higher benefits than in the transport sector itself. A solution can be the installation of low cost infrastructure like wells, which results in a higher benefit/cost ratio. It would be of great interest to research whether low cost measures like the planting of woodlots and the introduction of low consumption stoves would entail bigger effects[42].

Comparing the different transport interventions it can be concluded that motorised access is a necessary precondition for regional market integration, but it does not automatically stimulate the development process. The improvement of footpaths can be a very efficient and cheap measure to stimulate the marketing of villages within walking distance to regional markets, especially if traditional trading links exist. The increasing market integration entails the growth of production and marketing related transport tasks; in this phase the purchase of Intermediate Means of Transport can induce another sharp increase in agricultural production. The strong effects and the high benefit/cost ratio warrant the promotion of IMT. Traffic avoiding measures can be economically justified only if they are low cost interventions. Other non-transport effects probably entail bigger benefits. Comparing the absolute effects and the cost efficiency it can be safely stated that **non-motorised transport interventions have the same magnitude of impacts as interventions in the motorised sector.**

---

42 Low consumption stoves reduce the firewood consumption by 40 %, thus women would save annually 140 hours for firewood collection. The benefit/cost ratio can be estimated at about 9.

5 System Model: Nexus between Transport and Rural Development

The previous chapters described the various impacts of a single project conducted to improve the transport in a peripheral region of Tanzania. Each transport intervention had various effects and it was difficult to separate these effects from general changes or to assess the synergetic impacts of combined transport interventions. In this chapter an econometric model is set up in order to assess the nexus between transport interventions and the observed development.

Regional development in Makete can be described as a shift from a subsistence economy towards a market orientation. During this process the increasing production entails growing time requirements for labour and production- and marketing related transport activities. The limited time budget might set restrictions for the further increase of productive activities. On the other hand the rising cash income gives an opportunity to use more non-labour inputs like seeds and fertiliser, which entail a further growth in production. It is difficult to judge the effects of the various interrelations, feedbacks and restrictions. The goal of this chapter is to present a model, which visualises these interrelations by using a systems dynamics approach. The software used was developed by the Michigan Institute of Technology and its most popular applications were the world development scenarios published by the Club of Rome.

The main idea is to simulate the process of a growing market orientation of a predominantly subsistence oriented region over a period of 20 years. The initial situation assumes complete isolation of the region. The scenario technique is used to assess the impacts of various transport investments: footpaths, feeder roads, local tracks, IMT and transport avoiding measures. **The main purpose of the model is to compare the relative effects of these scenarios on regional production, marketing, disposable income and time budget.**

5.1 Basic Features of the Software: Two Examples

The basic feature of the systems dynamics approach is to assess the interrelations and feedback processes between the system elements during a given period. Initially a number of simple equations is set up to define the relationship between the system elements. By calculating these equations step by step for every period of the modelling time (e.g. one year) the systems approach is able to assess the various interrelations and feedbacks of the variables. Even simple equations can result in structures which are so complicated that a mathematical solution is often not possible (FORRESTER 1972 p. 85).

The software works in such a way that first the system relations are graphically visualised and later on the equations are defined. The main graphical ele-

114

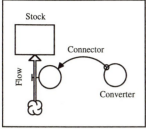

Fig.5.1-1: Basic elements

ments are stocks and flows, converters and connectors, which are plotted in Fig. 5.1-1. Stocks are reservoirs, which change only if something flows in or out. A flow transfers every period material into or out of the stock. Converters are "catchalls" which convert inputs into outputs. Connectors are used to transfer information from stocks, flows or converters to other converters or flows.

The example of a natural population growth describes a simple feedback process. On the left hand side of Fig. 5.1-2 the small model is visualised, in the middle sction the equations are given and on the right hand the output is plotted. The stock "Population" describes the number of people in a region, which was initially set at 20,000 inhabitants. Every year the new born children (flow "Births") are added and the "Deaths" are subtracted from the number of inhabitants. The number of births and deaths are regulated by the "Fertility" and "Mortality" rates (converters). Every year 5 % of the population give birth to a child and 3 % of the inhabitants die. In the first year the population grows by 400 inhabitants because 1000 children were born and 600 people were dying. The result can be described as an exponential growth of the population at an annual 2 %, which reaches nearly 30,000 inhabitants after 20 years. This example constitutes a **positive feedback loop**, which is a self reinforcing process because a growing stock (population) causes a bigger increase of the flows (births and deaths), which results in a bigger stock in the next period.

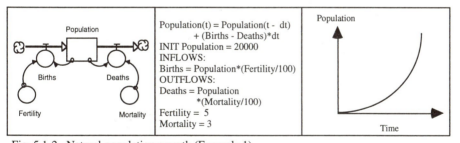

Fig. 5.1-2 Natural population growth (Example 1)

The next example in Fig. 5.1-3 shows the growth of cultivated area during a process of market integration. In the initial period 5 acres are under cultivation. The maximum acreage which one household is able to cultivate is set at 15 acres (converter "Max Acres"). During the development process the farmers will not immediately take the whole 15 acres under cultivation, but the households will clear new land every year at a special "Rate". The model assumes that annually

20 % (converter "Rate") of the difference between maximum and actual acreage are cleared (flow "Clearing"). This implies that every period a smaller acreage is cleared; in the first year 2 acres are taken under cultivation in the last year only 0.03. The curve of the "Acres" shows an asymptotic approximation towards the defined maximum acreage. After 20 years the cultivated area has grown from 5 to 14.9 acres. This process constitutes a **negative feedback loop**, which seeks to maintain conditions in line with target values.

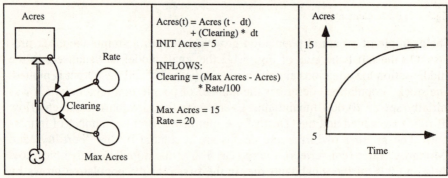

Fig. 5.1-3   Growth of agricultural area (Example 2)

Systems dynamic models combine various positive and negative feedback loops and assess the outcomes of their interactions[1]. As an example a combination of the above described positive and negative feedback loops shall be given: a growing population will clear fallow land until the whole arable land is under cultivation. If the population continues to grow, a decreasing per capita acreage will either lead to out-migration or to decreasing fertility rates due to nutritional deficits; the exponential population growth will turn into an S-shaped curve. This process can be simulated if the negative and the positive feedback loops are combined in one model. For example, the maximum acreage could be defined as function of the population and the fertility rate be dependent on the acreage per capita.

5.2   Description of the Model

The model describes the nexus of production and transport as it was observed in Makete. The main system features are given in Fig. 5.2-1. The agricultural production, which is the salient variable of the system, is determined by the following inputs: labour, cultivated area and amount of fertiliser used[2]. The biggest share of the products is consumed by the farming households and only a small

---

1   For further reading: FORRESTER (1972) and GOODMAN (1974).
2   The production function was estimated in a multiple regression described in Chapter 5.2.3.

share is traded on markets. Marketing revenues reduced by the input costs determine the agricultural income of the region. A small positive feedback loop symbolises an income multiplier: a share of the agricultural income will be spent on locally produced consumer goods, which increase the non-agricultural income of other housheolds in the region. The main negative feedback loop is caused by the transport activities, which are determined by the transports necessary for subsistence, crop production and crop marketing. A rising transport burden reduces the disposable time of the time budget. If more time is used for transport activities, less time can be spent for labour in the fields. This feedback loop establishes an equilibrium between the time needs for labour and transport. The number of working hours is rising as long as enough time is disposable. Increasing labour makes the cultivation of more plots possible and leads to a bigger acreage. A positive feedback loop exists between the amount of fertiliser and the income. If the income rises more fertiliser can be purchased in the next period. The model contains several other loops which are of minor importance.

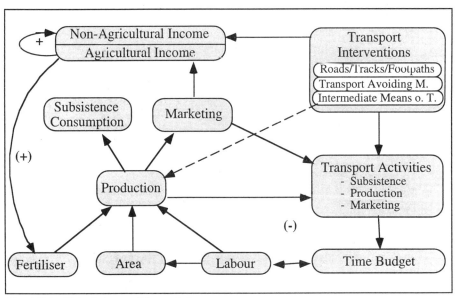

Fig. 5.2-1 Main features of the model

Transport interventions influence the transport patterns of the household and modify the time budget, which leads to a changing production. Some of the interventions have direct impacts on the household's income situation or the agricultural productivity. Five scenarios will be developed to compare the impacts of different changes in the transport system.

5.2.1 Main Assumptions

The following assumptions had to be undertaken in order to establish the model:

(i)   At the outset the region is completely isolated from abroad, the economy is basically relying on subsistence agriculture and only a small share of the products is sold in local markets in order to cover the regional demand. A simulation of the development without external marketing shows that the internal demand cannot induce a significant increase of the income. BOSERUP (1981) argues that agrarian non-market societies are unwilling to intensify their labour expenditure until population pressure and human survival needs make it imperative. New transport links and the operation of markets bring agricultural innovations to rural populations that may be adopted for other reasons than population pressure. The simulation assumes that transport investments connect the region with the rest of the world and induce a shift towards a market economy, which entails a growth of agricultural production.

(ii)   The external demand for agricultural produce is unlimited. Tanzania imports food crops because the internal production cannot satisfy the demand. It is assumed that regional production has no influence on the producer prices (WILSON 1973 p. 208).

(iii)   The government conducts an agricultural policy which favours a national food production and secures producer prices, which give sufficient incentives for the farmers. An empirical study in Tanzania 1969-1987 by ERIKSON (1993) shows that peasants respond to price incentives in general[3], but this effect was partly neutralised by the rationing of the consumer goods market. DIERKS (1995 p.46) observed positive price elasticities for various products in Makete between 1987 and 1994 . The improvement of the marketing conditions even caused production increases of other crops, for which the real prices declined slightly.

(iv)   A free transport market exists, which allows the free purchase of vehicles and unhindered service an all roads, assuring the evacuation of all crops offered by the farmers.

(v)   The sectoral division of labour is not changing significantly during the observed period. This assumption probably does not reflect the real development, because increasing productivity in the agricultural sector would probably entail a growth of other sectors. This assumption was set in order to keep the influences of other factors low.

(vi)   The negative experience during the socialist decades leads the farmers to conduct a risk adverse strategy, which primarily secures the family's sub-

---

3 Compare KILLICK (1993), pp 203 and 207

118

sistence by its own production (BRYCESON 1990, p.15). Reactions to market incentives are delayed during the first six years.

(vii) The time saved by transport interventions will be entirely used for direct productive or production related transport activities[4].

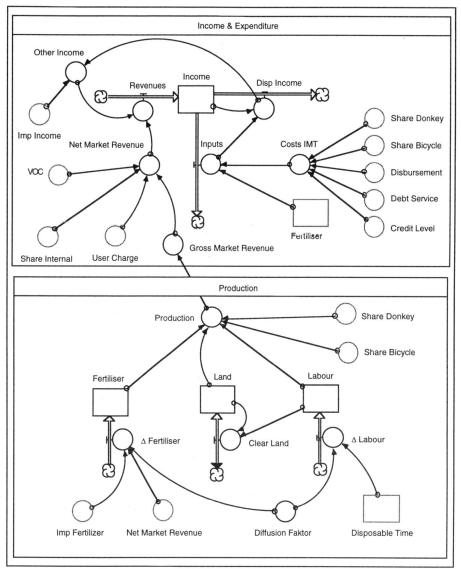

Fig. 5.2-2   The system of income, expenditure and production

4   Compare however the deliberations in Chapter 2.4.2.

5.2.2 Income and Expenditure

A visualisation of Income and Expenditure is given in the upper box in Fig. 5.2-2. The "Revenues" of the household consist of the "Net Market Revenue" from agricultural products traded and "Other income" from non-agricultural sources including regular wages, income from artisan work or trading and cash remitted by relatives. The "Net Market Revenues" are dependent on the transport costs of carrying the products to the market. They are obtained by subtracting the transport expenditure (Vehicle Operating Costs "VOC" and "User-Charges"[5]) from the "Gross Market Revenue", which is the result of the production process that will be explained in the next chapter. The addition of "Net Market Revenues" and "Other Income" equals the total "Income" of the household. Before the "Disposable Income" is obtained the costs for the "Inputs" fertiliser and for IMT (Scenario 5 only) have to be subtracted.

The saving rate of a subsistence society is very low[6]. Therefore it is assumed that the households spend all their cash completely until the next harvest. An analysis of the expenditure patterns in Makete showed, that 10 % of the expenditure is spent for regionally produced consumer goods and services[7]. The connector between "Disposable Income" and "Other Income" signifies that an increase of the income results in a growth of "Other Income" in the following year. This small feedback loop causes a slight increase of the total income during the observed period of 20 years. It cannot be the engine for an autonomous regional development process.

5.2.3 The Production Process

The production process is visualised in the lower box in Fig. 5.2-2. The households have their main source of cash income from the "Net Market Revenue", which is determined by their agricultural "Production". The amount of harvested products depends on how much input the households use: the farmers have the possibility to change the number of working hours in the fields ("Labour"), the area used for crop cultivation ("Land") and the amount of "Fertiliser" measured in kg. If the total value of the agricultural products is reduced by subsistence consumption, which is assumed to be constant during the simulation period, then the "Gross Market Revenue" mentioned in the previous chapter is obtained.

---

5 "Share Internal" indicates which share of the products is not transported to markets because it is sold within the village (Chapter 5.2.4). The VOC are set at 50 ¢/tkm. The costs include a partly empty return voyage, higher costs for the travel on an earth road, evacuation of the crops with Pick Ups and small trucks and the profit of the vehicle owner. User charges are explained in Chapter 5.4.

6 Anybody who has ever tried to change a bill worth $ 10 knows about the lack of cash in rural areas of Africa.

7 This is made up as follows: 2 % regionally produced consumer goods, 2 % taxes and fees, 4 % social expenditure and 2 % other local expenses.

120

Thus an increase of the inputs will automatically result in a growth of the "Gross Market Revenue" and "Disposable Income".

It is assumed that the households react to the changing marketing conditions by increasing their agricultural production. Because the farmers have practically no assets, they only have the possibility to work longer in their fields. The increase of their labour time is determined by their "Disposable Time"[8] budget for transport and labour purposes, which will be defined in Chapter 5.2.5. It is assumed that every year the household increases the amount of "Labour" used in the fields by $1/6$ of their "Disposable Time"[9]:

$$\text{"}\Delta \text{ Labour"} = 1/6 * \text{"Disposable Time"}$$

Fig. 5.2-3 shows that this negative feedback loop causes an asymptotic approximation of the "Labour" curve. The limiting value is determined by the initial "Disposable Time" reduced by the increasing time requirements for transport activities caused by the growing production. This negative feedback loop has a strong influence on the whole model.

The household's "Labour" time in the fields is the main determinant for the growth of the agricultural production. It is assumed, that the agricultural area under cultivation ("Land") is dependent on the "Labour" input; if farmers increase their working time in the fields, the number of acres grows synchronous with the increase of the "Labour" time[10].

The Makete survey demonstrated that an average household spends 10 % of its "Net Market Revenues" on the purchase of fertiliser[11]. Here a positive feedback loop exists: the growing revenues, resulting from the longer working time in the fields, allow higher expenditures for the purchase of fertiliser, which will cause another increase of production.

The Fig. 5.2-3 shows the growth of inputs in Scenario 2, which will be defined later on. All inputs show an asymptotic approximation to a limiting value, which is mainly determined by the limited time budget. Depleting time reserves will set restrictions on the households to further increase their labour in the fields; the growth process slows down. Restrictions can also be assumed due

---

8   The "Disposable Time" is set for the initial period. This amount is reduced in every period by the increasing time requirements for trips and for labour on the fields. See also Chapter 5.2.5.

9   The factor 1/6 only determines the speed of the growth process but does not change the results from the scenarios. The factor was set in order to deplete completely the disposable time budget during the modelling period for all scenarios.

10 This is achieved by clearing land if the labour input per acre rises above the Makete average.

11 A linear regression (Multiple $R^2 = 0.5$) shows that the amount of fertiliser grows with the revenues but decreases with the acreage under cultivation. In Bulongwa, where land is available in abundance no fertiliser is used, while in Matamba fertiliser compensates the smaller acreage. In the model it makes no sense to decrease the use of fertiliser with increasing acreage. Therefore the amount of fertiliser will be linked directly to the "Market Revenue" using the mean expenditure for fertiliser observed in Makete.

121

to the risk averse behaviour of the farmers. After the transport interventions not all farmers take advantage of the new opportunities. During the first third of the modelling period the growth process is slowed down by the variable "Diffusion Factor"[12], which regulates the "Labour" and "Fertiliser" inputs.

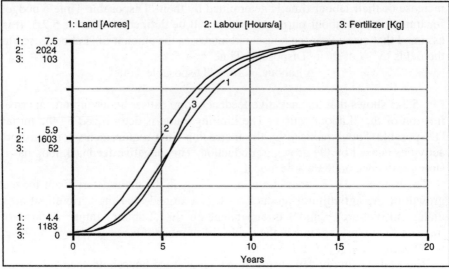

Fig. 5.2-3   Increase of inputs in Scenario 2

Estimation of the Production Function

The Production function describes the nexus between the inputs and the total output of the agricultural production. The input variables "Labour", "Area" and "Fertiliser" were achieved as the results of a multiple regression using the data from the 1994 Makete survey.

A data problem occurred because the measurement of the labour input was subject to uncertainties:

- The number of labour days was assessed by multiplying the working periods with the number of trips. Small misjudgements might lead to big mistakes.
- The duration of the labour days was not measured.
- A few households employ labour in their fields, which was not registered during the survey.
- Some households might be reluctant to give correct data about their production.

---

12 It is assumed that during the first year only 1/6 of the farmers react to the market incentives. This amount increases annually by 1/6 until the sixth year when all farmers react as presumed.

In order to eliminate these problems the data set was reduced by the extreme values of the ratio of the crop production per labour day. The frequency histogram given in Fig. 5.2-4 shows that the values above 3.6 $/day can be regarded as extreme values or outliers. The number of extreme values comprises 8 % of the whole sample. Another 8 % of the cases were deleted on the lower end of the frequency distribution. Thus, the number of valid cases is reduced by 16 % to 191.

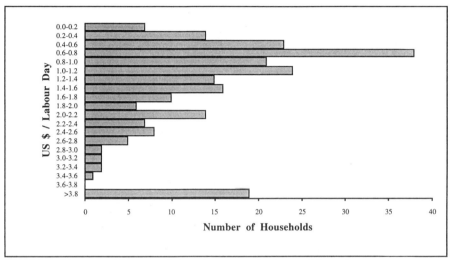

Fig. 5.2-4   Frequency histogram of the ratio crop production per labour day

A non-linear production function of the Cobb-Douglas type was chosen, which has the following general form:

$$Y = k * A^{\alpha} * B^{\beta} * C^{\chi} \ldots$$

Y	= Agricultural output measured in Dollars
A, B, C, ...	= Independent variables: Area, Labour, Fertiliser, Dummies
$\alpha, \beta, \chi, \ldots$	= Coefficients to be estimated in the regression, with $\alpha, \beta, \chi > 0$
k	= Constant to be estimated in the regression

The production function is estimated according to the logarithmic function:

$$\ln Y = \ln k + \alpha * \ln A + \beta * \ln B + \chi * \ln C \ldots$$

The dependent variable is the agricultural output measured in US$. The relevant independent variables are the following inputs: agricultural area measured in acres, the number of working days on the fields and the amount of fertiliser measured in kg. Dummy variables were created for households possessing bicycles, donkeys or several IMT. The regression was conducted in a stepwise

123

method, which produced significant results. The adjusted R^2 used for multiple regressions amounts to 0.65. If some single villages are regarded the outcome is significantly higher. The F-significance, testing the R^2 against 0 is very satisfying for all of the regressions.

	All Villages	Bulongwa	Matamba	Mpangala	Utengule
Adjusted R^2	0.65	0.58	0.70	0.84	0.89
F-Significance	0.0000	0.0000	0.0000	0.0000	0.0000
Number of Cases	191	77	108	40	11

Tab. 5.2-1 Results from log-linear regressions

Variables	Coefficient α, β, χ	Standard Regression Coefficient	T-Significance	Tolerance
Labour [days]	0.440365	0.455838	0.0000	0.563966
Land [acres]	0.372422	0.324492	0.0000	0.591773
Fertiliser [kg]	0.049917	0.169441	0.0003	0.863331
Dummy Donkey	0.448120	0.183601	0.0001	0.865809
Dummy Bicycle	0.289104	0.160612	0.0005	0.881359
Dummy IMT	0.726777	0.145727	0.0008	0.974751
Constant k	9.294093		0.0000	

Tab. 5.2-2 Coefficients and statistical tests for the regression

The coefficients and the constant show a very high T-significance and the relatively high tolerance values seem to exclude the possibility of a collinearity of the variables. The Durbin Watson-Coefficient which is an indicator for the autocorellation, is located in the acceptable interval[13] between 1.5 and 2.5. In Fig. 5.2-5 the cumulated frequency of the residuals are compared with the expected normal distribution, which is represented by the diagonal on the graphs. The graph visualises, that the residuals of the estimated Cobb-Douglas function are almost normal distributed.The Production function plotted in Fig. 5.2-6 describes the growth of the production of different household types according to the results from the regression. If house-

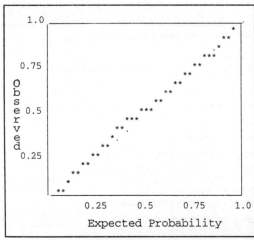

Fig. 5.2-5 Normal probability plot of observed and expected residuals

---

13 BROSIUS (1995) p.491, the Durbin Watson-Coefficient was calculated at 1.85.

124

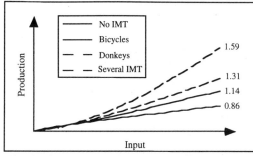

Fig. 5.2-6   Production function for different
households in Makete

holds which do not possess an IMT increase their inputs by the factor λ, their production will grow by $\lambda^{0.9}$. Households owning a bicycle will increase their production by $\lambda^{1.1}$, households with donkeys by $\lambda^{1.3}$ and with several IMT even by $\lambda^{1.6}$. This means that **the possession of donkeys or bicycles will enable the household to change its productivity from decreasing to increasing returns to scale.**

The question arises, if the growth in productivity stems only from the possession of the IMT or whether only active households which already have high productivity are able to purchase these means of transport. On the other hand it can be argued that the IMT enable the farmers to produce more efficiently:[14]

• Reduced effort and drudgery of human porterage might increase the labour productivity.
• Pest damage and spoilage due to transport at crop harvest time is reduced.
• It is possible to cultivate further distant plots, where fertility might be higher.
• Distant markets where producer prices are higher are more easily accessible.

Because the sample of households with several IMT is fairly small (10 cases) only the production functions of bicycle and donkey posessing households will be used henceforth.

5.2.4   The Transport Sector

The transport sector, given in Fig. 5.2-7, was calibrated by the data collected in Makete. The most important variable is "Trans Time", which represents the total time used for the household's transport activities. It is the sum of the time used for market trips ("Time Market"), the time for the trips to the fields ("Time Fields") and the other transport ("Other Time"), which consists mainly of transport for subsistence tasks like water and firewood collection.

The trips to the fields are determined by the number of working days ("Labour") and the distance from the homestead to the fields ("Dist Field"); the latter grows with the enlarging cultivated area ("Land")[15]. The transport to the markets is more difficult to assess: the Makete survey showed that a part of the

---

14 Compare AIREY (1992)
15 Result of linear regression of acreage and distance to the fields:
Distance Fields = 2.89 + 0.14 * Acres

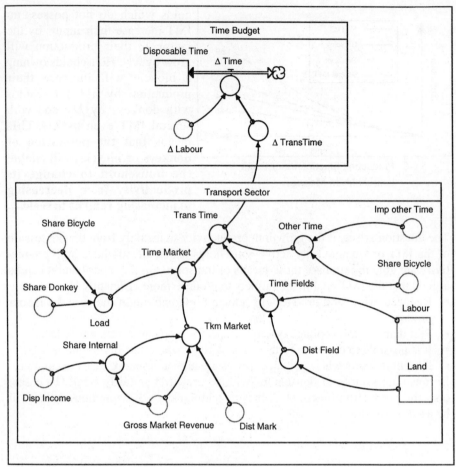

Fig. 5.2-7   The transport sector and the time budget

"Disposable Income"[16] is spent in the village to purchase food crops from other farmers. Therefore households market a share of their agricultural products internally ("Share Internal") and transport the remaining amount to external markets. The tkm for market transport ("Tkm Market") can be achieved by multiplying the weight of products marketed ("Gross Market Revenue") with the distance to the markets. It is assumed that the internal marketing distance is the average distance to the village centre. The distance to the external market or to the collection point ("Dist Mark") varies with the scenarios. The "Tkm Market" is the basis to estimate the time for marketing trips ("Time Market") by using the

---

16 It was estimated that in Makete 12 % of the expenditure was spent for locally produced food crops.

126

"Load" factors for different transport modes. In the Scenarios 1-4 all products are transported by headload with an average "Load" of 20 kg per trip. In Scenario 5 donkeys or bicycles are used for many transport purposes and the average load can be increased to 40 kg per bicycle and 60 kg per donkey. It has to be assumed that not all the crops are transported with the IMT: only 40 % of the products are carried by the households possessing a bike, but 80 % by households owning a donkey. The variables "Share Donkey" and "Share Bicycle" indicate which percentage of the households possess an IMT. The time which households use for subsistence transports ("Other Time") can be influenced by the possession of bicycles and transport avoiding measures ("Imp Other Time"). The use of donkeys for subsistence transport is plausible, but was not observed in Makete.

The households in the model region increase their marketing of agricultural products during the observed period. This expansion entails growing transport needs for production and marketing related transports. Fig. 5.2-8 shows the change of the total transport time ("Trans Time") in Scenario 2. The time used for subsistence trips ("Other time") which dominates total transport time remains constant, while the time for market trips and trips to the fields increases and entails a growth of the total time devoted for transport ("Trans Time").

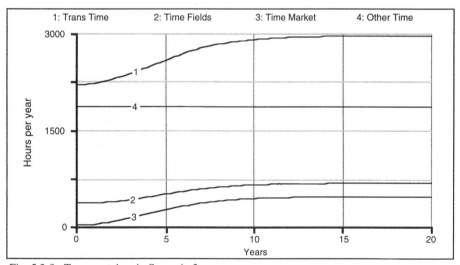

Fig. 5.2-8 Transport time in Scenario 2

The different transport interventions in the various scenarios discussed later on have direct impacts on the following variables:
- "Dist Mark": the distance to the markets and collection points are changed by the construction of roads.
- "Imp other time": subsistence transports are reduced by transport avoiding measures.
- "Share Bicycles", "Share Donkeys": the purchase of IMT is promoted.

A change of the variables has an impact on the total time used for transport purposes ("Trans Time") which entails a change of the "Disposable Time" budget. With the help of these changes the whole production system is influenced.

5.2.5   The Time Budget

The "Disposable Time" budget plotted in Fig. 5.2-7 is the steering element in the whole model. It is assumed that every household has a constant time budget which is **exclusively used for the labour in the fields and for transport purposes**. The time for the household's non-transport-tasks and for leisure time is excluded from the "Disposable Time" budget. The time budget is set at 5,000 hours per year. A detailed discussion of the assumptions including sensitivity tests is given in Chapter 5.4. This budget is reduced by the time requirements for transport and labour in the fields. In the first year before the transport interventions are undertaken a household uses 3,400 hours for labour and transport in order to cover its subsistence needs. This implies that 1,600 hours are still disposable. The increasing production in the following years entails a growth of the transport and labour time: every year of the simulation period the increased time requirements for labour ("Δ Labour") and transport (Δ Trans Time) are subtracted from the "Disposable Time" budget. Fig. 5.2-9 shows the depletion of the "Disposable Time" budget, while the amount of time used for labour and transport increases during the development process[17]. The effects of the different scenarios are achieved by distributing the disposable time between labour and transport. It can be stated that in none of the scenarios does the labour time exceed the household's time for transport activities!

The depletion of the time budget is the reason for the reduced growth of labour and transport time. Fig. 5.2-3 shows that the "Disposable Time" determines the growth of "Labour" in the fields. This is the most important feedback loop in the system, which regulates the production system. A change in the transport system reduces the time requirements for transport and leaves more time for directly productive labour. The model shows, that different transport

---

17 It should be mentioned that the sum of "Disposable Time", "Trans Time" and "Labour" remains constant at 5,000 hours. The growth of "Δ Labour" was regulated in a way, such that for all scenarios the disposable time budget is completely depleted after 20 years.

128

interventions have different impacts on the time budget and thus on production and income.

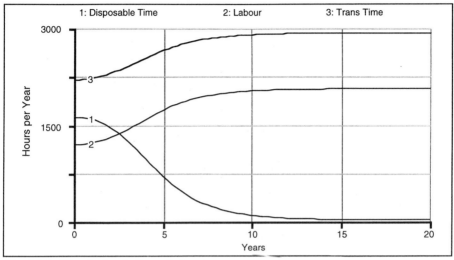

Fig. 5.2-9   Time budget in Scenario 2

5.3   Impacts of Transport Interventions

Five scenarios were developed to assess the impacts of different transport interventions in a region which is initially completely isolated and primarily subsistence oriented. Only a small share of agricultural production is traded on the village markets to satisfy local demand which is caused by the non-agricultural income. Without any modification of the transport system no change of the production and marketing patterns would occur and the economy would only increase with the growing population. The model region was designed with an idealised spatial structure based on the data from the Makete district. A sketch of the region and the main features of the scenarios are listed in Fig. 5.3-1. The region is made up of 19 villages of the same size which are equally distributed over the area and where 20,500 persons live in 4,180 households.The effects of the scenarios are presented for an average household in the region.

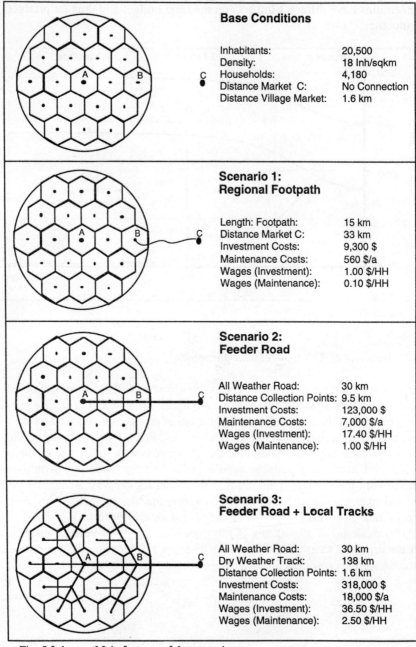

Base Conditions

Inhabitants:	20,500
Density:	18 Inh/sqkm
Households:	4,180
Distance Market C:	No Connection
Distance Village Market:	1.6 km

Scenario 1:
Regional Footpath

Length: Footpath:	15 km
Distance Market C:	33 km
Investment Costs:	9,300 $
Maintenance Costs:	560 $/a
Wages (Investment):	1.00 $/HH
Wages (Maintenance):	0.10 $/HH

Scenario 2:
Feeder Road

All Weather Road:	30 km
Distance Collection Points:	9.5 km
Investment Costs:	123,000 $
Maintenance Costs:	7,000 $/a
Wages (Investment):	17.40 $/HH
Wages (Maintenance):	1.00 $/HH

Scenario 3:
Feeder Road + Local Tracks

All Weather Road:	30 km
Dry Weather Track:	138 km
Distance Collection Points:	1.6 km
Investment Costs:	318,000 $
Maintenance Costs:	18,000 $/a
Wages (Investment):	36.50 $/HH
Wages (Maintenance):	2.50 $/HH

Fig. 5.3-1   Main features of the scenarios

130

Scenario 1: Footpath Construction

Initially no transport link between the region and the external market C exists. It is assumed that a natural barrier like a river or a steep escarpment, as in the case of Utengule, obstructs any trade between the region and the market C. The distance between village B and the market C comprises 15 km; the same length as the distance between Utengule and Ng'yekye. The construction of a footpath simulated in Scenario 1 causes an increase in the transport to the market place. The scenario calculates the behaviour of an average household in the region: the average distance to the market is 33 km, which is exclusively covered by walking. The participation of the villages will probably decrease with increasing distance to the market. The construction costs at $ 9,300 are relatively low as well as the wages earned by inhabitants of the region. Because there is no road access into the region, fertiliser cannot be purchased and thus will not be used as an agricultural input.

   Curve 1 in Fig. 5.3-2 shows that the labour input after a time of adaptation will increase exponentially. But the restrictions in the time budget limit the labour input to less than 1,900 working hours per year. The main reason are the growing transport needs especially for trips to the markets, which occupy nearly 700 hours per year (Fig. 5.3-3 curve 1). Fig. 5.3-4 shows that the construction of a footpath induces a growth of the total production of $ 70. The disposable income plotted in Fig. 5.3-5 could even increase slightly more due to the employment revenues during the construction phases and the regional income feedbacks.

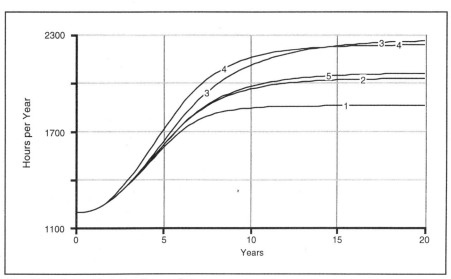

Fig. 5.3-2 Labour input in all scenarios

The Scenario 1 reflects the situation of the Bulongwa Region in 1994: the road access is very bad and a big share of the products are transported by headload over long distances to the external markets. The survey observed marketing revenues in Bulongwa of $ 48 which the model simulates after a period of four years after the footpath construction. After 10 years of simulation the revenue stagnates at $ 80 per household. The transport conditions and the limited time budget do not allow a further increase of the market production. New transport interventions are necessary to make another increase of the market production possible.

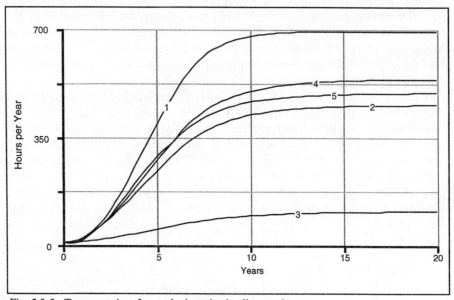

Fig. 5.3-3   Transport time for marketing trips in all scenarios

Scenario 2: Construction of a Feeder Road

This scenario simulates the construction of an all weather road, which leads from external market C to regional centre A (see Fig. 5.3-1). 30 km are constructed with labour based technologies and low cost standard. The investments amount to $ 123,000 and the annual maintenance to $ 7,000. Three points are installed on this road, where agricultural produce are collected and inputs delivered. The farmers still have to transport their products over an average distance of 9.5 km. Curve 2 in Fig. 5.3-2 shows that the labour input could be increased significantly compared to Scenario 1, which is mainly due to reduced transport time for marketing trips (Fig. 5.3-3). The growth of the inputs made it possible to increase agricultural production by $ 160, which is much stronger than the

132

growth in the previous scenario. The disposable income[18] (Fig. 5.3-5) did not grow as fast as the production, because the transport costs reduce the marketing revenues. It can be stated that the economy is stagnating after a rapid growth of the production of up to 10 % per annum during the first half of the simulation period. Time restrictions are the main reason for the declining inputs.

Scenario 2 can be compared with the situation in Matamba Region in 1994 where an all weather road gives access for motorised vehicles and allows the evacuation of agricultural produce. The average marketing revenues in Matamba amount to $ 122, which the model simulates 8 years after the road construction. After 15 years of simulation the revenues stagnate at $ 137. This signifies, that without further technological changes the regional development will be hampered in the near future.

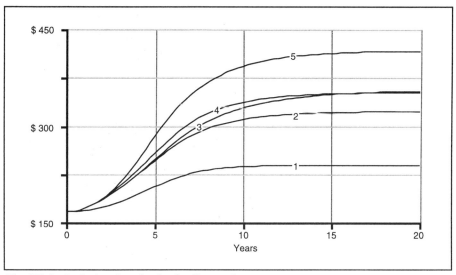

Fig. 5.3-4   Agricultural production in all scenarios

Scenario 3: Motorised Access to all Villages

The third scenario assumes that every village receives access to a dry-weather track, while the regional centre is accessible by an all-weather-road as assumed in Scenario 2. The low-cost-construction of 138 km of local tracks and 30 km of the feeder road costs $ 318,000 and annual maintenance amounts to $ 18,000. The farmers can market all their products in the village centre, which is on average 1.6 km away from their homestead. This scenario computes the least time

---

18 The income curves for the scenarios 2 to 5 show a decline after the first year, which is due to declining employment after the termination of the construction phases.

requirements for marketing trips (Fig. 5.3-3) and allows an increase in labour time in the fields (Fig. 5.3-2). After 20 years, production increased by $ 189 and disposable income grew by $ 146. The higher transport costs reduce the net benefits of the Scenario 3: compared to Scenario 2 the disposable income increases by only $ 18 per household. The question arises as to whether the higher investment and maintenance costs for the local tracks can be warranted or whether other investment opportunities with higher rates of return exist. The following two scenarios will try to answer this question.

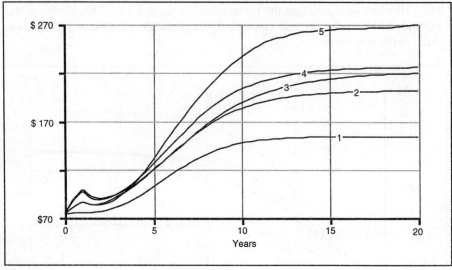

Fig. 5.3-5 Disposable income in all scenarios

Scenario 4: Transport Avoiding Measures

Scenario 4 tries to relieve the household's time budget by reducing the household's transport for subsistence tasks. Every village receives low cost wells, which reduce the average walking distance to the water source as observed in Makete. The number of trips for firewood collection are reduced by 40 % if low consumption stoves are introduced. Both measures cause a reduction in the subsistence transport time ("Other Time") of 388 hours per year. On top of that the feeder road constructed in Scenario 2 will be built as well. The total investment costs amount to $ 473,000 and annual maintenance comprises $ 10,000. If the costs are added over the whole simulation period (without discounting) then the total amount is comparable with the cumulated costs of Scenario 3.

The time savings by the reduction of subsistence transport are to 55 % used to increase the labour time, which gives rise to production growth and entails an increase of production related transport activities. The total production grows by

134

$ 186, which is slightly lower than the increase induced in Scenario 3 but well above the increase in Scenario 2 (Fig. 5.3-4). The model shows that transport avoiding measures can have the same impacts on production as the construction of local roads. If the disposable income is regarded, the transport avoiding measures have a slightly stronger impact than the track construction due to lower transport costs. The impacts on the health- and environmental situation cannot be assessed in monetary terms.

Scenario 5: Promotion of Intermediate Means of Transport

In Scenario 5 the effects of the promotion of IMT are assessed. The precondition is the construction of a feeder road, as simulated in Scenario 2. In addition, donkeys and bicycles are promoted by the provision of credit. A revolving credit fund is installed, which provides credit for the farmers, who want to purchase a donkey or a bicycle.The field study shows that 30 % of the households want to purchase a donkey and 60 % a bicycle. The main restriction seems to be lack of funds. 82 % of the households that prefer a donkey and 92 % of the households wishing to purchase a bicycle state that the IMT are too expensive for their small budgets. While the price for a donkey is estimated at $ 88 the willingness to pay (WTP) comprises only $ 20. Bicycles cost $ 74 and the WTP is estimated at $ 15. Scenario 5 assumes that the IMT will be credited at 75 %. The purchase of IMT in the model is related to the development of the "Marketing Revenues". The willingness to pay observations already mentioned in the Chapters 4.4.1 and 4.4.2 were set in relation to the marketing revenues and a demand curve was derived for the donkeys and bicycles. It is assumed that the IMT can be used for ten years until they break down or die. In this case another IMT will be purchased using the credit system again.

Credit Level	Share Bicycle	Share Donkey	Increase of Disposable Income	Annuities Donkey Households	Annuities Bicycle Households	Credit Fund
0 %	13 %	2 %	$ 143	0	0	0
50 %	29 %	11 %	$ 172	$ 12	$ 10	$ 34,000
60 %	34 %	13 %	$ 179	$ 15	$ 12	$ 53,000
70 %	41 %	15 %	$ 189	$ 17	$ 14	$ 73,000
80 %	46 %	21 %	$ 204	$ 18	$ 15	$ 98,000
90 %	50 %	27 %	$ 219	$ 22	$ 18	$ 133,000

Tab. 5.3-1 Effects of different credit levels at the end of the simulation period

The growing revenues during the development process will enable an increasing number of the households to purchase an IMT. In Scenario 5 the share of donkey possessing households increases from 0 % to 18 % while the share of bicycle owning households reaches 44 % at the end of the simulation period. The possession of IMT causes a shift of the production function from decreasing to

135

increasing returns to scale, which gives rise to a rapid growth of the agricultural production. At the end of the simulation period the production per household increased by $ 250 (Fig. 5.3-4), which is $ 60 more than in the best road scenario (Scenario 3). The disposable income increased by nearly $ 200 (Fig.5.3-5), which is $ 44 more than in Scenario 4. The strong impacts from the IMT stem partly from reduced time requirements for production and marketing related transport, while a considerable share is caused by the change in the production function.

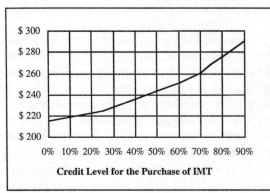

Fig. 5.3-6   Impacts of the credit level on disposable income after 20 years

Scenario 5 assumes a credit level of 75 %. The variation of this level can influence the results significantly. Table. 5.3-1 shows the effects of different credit levels. If the IMT are simply promoted but no credit system is installed, than after 20 years 13 % of the households would be able to purchase a bicycle and only 2 % a donkey. The disposable income would grow by $ 143, which is $ 15 more than the increase in Scenario 2. Stronger effects can be achieved if the credit level is increased. If 90 % of the price could be covered by credits then 50 % of the households would own a bicycle and 27 % a donkey. This would increase the disposable income by $ 219, which is $ 90 more than in Scenario 2 or $ 72 more than Scenario 3. Fig. 5.3-6 plots the effects of different credit levels on the disposable income at the end of the simulation period.

One of the main problems connected with small scale credits are the high overhead costs. Therefore a real interest rate of 12 % was assumed[19]. Another problem is the low repayment quota. Therefore it is assumed in the model that only 80 % of the credits are paid back. The Grameen Bank in Bangladesh seems to be a good example how these high costs can be externalised[20]. The responsibility for the credit distribution and the debt service payments lies within a group of creditors. Group pressure and social responsibility towards the other members seems to be the main reason for the high repayment quota of over 98 % in Bangladesh.

---

19 The real interest rates of small scale credit schemes for IMT range between 3.5 % in Burkina Faso and 11 % in Sri Lanka and Bangladesh (International Forum for Rural Transport and Development, Forum News, Vol. 2, June 1994).
20 See Neue Züricher Zeitung 24.6.1995 "Auch arme Menschen sind kreditwürdig".

The West African 'Tontine', a traditional female saving club[21], could be an appropriate form of organising the credit system in Africa. Credit distribution to women could solve many of the problems concerning IMT:

- Nowadays in 63 % of the households men have the control over the resources (JENNINGS 1992, p 27). Jennings quotes a Makete women: "Why would men buy a donkey when they can buy another wife to do the work".
- The IMT are possessed by men and mainly used for the purpose of cash crop transport, but only in a few cases to reduce the transport burden of the female tasks (see Chapter 4.4). During non-harvest periods the donkeys were left in the mountains. Ladies' bicycles could not be found in Makete.
- The experience with saving groups shows that the reliability of women in money matters seems to be much higher than for men.

The simulation assumes a period of repayment of 5 years after the purchase of the IMT, which results in the annuities given in Tab. 5.3-1. The annuities are deducted from the income as described in Chapter 5.2.2. The debt service seems to be low in absolute terms, but it is quite high if it is compared with the low cash income. But the high production increase after the purchase of the IMT makes the debt service possible. It has to be recalled that households possessing donkeys in Makete had roughly twice the income of comparable non-donkey-households (Chapter 4.4.1).

The debt service is paid into a revolving fund, which is used to give new credits to other non-IMT-households. Assuming a credit level of 75 %, the maximum cash need of $ 84,000 would be reached after six years. If no credits are distributed to replace old IMT[22], the fund would reach positive values after 12 years and at the end of the modelling period a surplus of more than $ 16,000 can be accumulated. Tab. 5.3-1 shows that increasing credit levels entail a growing need of start capital for the credit fund. A credit level of 90 % necessitates $ 133,000, which is still much lower than the investments for local tracks (Scenario 3) or for transport avoiding measures (Scenario 4).

5.4   Sensitivity Testing of the Time Budget

Time restrictions are the most important constraint for the simulated development process. The Makete survey shows that annually 1,420 hours can be regarded as labour time, while 2,439 hours were used for transport activities. The total "Disposable Time" budget sums up to 3,900 hours per year. A comparison with other African studies (Tab. 5.4-1 and Tab. 2.3-1) shows that the labour

---

21 The 'Tontine' is a traditional female saving group in West Africa, which provides credits for commercial or social purposes to its members. The money stems from individual contribution of the participants. The repayment of the debt is enforced by the group pressure.

22 In the model it is assumed that an IMT can be used for 10 years and the replacement is financed with a new credit. In this case the credit fund will not reach positive values during the simulation period.

time in Makete ranges at the end of the scale. The market production in Makete is still very low and an increasing market integration would imply a growth of the labour time in the fields. If it is assumed that the daily budget for transport and labour per able-bodied person comprises 7 hours during 310 days of the year, **then the disposable time per household can be set at 5,000 hours/year**[23]. An increase of more than 1,000 hours per household seems to be quite strong, but it has to be mentioned that already one quarter of the households in Makete are using more than 5,000 hours for transport and labour.

Hours/Year	Labour Time for Crop Cultivation			Transport time			Total	Study
	Male	Female	House-hold	Male	Female	House-hold		
Makete 1994			1420	503	1562	2439	3859	Makete Survey
Makete 1986/87				531	1648	2475		Barwell/Malmberg
Tanga						2083		Dawson et al 1993
Cameroon 1962-64	1077	1355	2432*	1300	1542	2842*	5274*	Tissandier 1970
18 Field Studies	825	1100	1925*					Boserup 1989
Togo 1981			1233					Midhoe 1982
Gambia	740*	920*	1660					Cleave 1974
Uganda 1963/65			2200					Cleave 1974
Malawi 1972	665*	1715*	2380					Dasgupta 1977
Kenya 1956/57			1911					Clayton 1960
Ghana 1970	992*	833*	1825*					Wagenbuur 1972
* Estimate								
Sources: BARTH/HEIDEMANN 1987, BARWELL/ MALMBERG 1989, LEVI 1982, DAWSON BARWELL 1993, Boserup 1989, Makete Survey 1994								

Tab. 5.4-1 Time budget for labour on the fields and transport

The annual time used in Makete for transport and labour amounts to 3, 900 hours, while in the model the budget was set at 5,000 hours by using crude assumptions. The sensitivity analysis in Fig. 5.4-1 plots the change of the disposable income during the simulation period under different time restrictions in all scenarios. The graph shows that the setting of the time budget has impacts on the level of production and therefore on the disposable income. The main purpose of the model is not to estimate exactly the absolute regional effects, but to show the relative impacts of transport interventions. However strong the time restrictions might be, the ranking of the scenarios is in general not changed. With increasing time budget the effects of the construction of motorable tracks (Scenario 3) are gaining compared to the transport avoiding measures (Scenario 4).

---

23 Assumptions: 2.3 persons per household, no labour on Sundays.
   The time budget of a comparable European household can be estimated as follows:
   2.3 persons * 240 working days * (8 hours work/day + 1 hour transport to/from work) $\approx$ 5,000 hours/a.

138

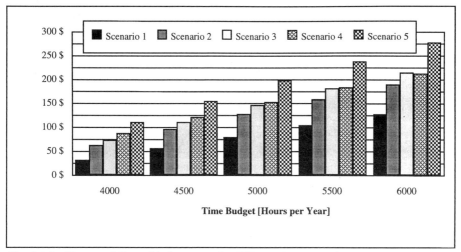

Fig. 5.4-1 Change of disposable income under different time constraints.

While the model used annual time limits in reality seasonal variations occur, which might set stronger restrictions than simulated in the model. The variation of the time requirements are examined for the last year of the simulation period (year 20). Fig. 5.4-2 shows the annual variation of the monthly time requirements per household for labour in the fields (Curve 1) and for all transport activities (Curve 2) in Scenario 2. During most of the year more time is used for transport than for labour. The agricultural calendar causes an uneven distribution of the annual time requirements; time restrictions occur especially during harvesting periods, when the crops have to be transported to the marketing places[24] (curve 3). The labour time and the time for the trips to the fields (curve 4) do not vary as strongly as the total time needed for transport purposes.

Fig. 5.4-3 plots the total time per person and day used for transport and labour in the fields in every scenario. Scenario 1 has the strongest variation of time needs. Especially during the harvesting periods the long walking trips to the external market are causing high time requirements, which in June nearly reach 9 hours per day. The creation of motorised access to every village in Scenario 3 reduces the annual variations of the time exigency, which ranges only between 3.5 and 7.8 hours per day. The motorised access on the tracks cuts off the peak transport loads by shortening the trips to the marketing points

---

24 The annual time distribution was achieved by combining the agricultural calendar (BARWELL / MALMBERG CALVO 1987, pp 52) with the results from the field study. Because no data on the annual variation of the marketing trips were collected, it is assumed that the households market their products just after harvesting them. Missing storage facilities and risk reduction from pest damage are the main reasons for this behaviour.

during harvesting periods. The scenarios 2, 4 and 5 range in-between the scenarios 1 and 3.

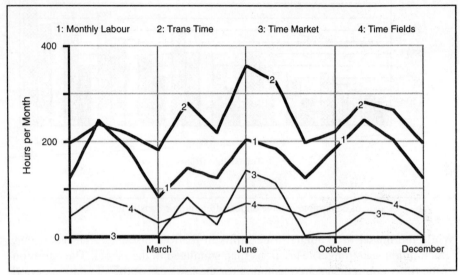

Fig. 5.4-2   Annual variation of the transport and labour time in Scenario 2

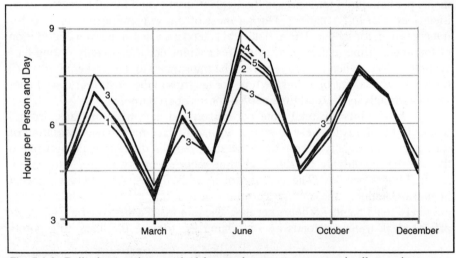

Fig. 5.4-3   Daily time requirements by labour and transport per person in all scenarios

The introduction of IMT has remarkable effects: even though households in Scenario 5 market 1.2 tons more crops than farmers in Scenario 2, the daily transport time during peak marketing seasons only differs by 10 minutes. The use of IMT reduces the number of trips needed for the evacuation of crops from the fields and for their transport to the markets. The simulation explains the intensive use of the IMT during the harvesting periods observed in Matamba. The construction of motorable tracks has the strongest effects regarding the time requirements during the harvesting season in June and July.

5.5   How can Road Investments and Maintenance Be Financed?

There is no doubt that roads and IMT are crucial for the regional development of peripheral regions, but someone has got to pay! One of the most salient features of the transport system in most Sub Saharan African Countries is the lack of maintenance of the existing road network[25]. The main reason is the lack of funds, which make adequate maintenance of the whole network impossible. This chapter will try to assess the possibility to finance the rural roads locally.

THERKILDSEN/SEMBOYA (1992) conducted research on the resource mobilisation in rural districts of Tanzania. The financial situation is so bad that most local infrastructures such as primary education, health services and rural roads are collapsing. The village and local governments have not been successful in raising their own revenues. The country wide collection ratio[26] of 50 % for the local governments can be explained by the poor administrative endowment and their bad performance. Declining revenues of the financial administration were related to corruption, mismanagement and wastage (p. 1103). The village government revenues stem from a share of the per capita development tax. These local revenues are earmarked for investment purposes and cannot be used for recurrent expenditures to maintain the local services. Due to the bad quality of theses services[27] people are reluctant to pay the development tax. In the long run the central government will not be able to solve the financial crisis of the districts and village governments. It is doubtful as well that the international donors would be willing to give long term subsidies for the recurrent district budgets.

In Tanzania many villagers had to participate in unpaid self help activities. THERKILDSEN/ SEMBOYA report that every village has 4-5 Self Help Projects and on top of that annually every person works 10-15 days only for road maintenance. JENNINGS (1992, pp 32) states that women accounted for 80 % of the Self Help activities of the MIRTP, which, despite the potential benefits, "substantially increased the workload of women"[28] and "seriously undermined the agricultural production". The unequal participation of the villagers is another point of criticism. The example of the Matamba-Chimala road (Box 5-1) shows that the unpaid Self Help labour is often related to economic inefficiencies.

---

25 Compare Chapter 2.4.3.
26 Ratio between actual tax collection and potential tax revenue.
27 For further reading see EDLING / FISCHER (1991).
28 JENNINGS estimates the workload at more than 20 hours per week.

Therefore in Matamba a local tax was preferred to Self Help labour. It can be argued in favour of the Self Help projects that they reduce the possibility of public funds being misused.

Box 5-1: Self Help Maintenance of the Matamba-Chimala Road

The rehabilitation of the Matamba-Chimala Road was initiated by the Matamba Ward as a Self Help project. The Self Help labour entailed a lot of economic inefficiencies like long walks from the homesteads to the escarpment (3 hours one way), which had to be undertaken every day. On top of that the work had to be done during periods where agricultural activities were required. The high opportunity costs of agricultural labour was the main reason why the Matamba Ward Council decided to raise a local road tax in order to pay hired labour, which was to be used instead of Self Help Labour. A tax of 40 ¢ per able bodied person was planned. In 1994 only one sixth of the expected revenue could be collected. Administrative changes were given as the reason for the poor collection ratio. The missing funds were partly replaced by the Lutheran church, but still the maintenance work could not be done properly by the end of the rainy season. Nevertheless the road was still in a "good" condition according to the judgement of a district council driver.

A road toll station was installed in Matamba, where all vehicles have to pass.

A means to solve the financial problems of the communities could be the levy of user charges, which should be designed as follows:
- The charges should cover the full investment and maintenance cost and the costs for the collection of the charges,
- the revenues should be earmarked for a special purpose,
- the charges should be simple and inexpensive to collect,
- users pay only according to their utilisation, and
- a locally elected commitee or institution should control the adequate use of the revenues.

Nowadays user charges are already collected for the grinding mills by the churches who operate the mills. It can be doubted whether these charges cover the full costs of the mills[29]. Water supply is given free of charge. Nevertheless it would be possible to collect a charge for the provision of clean water, which at least covers the maintenance costs[30]. The construction and maintenance of foot-

---

29 Often the prices are set not by economic but by social deliberations. The sustainability of the projects can be only secured by continuous external aid from the international donors.
30 In the case of Makete, where piped water systems were installed maintenance could be covered by $ 4.6 per household and year. The total investment costs (10 years writing off, interest rate 0 %) would be too expensive for the households ($ 40/year). Wells and hand pumps, which are much cheaper would imply annual charges of $ 8.

paths is so cheap, that it makes no sense to install a toll station. As long as the path is only used by one village, the maintenance can be conducted using self help labour. The willingness to participate in Self Help activities declines as soon as users from other villages walk on the path without participating in the maintenance. In this case it should be possible to collect the charge together with the market tax at the marketing place.

Since July 1991 in Tanzania a national road fund has existed, into which a share of the fuel tax (10 ¢/litre) is paid in order to secure the maintenance of the road system. 20 % of the road fund is reserved for rural roads. Experience from the Makete District shows that these funds are not sufficient to maintain the road network[31]. The district council in Makete does not pay the communities regularly in order to secure the maintenance of the transport network, but funds are released "according to the requirements". In some cases the spheres of responsibility between district council and regional engineer are not clearly delimited; the missing maintenance of the regional roads forced the district council to use their scarce funds to maintain regional roads in order to keep the external communication working. Often local roads, which were maintained by the village or ward authorities were in better condition than regional and district roads. The basic feature of successful systems seems to be the local interest in a road and the efficient control and enforcement of its maintenance.

Scenario	User charge per ton	Budget Road Fund	Reduction Disposable Income*
	$/ton	$	%
1	0.00	0	-
2	4.01	178,000	- 3.6 %
3	9.27	479,000	- 9.7 %
4	3.42	181,000	- 3.4 %
5	2.62	185,000	- 3.8 %

* User charges for water supply not included

Tab. 5.5-1   Road user charges

The collection of road user charges can be a solution to the above mentioned financial problems. In the case of the model region, which has spatial structures similar to Matamba, a road toll station could be installed at village B (Fig. 5.3-1), where all the incoming and outgoing traffic has to pass. Here a road tax can be levied according to the weight transported. A locally elected committee could take over the control of the revenues and the maintenance works. The following assumptions are taken:

- The construction of the road is financed by a credit (real interest rate of 8 %).
- Annual maintenance is paid by this fund.
- Road user charges are paid into the fund.
- The charges are designed in such a way that after 20 years the debt is completely repaid.

---

31 The district network consists of 190 km of district roads and 500 km of feeder roads. In 1994 the district received $ 10,000 from the national road fund, which is 14 $/km. The funds were used to improve 20 km of roads and repair two bridges.

Tab. 5.5-1 shows the necessary charges to fulfil the above listed requirements. Scenario 2 and 4 make user charges of 3-4 $ per ton of exported products necessary. In Scenario 3 user charges of 9 $/ton would need to be raised, in order to finance the construction and maintenance of 140 km of local tracks. The donkeys in Scenario 5 have strong impacts on the market production; less than $ 3 per ton would have to be charged. It has to be mentioned, that if only the maintenance works are financed by the road fund, the whole system would be sustainable at 35 % of the named charges. The next column in Tab. 5.5-1 indicates the necessary initial budget of the road fund to finance construction, maintenance and interest. While all the scenarios range around $ 180,000 the initial budget for Scenario 3 amounts to $ 480,000.

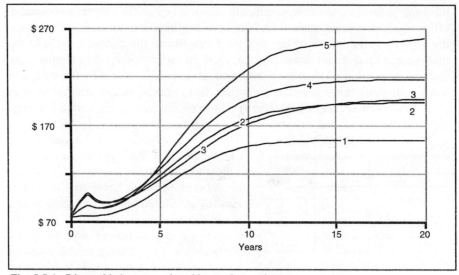

Fig. 5.5-1 Disposable income reduced by road user charges

It can be assumed, that the traders will completely pass on the road user charges to the farmers. Therefore producer prices will be reduced by the road charge and lead to a reduction of the household's disposable income, listed in the right column of Tab. 5.5-1. A general reduction in the disposable income of 4 % in the Scenarios 2, 4 and 5 and of 10 % in Scenario 3 can be stated. The development of the disposable income is plotted in Fig. 5.5-1, which shows that the households in Scenario 3 now have the same income as the households in Scenario 2 (compare Fig. 5.3-7). The question arises as to whether the producer prices in Scenario 3 have reached a level, where the farmers react by producing smaller quantities and whether they are willing to pay this high price for the non-monetary benefits.

5.6   Conclusions

In this chapter the empirical evidence observed in Makete District is used to built a model, which simulates the effects of rural transport interventions using a systems dynamic approach. An ideal region was assumed, which is initially completely isolated from external markets. Over a period of 20 years five scenarios assess the effects of different transport interventions, which are listed in Tab. 5.6-1. The main restrictions are the limited time budget of the households, the availability of fertiliser and the access to credits.

Initially the model region is completely isolated and the agricultural production is used to satisfy the subsistence needs. The regional economy stagnates because the low internal demand is not able to generate a significant growth. This process is induced by the construction of a **Footpath**, which gives access to an external market. Because the market is still within walking distance some villages begin to increase their production and sell crops outside the region. The disposable income increases on average at annually 3.8 %. The low construction and maintenance costs make it possible to obtain a high rate of return[32]. The rate seems to be quite elevated, but the initial situation with an assumed complete isolation of the region has to be taken into account[33]. It can nevertheless be stated that the production is very quickly restricted by the limited time requirements for the long walking trips to the external market and the lack of fertiliser, which is not available without motorised access. The construction of a footpath seems to be an efficient transport intervention, if

• the region has no motorised access,
• markets are within walking distance,
• funds available for road construction are not sufficient or
• a risk averse investment strategy is preferred.

The construction of a low cost **Feeder Road** to the regional centre reduces the time requirements for the evacuation of crops and makes fertiliser available, both of which cause a stronger increase in production than in the previous scenario. Increasing trips to the fields and to the collection points reduce the disposable time budget and set limits to the production. Income increases annually by 5.2 %. If a low cost road is built the rate of return amounts to 56 %. Of course here as well as in the previous scenario the good initial conditions favour a high rate of return. The construction of a feeder road is the basis for all the following scenarios and the effects always have to be regarded in relation to this scenario.

---

32 The economic rate of return compares investment and maintenance costs with the benefits from the increased disposable income. In the case of scenario 5 and 6 the IMT and the Transport Fund are included.
33 Probably the model overestimated the production increase for the footpath scenario, because no functional relation between distance to the market and market production could be implemented. The long walking distance would probably set stronger restrictions than in the other scenarios.

Scenario	Main Features	Costs		Without User Charges		With User Charges	
		Initial Invest- ments *	Annual Mainte- nance	Annual Income Growth	Economic Rate of Return**	User Charges	Reduction Disposable Income***
		$ / Inhabitant		%	%	$/ton	%
1	Footpath	0.46	0.03	3.8 %	114 %	0.00	-
2	Feeder Road	6.00	0.34	5.2 %	56 %	4.01	- 3.6 %
3	Feeder Road + Local Tracks	15.51	0.54	5.6 %	37 %	9.27	- 9.7 %
4	Feeder Road + Wells + Stoves	23.07	0.49	5.8 %	32 %	3.42	- 3.4 %
5	IMT Fund + Feeder Road	15.00	0.34	6.7 %	58 %	2.62	- 3.8 %
6	Succession of interventions	Not comparable		7.5 %	102 %	6.11	- 7.1 %

*	The initial endowment of the IMT Fund is added to the total investments for road construction
**	Benefits: change of Disposable Income, Costs: investments, maintenance, IMT Fund, Transport Fund
***	Compared to the same scenario without user charges. Scenario 4 and 6: user charges for piped water supply not included.

Tab. 5.6-1 Salient results of the scenarios

The third scenario tries to reduce the time constraints by supplying every village with a motorised access. The construction of a network of **Motorable Tracks** combined with the above described feeder road causes a reduction in the transport to markets and gives rise to another increase of production. The disposable income grows by annually 5.6 %, which is faster than in the previous scenario, but due to the high investment and maintenance costs the rate of return reaches only 37 %. Of course the roads would have other non-economic impacts, which cannot be monetarised here: reduced drudgery for market trips, access for ambulances and mobile health services.

In the fourth scenario the effects of **Transport Avoiding Measures** are simulated. All villages receive wells, water pumps and low consumption stoves, which reduce the time budget for subsistence transport. Production reaches the same level as in the previous local-track-scenario, but the lower VOC cause a slightly higher disposable income. The high investment costs reduce the rate of return to 32 %, which is below that of the previous scenario[34].

The biggest effects after the construction of a feeder road can be achieved by the promotion of **Donkeys and Bicycles**. The main reason why farmers are nowadays not purchasing the IMT is the high price; without any access to credits only 15 % of the households in the scenario 2 would be able to purchase an IMT. Therefore a revolving credit fund for the purchase of IMT is implemented.

---

[34] If instead of the rate of return the net present values was compared, then only a depreciation rate higher than 4.6 % would favour the tracks scenario.

146

A credit coverage of 75 % would, after 20 years, give 62 % of the households access to IMT. The IMT have two general effects: they reduce the transport time and they increase the productivity from decreasing to increasing returns to scale. These effects induce a strong growth in production. The growth of the disposable income (6.7 % p.a) exceeds the growth of all the previous scenarios. The rate of return can be estimated at 58 %. The model shows, that the purchase of an IMT even with a real interest rate of 12 % and a repayment within 5 years can be very profitable for the farmers. One of the main problems of these types of funds are the high overhead costs and the low repayment morale. Even if it is assumed that only 80 % of the credits are paid back, the fund will grow during the simulation period and reach positive values after 12 years if no credits are distributed to replace old IMT. At the end of the modelling period a surplus of more than $ 16,000 can be accumulated, which could be used for other development activities or to finance the high overhead costs of the credit system. It seems to be sensible to design the credit system primarily for women in the form of a revolving fund. The West African savings clubs, called 'Tontine', could be an appropriate institution to organise distribution of credits and collection of the debt service payments.

Someone has got to pay! In consideration of the desperate public financial situation in many Sub-Saharan African countries there is little hope that new rural roads can be financed by the recurrent budgets. A step towards a sustainable system could be taken if village governments, wards or districts were permitted to levy road user charges at special road toll stations. The model assumes that revenues are collected in a road fund, which has the goal of repaying the full investment, maintenance and credit costs (real interest rate 8%) of the project after 20 years . The user charges are listed in column 5 of Tab. 5.6-1. It is assumed that the user charges reduce the producer prices and therefore have an impact on the disposable income (column 6). A complete cost coverage of a feeder road would imply road user charges of $ 4 per ton and a reduction of the disposable income of 4 %. In the case of the construction of motorised track access to all villages user charges of 9 $/ton would have to be levied. This would reduce the disposable income of the households by 10 %. The income would reach the same level as if only a feeder road to the regional centre was constructed. The question arises as to whether the farmers are willing to pay this price for the reduced market transport and the non-monetary effects of the tracks.

An **Integrated Transport Approach** favours a combination of the above mentioned transport interventions as proposed in Fig. 5.6-1. The measures are financed with a Regional Transport Fund which is a combination of the Credit Fund for IMT and the Road Fund. The fund will be financed by an international credit with 8 % interest rate. In the initial phase, when the region is not accessible by motor vehicles a footpath to an external market is improved and credits are distributed for the purchase of IMT. If the farmers respond after a period of three years by increasing their market production, a feeder road to the regional centre is constructed. After six years of simulation the total debt reaches its maximum at $ 9.3 per inhabitant. A road user charge comprising 8 % of the producer price is levied on the exported products. The growing market production will enable the road users to repay the debt until year 9. Now the market production exceeds three tons and transport constraints hamper its further growth. After another two years enough user charges are collected to finance the construction of motorable tracks to every village. This investment entails another production expansion and the fund fills up faster in order to finance transport avoiding measures in the year 16. After 20 years the annual market production exceeds 4.2 t and the disposable income reaches $ 290, which implies an annual increase of 7.1 %. The income seems to be still very low, but it has to be compared to the reality in Makete, where in 1994 the revenues amounted to less than $ 80.

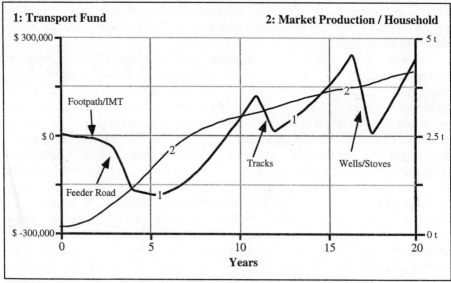

Fig. 5.6-1   Succession of various transport interventions (Scenario 6)

The model also shows, that with increasing production the investments have smaller productive effects due to decreasing returns to scale with the given production technology. At the end of the simulation period the invention of new agrarian technologies, like the use of ploughs with animal traction, high yielding varieties or irrigation schemes might entail a change of the production function. A further production increase necessitates another change of the transport technology, because the evacuation of crops can only be managed with animal drawn carts or small motor vehicles.

148

6 Appraisal of Transport Interventions

The new bias towards rural transport necessitates a widening of the approaches for the ex-ante appraisal of transport interventions. Conventional project assessments only emphasise motorised transport, often using crude appraisal methodologies. MANN et al. (1988, p.4) revised the assessment methodologies of transport projects in rural areas of Africa. They criticise that the majority of conventional transport demand studies are an 'addition of hypotheses and assumptions, using multiplicative factors and growth rates, which are not statistically secured'. The general procedure of the assessments is as follows:

(i)   Future traffic volumes are more often than not forecasted by simple extrapolation of existing traffic volumes.

(ii) The estimations of the project's benefits comprise mainly the reduction of Vehicle Operating Costs (VOC) and the increase of market production.

(iii) Alternative investments are compared by using cost/benefit analysis.

The assessments include various economic problems such as overvalued exchange rates, estimation of future inflation, the scope of the projects and the choice of the discount rate[1]. A comprehensive overview is given in ADLER (1987).

HOWE (1994, p.35) judges "the current state-of-the-art for surveying and forecasting local level rural traffic demands ... (as) extremely crude". The concern of many studies rarely goes beyond the routine prediction of motorised traffic and growth generation. While the biggest benefits in conventional assessments are usually generated by the reduction of VOC, the Makete Survey demonstrates (compare 4.7.2) that these benefits are relatively small compared to the other effects. The impacts of non-motorised means of transport and of transport avoiding measures are not taken into account. Therefore an appraisal of the different types of rural transport interventions should be based on a road **and** a household survey. This will change the planning methodology from a top down view, where the region is regarded as one entity, to a bottom-up approach, where the household is the basis for the conception of transport interventions. A sketch of the assessment methodology is given in Fig. 6-1.

(i)   The **road survey** observes the existing motorised transport on the main roads. The benefits can be derived if the reduced VOC are multiplied by the expected future traffic.

---

1 Especially the choice of the discount rate is crucial for the assessment, because future costs and benefits have a lower value than their present worth. A high discount rate favours projects which give fast returns on investment. Other problems occur with the calculation of shadow prices to overcome price distortions and with the choice of the methodology for the comparison of costs and benefits.

(ii) The **household survey** contains an assessment of household size and composition and an estimation of the future population growth, migration and change in employment. A crude assessment could distinguish between farmers, who receive their main cash income from marketing of agricultural products and non-farmers. Reference data from more developed regions can be used for the estimation of future employment patterns.

(iii) The household survey gives indication of the actual **market production** per household. The project may have direct impacts on the market production (e.g. by dissemination of IMT) or the reduced VOC give rise to future production increases (Producer Surplus Theory). Benefits from increased market production per household have to be multiplied by the expected future population.

(iv) The household survey reveals the actual **transport patterns** of rural households: trip generation for personal and freight transport purposes, distances and trip length. The increasing market production, which entails a further growth of the transport volume, has to be included in the estimation. The benefits per household are multiplied with the future number of households in order to obtain the total benefits.

(v)   **Direct income effects** comprise the wages paid during the construction phases, the income from lent IMT and the effect of hiring motor-vehicles for market transport.

(vi) The **comparison of the benefits** gives an overview of the absolute effects. The efficiency can be assessed by comparing costs and monetary benefits. The efficiency of time saving measures can be appraised by setting the annual time savings in relation to the annual costs or by adding the monetarised time values to the total benefits.

Because the conduct of household surveys is time consuming and costly the relevant information could be as well achieved with the methods of the 'Rapid Rural Appraisal' (CHAMBERS 1980). Instead of interviewing many households and later on having to compute large quantities of data, the information could as well be achieved from village representatives. HILLE and JAGD (1995, Annex 4) compared the results of village surveys with household surveys in Malawi. They conclude that in general the village surveys underestimated the average distances, while the use of IMT was overestimated. Concerning transport problems and improvements household surveys show a larger variety of responses, especially in regard to gender and poverty issues. Thus a 'Rapid Rural Appraisal' can only be a complement to a village survey.

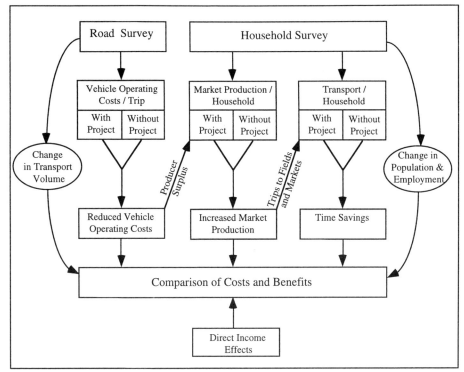

Fig. 6-1   Assessment procedure for rural transport interventions

Motorised traffic can be evaluated by traffic countings or road side passenger interviews. Countings on markets and central facilities like grinding mills could be helpful to evaluate the modal split, the trip distance and the catchment area. It is not necessary to evaluate exact data, but to estimate the magnitude of the impacts of future transport interventions. On the household level the time savings, which can be achieved by reduced number of trips and decreasing trip length are relevant. The changes in the household's transport patterns can be derived from the experience of other projects. Because IMT households have different transport patterns, the number of households possessing IMT should be estimated. Every intervention has its own area of influence: while a road may serve a whole region, a grinding mill serves a village and a bicycle is only used by one household. Often it is useful to define the area of influence by the distance of 90-95% of the users.

If it is planned to introduce several projects simultaneously, then interrelations between production, benefits from VOC, time savings and increased use of IMT might entail the calculation of feedback loops.

151

6.1 Benefits from Reduced Vehicle Operating Costs

The reduction of Vehicle Operating Costs (VOC) depending on vehicle type and road surface has been intensively researched in developing countries (ADLER 1987, pp 30). More difficulties are related to the estimation of future transport volumes, which determine the total benefits. ZACHCIAL (1985) criticises that the existing traffic is often simply extrapolated with assumed growth rates, which determine the results of the analysis. ADLER (1987, p. 25) counterargues that an overestimation of traffic would not entail strong consequences since "road transport is nearly always growing rapidly in developing countries" and it is only a question of time until the estimated volumes are reached. HOWE (1990) opposes that countries experiencing a severe shortage of foreign exchange may not be able to expand the size and usage of their vehicle fleet and therefore no extra traffic would appear. The vehicle possession in Sub-Saharan Africa stagnated during the last decade[2]. The provision of roads does not automaically stimulate the growth of the transport volume, if the future vehicle supply is not secured. GAVIRIA et al (1991, p 47) report that the observed increases in transport volume in Kenya during the Rural Access Roads Program were not encouraging. The estimates of expected agricultural benefits grossly overestimated the vehicle traffic on the roads. The authors criticise that rural roads are often overdesigned due to an overestimation of future transport volumes.

This discussion shows that future motorised transport volumes have to be assessed more carefully. Basis for this estimation can be the data collected in the road and the household survey. The expected vehicle supply has to be taken into account if future transport volumes are estimated. HOWE (1992, p.34) states that usually **personal transport** is more important on rural roads than the transportation of goods. The future personal transport volume is dependent on the population growth, the expected incomes and the reduced fares due to lower VOC. HOWE (1992) estimates the price elasticity of transport demand at 0.6-2.0. Reduced VOC only entail a growth of personal transport, if the cost reduction is passed on to the users. The transport markets are more often than not dominated by monopolistic enterprises, which rather increase profits than reduce the fares. A model for the forecast of personal transport was developed by MAYWORM (1982). The model (Box 6-1) assumes that future traffic is dependent on road surface, income, and the potential monthly travel. The latter can be estimated with the existing trip rates, the distance to the activity centre and the population living in the zone of influence.

The future **goods transport** volume is dependent on the estimated production increase per household and the changing number of inhabitants in the catchment area. The next chapter gives an overview of how the production increase can be assessed. It has to be taken into account that many households within walking

---

2 The Republic of South Africa is excluded. Compare Chapter 2.3

distance of markets prefer to transport their products by headload in order to save on transport costs. It can be assumed that empty goods vehicles entering the region to evacuate the agricultural products carry consumer goods, agricultural inputs and persons.

Box 6-1: Forecast of Personal Transport According to MAYWORM (1982)

$$AMT = f (Road, Income, PMT)$$

AMT	= Average Monthly Travel on the Rural Road (Person Trips)
Road	= Indicator for the Type of Road Surface
Income	= Average Annual Household Income in the Zone of Influence
PMT	= Potential Monthly Travel

$$PMT = f \left(\sum_i \frac{TRRATE_i}{D_i^{\alpha}} * POP \right)$$

$TRRATE_i$	= Average Potential Monthly per Capita Trip Rate from the Zone of Influence to the Activity Centre
D_i	= Distance from the Centre of the Zone to the Activity Centre
POP	= Total Population Living in the Zone of Influence
α	= Real Number to be Estimated

6.2 Benefits from Increased Market Production

The improved transport situation will probably entail an increase in the agricultural market production. The possible benefits have to be evaluated on the household level according to the type of transport investment and taking the agro-ecological frame conditions into account.

Marketing Increase Due to Road Investment

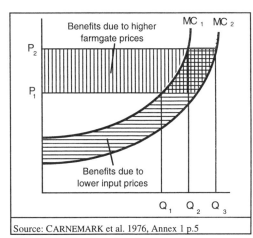

Source: CARNEMARK et al. 1976, Annex 1 p.5

Fig. 6-2   Producer Surplus

The Producer Surplus concept developed by the World Bank (CARNEMARK et al 1976) tries to assess the effects of reduced VOC on agricultural marketing. It is assumed that these reductions will be passed on to the producers, that all the products are marketed via the improved road and that a perfect competition exists. The considerations are visualised in Fig. 6-2. In a situation of complete competition the farmers offer their products according to the marginal cost curve MC_1. If the producer price is P_1 they offer Q_1 tons of products.

The reduced VOC will cause an increase in the producer prices to P_2, which entails a shift of the market production to Q_2. The benefits are represented by the area to the left of MC_1 between P_1 and P_2. On top of that the prices for inputs will decline due to lower transport costs: the supply curve shifts from MC_1 to MC_2 causing another increase of the market production to Q_3. The benefit area is located between MC_1 and MC_2. Both benefit areas represent the producer surplus[3]. The assessment requires an expert analysis using various input data, like crop production, market output, yields, production costs etc.

Even CARNEMARK et al admit that, if transport cost savings are not transmitted to producers, either because of government controls or due to non-competitive transport services, the development impact might be low. The static or declining transport fleet in Sub-Saharan Africa has created a situation, which favours the sellers of transport services and not the buyers. HOWE (1992, p.3) states that in many rural areas transport enterprises are not under pressure to transmit cost reductions to their clients. HINE (1993) corroborates that road investments had very low impacts on the producer prices. The Transport Research Laboratory observed that in Ghana producer prices increased by less than one percent after road improvements from earth to gravel surface. ADLER (1987 p.35) argues that transport costs are more often than not below 10 % of market prices and therefore the effects of reduced transport costs would be marginal. Mann et al. (1988) contradicts this by quoting studies in Zambia, Malawi, Zaïre and Somalia, where this share reached 25 % on distances below 150 km.

The model in Chapter 5 demonstrates that a strong growth of marketing can be expected if a road opens up a new area and creates access to markets. This might also be the case if an impassable road is rehabilitated. The empirical evidence from the Makete survey shows, that improved road access (e.g. in Ihela and Ngoje) does not necessarily give rise to increased agricultural production. Even though both villages had the best road access they were not performing as well as other villages; their marketing revenues were declining while other villages were able to increase their incomes. Other factors like agroecological regime, historical market orientation, availability of agricultural extension services etc. seem to be at least as important as motorised accessibility.

Marketing Increase Due to Possession of IMT

The empirical evidence in Makete shows, that IMT possessing households produce and market considerably more than households without any conveyance. The estimated production function shows that IMT-households have increasing returns to scale, while the returns are decreasing for non-IMT households. The

---

3 If the producer surplus approach is applied, then the reduced VOC have to be excluded from the total benefits in order to avoid double counting.

knowledge about the productive effects of IMT is still too small to allow conclusions for ex ante production assessments. Further research is therefore needed in this field.

Credit for the purchase of an IMT has a big advantage for the planner: it leaves it to the farmer to estimate whether the production increases will yield enough revenue to repay his loan. The household survey should contain a demand evaluation for IMT which could be the basis for the design of a revolving credit fund.

6.3   Benefits from Time Savings

Time valuations usually make up the biggest portion of the benefits in transport assessments of industrialised countries. Conventional assessment methodologies in developing countries usually ignore the individual time savings by the improvement of transport systems. They postulate that reduction of transport time entails no benefits for rural households, because leisure time is available in excess. Various studies on rural households show (Chapter 2.3) that the time budget is especially tight for women and time restrictions are regarded as a major constraint for an increase of agricultural production. The question arises as to whether and to what degree the 'saved time' will be used to increase agricultural production. The theoretical considerations in chapter 2.4.2 show, that saved transport time will most probably be used for welfare or production increasing activities. The model in chapter 5 demonstrates that a reduction of the transport time is a precondition for production increase. Further research in this field is needed to give a satisfying answer to this question. A valuation of transport time savings can be justified even if the saved time is not used for direct productive activities, because an enlarged time budget would probably be used to increase the welfare of the household. Therefore the effects of transport time reductions have to be included in the appraisal of rural transport interventions. The following time saving effects can be observed:
- Faster travelling due to infrastructure improvements (roads, paths, tracks) or new modes of transport (bicycles, motor vehicles).
- Reduced number of trips due to higher carrying capacities (motor vehicles, pack animals, wheelbarrows, footpath improvement etc.)
- Reduction of trip length by the improvement of the infrastructure endowment (grinding mills, water supply, woodlots, low consumption stoves etc.)

The estimations of the time effects have to be undertaken by comparing transport patterns of households with and without the regarded endowment. If no comparable households are available the experience from other projects has to be taken into account. It has to be noticed that compensating effects such as increased consumption of water after the installation of water supply might occur.

155

Before the 'saved time' is monetarised a comparison of the efficiency of different interventions can be undertaken by calculating the annual time savings in relation to annual costs (hours/$). This methodology allows a comparison on the time efficiency of different projects without attributing any monetary value to transport time. A monetarisation only makes sense, if other income or production effects occur and time savings represent only a portion of total benefits.

From the theoretical point of view the time valuations can be undertaken by sing the opportunity costs of labour: transport time for labour purposes can be valued with the marginal productivity of labour, which represents the value of the production output achieved by an additional working hour. The valuation of leisure time uses the consumers choice theory which assumes that the individual has the free choice between leisure and labour. Thus an equilibrium point is chosen where the last hour of leisure time has the same value as the last working hour (marginal rate of substitution). Therefore leisure can also be valued with the marginal productivity of labour.

The German Road Administration estimates the value of labour time and leisure time by using the National Income[4]. This methodology is not applicable in rural areas of Africa, because subsistence production is not included in the National Income Accounting and a distinction between the trips for leisure and for labour is difficult. The Makete survey allowed the estimation of a production function, which determines the marginal productivity of agricultural labour at 7 ¢/hour, while the average value comprises 16 ¢/hour and the minimum wage for government employees amounts to 11 ¢/hour. If the marginal productivity cannot be estimated a rough assessment might give an indication of the magnitude. If the total time one person is awake during one year (16 hours/day * 365 days = 5840 hours) is valued at the minimum wage of a government employee (232 $/year) then one hour would be worth 4 ¢. This value is well below the marginal productivity, which was chosen as the value of time in this study.

6.4   Other Benefits

Income can be directly generated by employment during the construction phase and by the wages paid for current maintenance works. The local benefits are higher, if labour based methodologies are applied. The Makete survey reveals that some farmers benefit from price differences between markets by transporting their products with hired vehicles to the high price markets. Other income is

---

4   It is assumed that half of the National Income is produced by economically active persons during their labour time, while the remaining half is produced without monetary compensation during non-working hours:
Value Labour Time = 0.5 National Income / (Labour Time * Active Persons)
Value Leisure Time = 0.5 National Income / (Awake Time * Non-Active Persons + (Leisure Time) * Active Persons).

generated by lending of IMT to other non-IMT households. An ex-ante estimate for both types of benefits are related to high unreliabilities.

The reduction of accident rates on roads and paths[5], the better access to services and the improved health situation after the installation of a water supply system generate benefits which are difficult to monetarise. The reduction of the accident rates are usually included in road assessments of industrialised countries. The German Road Administration values the prevention of a fatality in a road accident at 1.2 Million DM (1985 price level), which amounts to 40 times the GNP per capita. If this value were to be applied to Tanzania, the costs per fatality would amount to $10,000. Scandinavian Road Administrations attribute higher values to their transport victims by including contingency valuations for a 'human value'.

Environmental benefits might occur if woodlots are planted or low consumption stoves are introduced. The benefits from these interventions might be stronger than the transport related benefits, especially if the environment is in a critical situation, when erosion occurs, desertification menaces or firewood is in shortage.

6.5   Prioritisation of Transport Interventions

The scarcity of resources necessitates a prioritisation of transport investments. The choice, which transport intervention is most appropriate for which location depends on a variety of criteria:
*   **Effectiveness**: which intervention can generate the strongest effects?
*   **Efficiency**: which intervention has the strongest effect per unit of cost?
*   **Requirements**: in which location is the need for interventions strongest?
*   **Affordability**: can public and private households afford their contributions?
*   **Appropriateness**: does the local population accept the intervention?
*   **Sustainability**: can the adequate maintenance of the installations be secured?
The decision of which intervention should be implemented in which location is the core of a planning process, in which local decision makers and village representatives should be involved. If the quantification of project benefits is possible, transport interventions can be ranked according to their cost efficiency. If this is not the case, then standards have to be set up: e.g. maximum travel time to water supply, firewood, public services or central locations. In this case local needs more than economic considerqations determine the decision about investments.

---

5 Before the Utengule path was improved several fatal accidents were recorded and after the improvement, none. Two days after the evaluation team crossed a bridge consisting of a simple pole over a river, a villager died after falling from this bridge. The village representatives judged that sick persons could be transported to the hospital with an ambulance as the major impact of the track improvement to Unenamwa. Before the improvement several fatalities were recorded during the transport of pregnant women.

The methodologies of comparing costs and benefits[6] had been intensively discussed in the 1980s. If benefits can be monetarised the cost/benefit analysis is the most common method to rank transport investments. A comparison of the ratio of the discounted benefits and costs, of the Net Present Value or the Internal Rate of Return allows a ranking of the interventions[7]. A multi-criteria analysis (Scoring Model) is conventionally used if non-monetary benefits are included in the evaluation.[8] A number of problems are related to both methodologies; considerable need of data, unreliabilities in the estimation of monetary values for benefits which have no market price, subjective weighting of benefits in the scoring model, etc. Therefore ROTHENGATTER (1980) proposes the successive conduct of various tests in order to reduce the number of alternatives before utility functions are set up. Interactive procedures, developed by STRASSERT (1984) as an alternative to conventional cost/benefit assessments, comprise a stepwise comparison of advantages and disadvantages by the decision maker(s). BÖTTCHER (1995, p. 42) criticises that interactive assessments rely exclusively on the 'individual and collective competence of the decision maker(s)', because the transparency of the preferences is not given in the procedure.

The choice of the assessment methodology depends on the available financial means for the evaluation process and the competence of the decision makers. Problems might occur if the evaluation costs are becoming too high in comparison to the investment costs. Therefore BEENHAKKER and LAGO (1983) developed a couple of simplified screening and evaluation methodologies based on the Consumer Surplus (reduced VOC) and Producer Surplus Theory.

The German Kreditanstalt für Wiederaufbau KFW (1985) has developed a simple appraisal methodology for rural roads in Zimbabwe which is designed to be used by local planners. The investment costs for different types of roads are standardised according to the geological and morphological conditions. The region is classified according to agro-ecological zones and the potential benefits which might follow a road improvement are estimated. For each of the classes a representative area is chosen, where the expected increase in agricultural production per capita is estimated. A typical development path for population and production is assumed for every class. The total potential benefits, including reduced VOC, time savings, increase in production are estimated for every zone

---

6 A comprehensive discussion of cost/benefit assessment methodologies for transport projects is presented in DVWG (1980); FUNCK (1989) gives a short overview of the state of the art in Germany.

7 A detailed discussion about the advantages and diadvantages of these methodologies is given in ADLER (1987, pp 49).

8 CLEMENTS (1995) proposes the distribution of points for different poverty alleviating effects with the help of a defined capabilities-based poverty line.

and the per capita net present value is computed (An example is given in Tab. 6-1). The planner can now easily calculate the benefit/cost ratios for any road improvement in the region. This methodology could also be applied in principle in the case of other transport interventions like the promotion of IMT, the improvement of paths and transport avoiding measures. Potential benefit maps can give the regional planner a good overview of the local effects of different transport interventions.

Population Density	Flat and Rolling Terrain			Very Hilly and Broken Terrain		
[Inh./km^2]	Zone I	Zone II	...	Zone I	Zone II	...
0-5	Net Present Value of the per Capita Benefits					
5-10	Discount Rate: 6 %					
...	Time Horizont: 15 years					
Source: KfW 1985						

Tab. 6-1   Example of a standard benefit table for primary roads in rural areas

Often development projects include the target of poverty alleviation. The question arises as to whether assessment methodologies for these projects have to especially emphasise the poor population strata. Distributionally sensitive cost-benefit analyses could be an appropriate assessment tool because they value benefits to poor people higher than equal benefits to rich recipients (CLEMENTS 1995). It must however be questioned whether a special poverty oriented focus in rural areas is really necessary, because the income disparities within the rural areas in Sub-Saharan Africa are much lower than those between rural and urban areas. Thus a focus on rural development will automatically include a poverty orientation. On top of that it is difficult to implement project measures which focus primarily on the poor population and limit the number of wealthy beneficiaries.

The prioritisation of interventions which entail non-monetary benefits like improved access to education, administration and health services cannot be achieved with the above described procedure. In this case methodologies of regional science have to be applied, which help to plan the optimal spatial distribution of public services and central locations. The set up of desired accessibility standards for public services can be the basis for the planning process. It should be considered whether mobile services are more cost efficient in areas with low population densities. Possibly the improvement of footpaths and the promotion of bicycles will entail a better access to services than the construction of a road. AFFUM and AHMED (1995) tested the use of Geographical Information Systems for rural accessibility planning in Bangladesh. They calculate the ratio of observed impedance and ideal accessibility (Euclidean distances) which is used as an indicator for the performance of the transport infrastructure. The change of this ratio after road improvement depicts the relative improvement of accessibility.

The empirical evidence from many studies about the impacts of road improvements shows that the estimation of production and marketing changes is related to strong uncertainties. The low reliability of the predictions favours risk averse investment strategies:

- Choice of the cheapest investment opportunity related to the local needs. In an initial development phase the improvement of footpaths or construction of motorable tracks might be more appropriate than that of a wide feeder road.
- Spatial distribution of investments: build as cheaply and extensively as possible or undertake spot improvements on existing roads and wait for the response of the producers. If bottlenecks occur then further investments can be warranted in the responding regions.
- Choice of labour intensive construction methodologies in order to distribute the direct income effects more equally among the local population.
- Leave the risk assessment to the producers: a small scale credit system delegates the decision about the productive effects to the farmers. Probably the individual appraisal of the farmers is more reliable than the global assessment of a highly educated planner.

7   Summary

There is no doubt that transport infrastructure is essential for the development of rural areas in Sub-Saharan Africa. Consequently for a long time economic theory emphasised the positive role of transport infrastructure investments in the development process. This optimism faded away in the 1960s when empirical studies showed up the permissive character of transport investments. Infrastructure has henceforth been regarded as necessary, but not sufficient precondition for economic growth. Negative impacts might occur if formerly protected markets are exposed to international competition, if increasing human activity entails environmental degradation or if out-migration is stimulated by better access. The "New Growth Theory" inflamed again the discussion about the macroeconomic role of transport in the process of economic development.

This study contributes to the discussion from the regional perspective by assessing the impacts of a pilot project in the Makete District (Tanzania). For the first time a variety of integrated transport interventions were implemented. Two comprehensive household surveys before and at the end of the project form the basis for the assessment of the interventions. The results of the field study are used to calibrate an econometric model with a systems dynamics approach, which is meant to give more insights into the interrelations of the observed effects.

The empirical evidence in the Makete District shows, that **Road and Track Construction** entailed mainly positive effects, which are often emphatically affirmed by the rural population. Roads can stimulate agricultural production and save time which would have been used for the transport of crops to local markets. But the effects of roads are very much dependent on the existing local conditions. For example two survey villages with the best road access could not take advantage of the improved marketing possibilities. In the first village, which was a traditional source for migrant labour, the rural exodus increased and the agricultural production stagnated. The second village could not compensate for the breakdown of the regional pyrethrum market, while a neighbouring village with a worsening road access performed surprisingly well. The latter village profited from its traditional trading links and transported the whole market production on headload down a steep escarpment. The strongest impacts of the road investment were registered in a village, which is too far away from the market to undertake daily return trips and where heavy, low value products are cultivated. Here transport by headload would be too time consuming and tiring.

Agroecological and historical frame conditions very much seem to determine the effects of rural road investments. In order to reduce the unreliablilites of ex-ante-assessments, a risk reducing strategy should be applied: build as cheaply and extensively as possible. Further investments can be warranted later for the 'successful' roads, if farmers increase production and administrators show their ability to maintain the infrastructure. The construction and maintenance of rural roads would be most favourably undertaken with labour based construction technologies, because project funds and foreign currency are saved and local employment is created.

But roads are not enough! Even a good road access does not enable house-holds in Makete to undertake more than two motorised trips per year[1]. Rural households walk the overwhelming majority of the remaining 1860 trips, mainly for water and firewood collection and to the fields. Most of the rural transport activities take place in and around the villages on paths and trails. Women carry the greatest share of the loads on their heads which accumulate to considerable transport burdens in terms of tons, tkm and time. Not only the effort and drudgery of the transport activities, but also the time constraints especially during peak labour periods hamper the growth of agricultural production. A rural development strategy must take into account that expanding agricultural production entails growing transport activities to the fields and to markets, which increase existing transport problems. Road investments only influence the transport of goods to the markets, but the bulk of the household's transport burden does not change. An integrated transport approach is more appropriate to stimulate rural development. This approach takes into account

- the improvement of infrastructure, including roads, tracks and paths,
- the supply of conveyances available, including motor vehicles and Intermediate Means of Transport (IMT),
- the implementation of transport avoiding measures, e.g. water supply, woodlots, low consumption stoves,
- and the provision of transport services like bus-services, the location of motorised and non-motorised vehicles.

The field study and the system-model demonstrate that non-motorised transport interventions generate the same magnitude of effects as road investments.

The cheapest transport intervention was the improvement of a **Footpath** with regional importance leading down a steep escarpment to a regional market. Gang leaders and foremen were trained to conduct simple improvements on the path such as building wooden bridges and stairs, digging small ditches for drainage, constructing timber guard barriers and winding the path on steep slopes. The local population gave very positive feedback regarding the effects of the improvements; travel is much faster and safer, bigger loads can be carried and one third of the households is able to reach new places. The latter statement must not be underestimated because the path improvement is an appropriate measure to reduce rural isolation. Agricultural production in the catchment area

---

1 In the village with the best motorised access two trips per year are registered, while in the most remote village less than half a trip can be observed.

increased more strongly than in the remaining villages. The number of pedestrians using the path to reach a regional market is higher than that of passengers using the feeder road mentioned above. A considerable amount of traffic was generated by the footpath improvement. The absolute benefits from the improvement are nevertheless quite small, because the catchment area has a 'traditional', low market orientation. But the low construction costs attribute a relatively high benefit-cost-ratio to the footpath improvement.

Both the field study and the model show that in an initial phase, when the economy is exclusively relying on subsistence production and barter, a footpath improvement can give stimulus to regional development especially if 'traditional' trading links are ameliorated. Low costs and high efficiency favour this transport investment. The impact of a footpath is limited because the catchment area is restrained to half a day's walking distance. Therefore peripheral regions will hardly be affected at all by the improvement of footpaths before a road opens up the area. Footpath improvement might be the initial stimulus for a growth process if a village lies within walking distance from a road and if light high-value-crops can be produced.

Transport restrictions occur if agricultural production grows and bigger weights have to be transported. Road construction can only solve the problem of market related transport, but not that of transporting the harvested crops to the collection points. In this case **Intermediate Means of Transport** (IMT) can reduce the transport bottlenecks by more sizeable carrying capacities and a faster speed. The IMT have strong impacts on the welfare of their owners in that they enable the farmers to cultivate bigger fields and use more fertiliser, which gives rise to much higher production and income. The purchase of an IMT changes the productivity of the household from decreasing to increasing returns to scale. In Makete donkeys have more important effects than bicycles and wheelbarrows. Donkeys are mainly used to transport agricultural products and farm inputs, while bicycles mainly carry persons on external trips to markets, health facilities and grinding mills. The latter reduce the isolation of the households by enabling them to undertake more external trips.

The IMT were exclusively owned by men and thus not used for the female tasks of water and firewood collection. IMT-possessing households are comparatively wealthier and have higher productivity than non-IMT households. It could not be clarified if the purchase of an IMT was the reason or the consequence. Further research is therefore necessary in this field.

If these IMT are so effective, why are they not purchased? The reason for this is that the IMT are too expensive to be bought by households which primarily rely on subsistence production. In Makete a household had to spend its total annual marketing revenue to purchase a donkey or a bicycle. The model demonstrates that a revolving credit fund for the purchase of IMT in combination with a feeder road entails the biggest production and income increases. Even if a real interest rate[2] of 12 % is levied, the growth in income will more than compensate for the household's debt service. A credit system has the advantage that the decision about the viability is left to the farmer, who probably can estimate the future benefits better than a planner.

The credit fund would be sustainable even if a repayment quota of only 80 % is assumed. The Grameen Bank in Bangladesh demonstrates how an efficient credit system can be organised on the basis of rural saving groups with a much higher payment-moral. Since the effects of IMT would most probable be stronger if possessed by women, the credits should be primarily distributed to female saving clubs, like the West African "Tontine".

Box 7: Empowerment of Women in India

The Total Literacy Scheme has the aim of empowering women in Pudukkottai District, Tamil Nadu, India. Because mobility is one of the five pillars of the programme a revolving credit fund for 1,500 ladies bicycles was installed. The empowering impact of the scheme can perhaps be best gauged by one of the songs they sing while riding their bicycles:

> We have learned to ride the cycle sister,
> We have set in motion the wheels of life sister.
> We no longer beg our men
> To visit the hospital in times of need.
> Once confined to the kitchen,
> Now round the world we go with speed.

Nitya RAO, University of East Anglia, Norwich, in: International Forum for Rural Transport and Development, Forum News Vol. 2, Issue 3, September 1994

The female transport burden can also be reduced if **Transport Avoiding Measures** are undertaken. Women have to walk long distances to reach the sources of water and firewood or to carry their grains to the next grinding mill. The effects of a piped water supply and repaired grinding mills were observed in Makete. Even though after the installation of a piped water system the consumption of water increased, the total transport time per household decreased considerably. Grinding mills have a smaller impact, because less trips are annually undertaken. The benefit-cost efficiency for both interventions is low, because the investment costs are relatively high. These costs can be reduced if wells instead of expensive water pipes are installed. Other non-transport effects like improved health situation and reduced drudgery for hand-grinding occur. Woodlots and low consumption stoves would most probably entail the same magnitude of transport time reductions but cause a higher cost efficiency. Theoretical deliberations show, that time savings will probably be used either for

---

2 Nominal interest rate minus consumer price increase (inflation rate).

direct productive activities or to increase the welfare of the household e.g. by better child care or cooking. The model demonstrates that production and income effects of transport avoiding measures remain below the impacts of IMT.

The Sub-Saharan rural roads are in a bad condition due to lack of maintenance caused by institutional and financial constraints. Diseconomies occur, because every Dollar saved on road maintenance entails a three dollar increase in Vehicle Operating Costs. World Bank reforms include the implementation of independent road agencies under the control of a board of directors including private and public representatives. One of its main features is the financial independence of these agencies including the right to collect their own revenues. The construction of new infrastructure is difficult to finance in consideration of the constraints on African public budgets. The levy of user charges on new roads can be an adequate solution. The model shows that a 30 km feeder road, which gives access to a region with 20,000 inhabitants, can be financed entirely by road pricing under the following conditions:

- only the regional centre is connected with the external market,
- a low-cost-road is constructed using labour based technology,
- the investments are financed by international credit (real interest rate 8 %),
- road charges are used to pay the debt service and maintenance expenditures,
- the road charges are designed in such a way that after 20 years the debt is completely extinguished.

It can be assumed that traders deduct the road user charges from the producer prices they pay to the farmers. The model estimates that the charges reduce the disposable income of the farmers by 4 %. This amount seems to be a reasonable price to pay for an external access, which enables the farmers to export their products. If all villages in the region receive motorised access, then 138 km of motorable tracks would have to be constructed next to the feeder road. Even with a low cost-construction, the necessary user-charges would leave no extra benefits to the farmers. Thus in an initial stage of development the implementation of motorised access to all villages cannot be recommended.

The system model also shows, that the timely scheduling of different transport interventions is the most favourable scenario. In an initial period, when the economy is predominantly relying on subsistence, the improvement of footpaths to local markets and the promotion of IMT can be the starting point for economic development. When transport loads to markets grow, the construction of a low cost road access to the regional centre can improve the evacuation of crops. Road user charges contribute to the redemption of the debt and a decade after the road construction sufficient funds will be collected to finance local tracks to all villages. After two decades enough money can be raised to pay even expensive transport avoiding measures.

Why have these often inexpensive and efficient measures not been implemented by communities or districts? On the communal level the lack of decision competence, scarce funds and little local initiative can be suggested. On the district and national level the awareness about integrated transport planning is often low, while the international donors mostly favour the 'road and car' approach.

An integrated transport approach necessitates the development of new assessment methodologies for all types of the rural transport interventions described above. Future production increases and time savings are the main benefits which have to be assessed on the basis of household and road surveys. Several problems occur, which cannot be solved satisfactorily today: how can the future motorised transport be predicted? How can reductions in transport time be monetarised? How can the improved safety and health situations be included in the valuations? Which evaluation methodology is inexpensive and simple enough to be used by local decision makers? Future research is warranted in this field as well.

The Makete Project also demonstrates that the involvement of the local population in planning and construction is a step towards sustainability. The project components with strongly individual or communal interests were most successful. Ex-ante-evaluations should therefore appraise local needs e.g. the demand for IMT, as well as the willingness to give their own contribution to the project and the ability to adequately maintain the infrastructure.

The economic and social development of rural areas in Sub-Saharan Africa remains one of the most important tasks for the decades to come. In most rural areas labour intensive shifting cultivation is practised using hoes, little fertiliser and practically no improved seeds. In addition transport activities are very time consuming and therefore hamper the growth of production. A eurocentric transport approach, which focuses exclusively on motorised transport, does not reflect the production constraints of African rural households. This study demonstrates that the improvement of the local transport system in and around the village can free up forces which stimulate economic development. Reduced effort and drudgery in transport, decreasing time constraints and better access to public facilities and markets will most probably entail an expansion of agricultural production. Intermediate Means of Transport can increase agricultural productivity, reduce rural isolation and thus raise the acceptance of agricultural innovations. A productivity increase due to the use of ploughs, fertiliser and improved seeds is the next step towards a modern agricultural system. Growing rural incomes will lead to an expansion in the demand for consumer goods and thus create non-agricultural employment in commerce and in small scale industries. Transport improvement for rural households is an important precondition for this dynamic process, which can be the basis for the development of the whole national economy.

References

Transport Theories and Appraisal Methodologies

ABRAHAM, Günter G.(1993): Appropriate Means of Road Infrastructure and Transportation in Rural Areas: A Case-Study of Labour-Intensive Methods, in: THIMM, Heinz-Ulrich und Herwig HAHN (Ed): Regional Food Security and Rural Infrastructure, International Symposium in Gießen/Rauischolzhausen May 3-6, p. 207-222.

ADLER, HANS A: (1987): Economic Appraisal of Transport Projects, A Manual with case Studies, The World Bank, Baltimore and London.

AFFUM, Joseph K. and Farhad AHMED (1995): Use of GIS as a Decision Making Tool in Integrated Rural Transport Planning, University of South Australia, mimemo.

AHMED, Farhad, CARAPETIS, Steve and Map TAYLOR (1995): Rural Transport in Bangladesh: Impact of Non-Motorised Transport on Household's Activity Patterns, Paper presented at the International Conference of the Eastern Asia Society of Transportation Studies (EASTS), Manila 28-29 September.

AHMED, Raissudin und M. HOSSAIN (1990): Development Impact of Rural Infrastructure, International Food Policy Research Institute, Research Report No. 83, Washington D.C.

AIREY, Tony (1992): Transport as a Factor and Constraint in Agricultural Production, Local Level Transport in Sub Saharan Africa, Rural Travel and Transport Project, The World Bank, ILO, Ardington, Oxon.

ANDERSON, G. William und Charles G. VANDERVOORT (1982): Rural Roads Evaluation Summary Report, USAID Program Evaluation Report No. 5.

ANDERSON, Mary und Debby BRYCESON (1993): Reducing the Burden of African Women, in: Appropriate Technology, p.14-16

ASCHAUER, David Allan (1989): Is Public Expenditure Productive? in: Journal of Monetary Economics 23: 177-200.

BANJO, Adegboyega G. (1980): The Theoretical Basis for Travel Time Savings Valuation in Developing Countries, Department of Civic Design, University of Liverpool, Working Paper 15, Liverpool.

BARON, Paul(1980): The Impact of Transport on the Social and Economic Development in Less Developed Countries, in: Policy and Decision Making, Vol. 1 London, p. 47-53.

BARTH, Ursula and Claus HEIDEMANN (1987): Rural Transport in Developing Countries, - A synopsis of findings and a framework for studies, Karlsruhe.

BARTH, Ursula (1989): Frauen gehen lange Wege, Schriftenreihe des Instituts für Regionalwissenschaft (IFR) No. 36, Karlsruhe

BARWELL, I., EDMONDS, G.A., HOWE, J.D.G.F. and J. DE VEEN (1985): Rural Transport in Developing Countries, ILO, London.

BARWELL, Ian (1993): Final Synthesis of Findings and Conclusions from Village Travel and Transport Surveys and Related Case Studies, Local Level Rural Transport in Sub-Saharan Africa, The World Bank, ILO, Ardington, Geneva.

BARWELL, Ian und Jonathan DAWSON (1993): Roads are not Enough, Intermediate Technology Publications, London.

BARWELL, Ian, HATHWAY, G.K. und John HOWE (1982): Guide to Low-Cost Vehicles for Rural Communities in Developing Countries, Ardington.

BEENHAKKER, H.L., LAGO, A.M. (1983): Economic Appraisal of Rural Roads, World Bank Staff Working Papers No. 610, Washington.

BEENHAKKER, Henry L. (1979): Identification and Appraisal of Rural Roads Projects, Staff Working Paper No. 362, The World Bank, Washington D. C.

BERLINER SOMMERSEMINAR (1986): Verkehrsplanung in Entwicklungsländern; Mehr Straßen oder neue Wege?, Schriftenreihe des Instituts für Verkehrsplanung und Verkehrswegebau der TU Berlin, Heft 21.

BOSERUP, Ester (1981): Population and Technological Development, Oxford.

BOSERUP, Ester (1989): Woman's Role in Economic Development, London.

BÖTTCHER, Harry (1995): Multikriterielle Entscheidungskonzepte in den Sozialwissenschaften, Baden Baden.

BROSIUS, Gerhard and Felix (1995): SPSS Base System und Professional Statistics, Bonn.

BRYCESON, Deborah Fahy and John HOWE (1992): African Rural Households and Transport: Reducing the Burden on Women? International Institute for Infrastructure, Hydraulic and Environmental Engineering, IHE Working Paper IP-2, Delft.

BRYCESON, Deborah Fahy and John HOWE (1993): Women and Labour Based Road Works in Sub-Saharan Africa, International Institute for Infrastructure, Hydraulic and Environmental Engineering, IHE Working Paper IP-4, Delft.

CARAPETIS, S. , BEENHAKKER, H.L. and J.D.G.F. HOWE (1984): The Supply and Quality of Rural Transport Services in Developing Countries, World Bank Staff Working Papers No.654, Washington.

CARNEMARK, Curt, BIDERMANN, Jaime and David BOVET (1976): The Economic Analysis of Rural Road Projects, World Bank Staff Working Paper No.241, Washington.

CHAMBERS, Robert (1980): Rural Poverty Unperceived: Problems and Remedies, World Bank Staff Paper No. 400, Washington D.C.

CHAMBERS, Robert (1980): Rapid Rural Appraisal, Rational and Repertoire, Brighton.

CLEMENTS, Paul (1995): A Poverty-Oriented Cost-Benefit Approach to the Analysis of Development Projects, in: World Development Vol. 23, No.4, pp 577-592.

COOK, Cynthia, BEENHAKKER, Henry L. and Richard HARTWIG (1986): Institutional Considerations in Rural Roads Projects, World Bank Staff Working Papers No. 748, Washington.

COOK, Peter and Cynthia (1990): Methodological Review of the Analysis of the Impacts of Rural Transportation in Developing Countries, in: Transportation Research Record No. 1274, National Research Council, Washington, p. 167-178

COOTNER, P. (1963): The Role of the Railroads in US Economic Growth, in: Journal of Economic History, December, p.72.

DAWSON, Jonathan (1993): Improving Access for the Poor, in: Appropriate Technology, No. 1 June, p.1-4.

DE VEEN, Jan (1984): The Rural Access Roads Program, Appropriate Technology in Kenya, ILO Geneva.

DE VEEN, Jan (1991): Appropriate Use of Available Resources and Technology, in: The Road Maintenance Initiative, Sub-Saharan Transport Program, The World Bank, Washington D.C., p. 115-122.

DEGWITZ, Ulrich (1992): Rural Transport in Peripheral Areas of Southern Malawi, Universität Gießen.

DENNIS, Ron and John HOWE (1993): The Bicycles in Africa: Luxury or Necessity? Velocity Conference "The Civilised city: Response to New Transport Priorities" 6th-10th September 1993, Nottingham UK, International Institute for Infrastructure, Hydraulic and Environmental Engineering, IHE Working Paper IP-3, Delft.

168

DVWG (1980): Nutzen-Kosten-Untersuchungen im Verkehrswesen, Eine Zusammenfassung von Seminarveranstaltung und Workshop vom 19. bis 23. September 1977 in Karlsruhe, Schriftenreihe der Deutschen Verkehrswissenschaftlichen Gesellschaft B 49/1 und B49/2, Cologne.

EDLING, Herbert und Ernst FISCHER (ed.) (1991): Steuerverwaltung und Entwicklung, Baden Baden, pp 35-62.

EDMONDS, G. A. and Colin RELF (1987): Transport and Development, A Discussion Paper, ILO, Geneva.

EDMONDS, G.A. und J.J. van de Veen (1993): Technology Choice for the Construction and Maintenance of Roads in Developing Countries, ILO, Geneva.

EEKHOFF, Johann, HEIDEMANN, Claus and Günter STRASSERT (1981): Kritik der Nutzwertanalyse, Institut für Regionalwissenschaft der Universität Karlsruhe, Diskussionspapier No. 10, Karlsruhe.

FISCHER, Wolfgang (1983): Querschnittsanalyse zur Inspektion Straßenbau in Afrika, Bundesministerium für Wirtschaftliche Zusammenarbeit (BMZ), Bonn

FOGEL, R.W. (1964): Railroads and American Economic Growth, in: Econometric History, Baltimore.

FORRESTER, J.W. (1972): Grundsätze einer Systemtheorie, Wiesbaden. (engl.: Principles of Systems)

FRITZ, Joachim (1975): Integrierte Verkehrsplanung im ländlichen Raum von Entwicklungsländern, Berlin.

FUNCK, Rolf (1989): Verfahren der sozialen Bewertung von Straßenprojekten: Stand, Probleme, Entwicklungen, in: Roads and Traffic 2000, International Road and Traffic Conference, Berlin 6-9 September 1988, Vol. 3, Theme 3 Traffic Economy, p. 51-56.

GAUTHIER, HOWARD L. (1973): Geography, Transportation and Regional Development, in: HOYLE, B.S.: Transport and Development, London, p.19-31.

GOODMAN, Michael R. (1974): Study Notes in System Dynamics, Massachusetts.

GTZ (1984): Praxis der Verkehrsplanung in Entwicklungsländern, Das Beispiel Afrika.

HARRAL, Cell G. (1988): Road Deterioration in Developing Countries, Causes and Remedies, A World Bank Policy Study, Washington D.C.

HEGGIE, Ian (1994): Management and Financing of Roads; An Agenda for Reform, Technical Paper No. 275, Africa Technical Department Series, The World Bank, Washington D.C.

HEIERLI, Urs (1993): Environmental Limits to Motorisation, SKAT- Swiss Centre for Development Cooperation in Technology and Management, St. Gallen.

HEINZE, G. Wolfgang (1967): Der Verkehrssektor in der Entwicklungspolitik, Ifo-Institut f. Wirtschaftsforschung, Afrika-Studien 21, München.

HEINZE, G. Wolfgang (1973): Verkehrsinvestition als Instrument der Regionalpolitik in Entwicklungsländern, in: Schweizerisches Archiv für Verkehrswissenschaft und Verkehrspolitik, Nr.2, Zürich, p. 220-247.

HELLEINER, G.K. (1992): Structural Adjustment and Long-term Development in Sub-Saharan Africa, in STEWARD, Frances et al (Ed).: Alternative Development Strategies in Sub-Saharan Africa, p. 48-78, New York.

HERTEL, Sven (1991): Labour-Intensive Public Works in Sub-Saharan Africa, ILO, Geneva.

HILLE, Christine and Nic van der JAGD (1995): Findings from Household-level Rural Transport Survey and Recommendations for Household-level Survey Methodology, Pilot Integrated Rural Transport Project, Malawi, Centre for International Cooperation and Technology (CICAT), TU Delft.

HINE, John L. (1993): Transport and Marketing Priorities to Improve Food Security in Ghana and the Rest of Africa, in: THIMM, Heinz-Ulrich und Herwig HAHN (Ed): Regional Food Security and Rural Infrastructure, International Symposium in Gießen/Rauischolzhausen May 3-6, p. 251-266.

HIRSCHMAN, A.O. (1958): Strategy of Economic Development, Yale.

HOFMEIER, Rolf (1970): Die politische Ökonomie von Verkehrsvorhaben in Afrika, in: Afrika Spektrum 79/1, Hamburg.

HOWE, John (1980): The Future of Surface Transport in Africa, in: African Affairs Vol. 74, No.296 July, London, p. 314-325.

HOWE, John (1994): Enhancing Non-Motorised Transport Use in Africa - Changing the Policy Climate, International Symposium on Non-Motorised Transportation, Beijing, China May 23-25, IHE Working Paper IP-5, Delft.

HOWE, John (1994): Infrastructure Investment in Bangladesh: Who Really Benefits and How? International Institute for Infrastructure, Hydraulic and Environmental Engineering, IHE Working Paper IP-6, Delft.

HOWE, John und Peter RICHARDS (1984): The Impact of Rural Roads on Poverty Alleviation: A Review of the Literature, in: Rural Roads and Poverty Alleviation, ILO, Intermediate Technology Publications, p. 48-81, London.

HOWE, John (1990): Benefits of Rural Roads: Current Issues and Concepts.

HOYLE, B.S. (1973): Transport and Economic Growth in Developing Countries: The Case of East Africa, in: ibid.: Transport and Development, London, p.50-62.

JÄGER, Adolf (1972): Die Verkehrsthematik in der Entwicklungspolitik, München.

JIMENEZ, Emmanuel (1994): Human and Physical Infrastructure: Public Investments and Pricing Policies in Developing Countries, The World Bank, Washington D.C.

KAIRA, Charles K. (1993): Der Transportbedarf der ländlichen Bevölkerung in Entwicklungsländern, Ansätze zu einer Verbesserung der Verkehrsplanung, Schriftenreihe des Instituts für Regionalwissenschaft Heft Nr. 21, Karlsruhe.

KILLICK, Tony (1993): The Adaptive Economy, Adjustment Policies in Small Low Income Countries, Economic Development Institute of The World Bank, Washington.

KOCHENDÖRFER-LUCIUS, Gudrun (1989): Ländlicher Wegebau- Ein Beitrag zur Agrarentwicklung? IFO-Institut f. Wirtschaftsforschung, Afrika-Studien, München.

KREDITANSTALT FÜR WIEDERAUFBAU KFW(1985): Ländliche Entwicklung im Rahmen der finanziellen Zusammenarbeit mit Entwicklungsländern, Frankfurt/Main.

KROH, Wolfgang (1987): Kosten- und Finanzierungsaspekte des Straßenverkehrs in Entwicklungsländern, in: Verkehr in Entwicklungsländern, 8. Daimler-Benz Seminar, 20/21 November 1986, Berlin.

LEE, Joo-Young und Ludger VONNAHME (1985): Der Einfluß des Verkehrssystems auf die sektorale und regionale Entwicklung der Republik Korea, Schriftenreihe zur Industrie- und Entwicklungspolitik, Berlin.

LEVI, John (1982): Economics of African Agriculture, London.

LEVY, Hernán and Patrick O. Malone (1988): Transport Policy Issues in Sub-Saharan Africa, Report of a Series of Roundtables held in Rome, Italy, April 1-18, 1986, An EDI Policy Seminar Report No. 9, The World Bank, Washington D.C.

LIST, Friedrich (1837): Die Welt bewegt sich, über die Auswirkungen der Dampfkraft und der neuen Transportmittel..., Pariser Preisschrift, nach der französischen Handschrift, übersetzt von Eugen WALTER, 1985, Göttingen.

MALMBERG-CALVO, Christina (1994): Case Study on Intermediate Means of Transport: Bicycles and Rural Women in Uganda, The World Bank, SSATP Working Paper No. 12, Washington.

MANN, Hans-Ulrich, ZACHCIAL, Manfred, GÖTZ, Bettina und Hans Dieter HARTMANN (1988): Verbesserung der Prognoseverfahren für die Verkehrsnachfrage in ländlichen Räumen afrikanischer Länder, Köln.

MASON, Melody und Sydney THRISCUTT (1989): Road Deterioration in Sub-Saharan Africa, in: PTRC Transport and Planning Annual Meeting, Brighton, p. 19-42.

MAYWORM, P.D. (1982): Personal Travel Demand Forecasting on Rural Roads in Developing Countries. Transportations and Water Department, The World Bank.

MELKIZEDECK and E. SANARE (1986): An Overview of the Performance of the Public Transport Corporations in Developing Countries, in: GTZ: Future Aspects of Transportation in Third World Countries, International Seminar for High Government Representatives and General Mangers of Public Transport Corporations of Developing Countries, Minden, p. 229-264.

MELLOR, John (1985): The Changing World Food Situation, Washington.

METSCHIES, Gerhard (1985): Der nicht motorisierte Verkehr aus der Sicht der Förderinstitutionen, in: Verkehr in Entwicklungsländern, 8. Daimler-Benz Seminar, 20/21 November 1986, Berlin

METSCHIES, Gerhard (1992): Gut, besser, ausbessern, in: GTZ-Info, Zeitschrift für technische Zusammenarbeit, No. 5, Eschborn.

MIEDEMA, J.W.H. (1995): An Attempt at an Improved Prioritization Method, Pilot Integrated Rural Transport Project in Malawi, Delft University, Department of Infrastructure, Delft.

MILLARD, R.S. (1973): Der Straßenverkehr in den Entwicklungsländern, in: Internationaler Kongreß für Straßenwesen, Wiesbaden, pp 5.

MÜLLER, Meike (1994): Die ökonomische Bewertung von Entwicklungshilfeprojekten im Verkehrssektor, Diplomarbeit am IWW, Karlsruhe.

MYRDAL, Gunnar (1974): Ökonomische Theorie und unterentwickelte Regionen, Stuttgart.

RABENAU, Kurt von (1993): Rural Road Construction and Agricultural Production in Developing Countries, in: THIMM, Heinz-Ulrich und Herwig HAHN (Ed): Regional Food Security and Rural Infrastructure, International Symposium in Gießen/Rauscholzhausen May 3-6, p.267-276.

RIVERSON, John and S. CARAPETIS (1991): Potential of Intermediate Means of Transport in Improving Rural Travel and Transport in Sub-Saharan Africa, Transport Research Record, May 1991

RIVERSON, John, GAVIRA, Juan und Sydney THRISCUTT (1991): Rural Roads in Sub-Saharan Africa, Lessons from World Bank Experience.

ROTHENGATTER, Werner (1980): Bewertungen von Investitionsalternativen durch sukzessive Entscheidungsfilter, in DVWG: Nutzen-Kosten-Untersuchungen im Verkehrswesen, Schriftenreihe der Deutschen Verkehrswissenschaftlichen Gesellschaft B 49/2, Cologne, p. 256-289.

SANDHU, David (1992): Who Pays the Highwayman? in: World Highways, Nov/Dec, p.23-28.

SIEBER, NIKLAS (1988): Raumnutzungskonflikte im Waldland Süd-Kameruns, Hausarbeit für die 1. Staatsprüfung für das Lehramt, Hamburg.

SMITH, Ian (1991): Road Financing and Pricing in Developing Countries, in: The Road Maintenance Initiative, Sub-Saharan Transport Program, The World Bank, Washington D.C., p. 41-49.

STRASSERT, Günter (1984): Entscheidungen über Alternativen ohne Super-Zielfunktion: Schrittweise und Interaktiv, Diskussionspapier Nr. 14, Institut für Regionalwissenschaft der Universität Karlsruhe, Karlsruhe.

TAAFE, Edward J., MORILL, Richard L. and Peter R. GOULD (1970): Verkehrsausbau in unterentwickelten Ländern - eine vergleichende Studie, in BARTELS: Wirtschafts- und Sozialgeographie.

THERKILDSEN/SEMBOYA (1992): Short-term Resource Mobilisation for Recurrent Financing of Rural Local Governments in Tanzania, World Development, Vol. 20, No. 8, p. 1101-1113.

TIMMER, Peter (1988): The Agricultural Transformation, in: CHENERY, Hollis and T.N. SRINIVASAN (ED.): Handbook of Development Economics, Vol. 1, Handbook in Economics 9, Amsterdam, New York, Oxford, Tokyo, p. 276-331.

TINGLE, E.D. (1977): Rural Road Planning in Developing Countries, in Transport Decisions in an Age of Uncertainty, Proceedings of the World Conference on Transport Research, The Hague.

UNITED NATIONS Transport and Communications Decade UNCTADA II (1990): Roads Sub-Sector Working Group, Strategy Paper.

VIESER, Dirk (1992): Probleme der wirtschaftlichen Rechtfertigung von Straßenbauvorhaben in Entwicklungsländern, in: Mäding, Heinrich et al (Ed).: Wirtschaftswissenschaft im Dienste der Politikberatung, p.335-341, Berlin.

VOIGT, Fritz (1959): Die gestaltende Kraft des Verkehrsmittels im wirtschaftlichen Wachstumsprozeß, Bielefeld.

VOIGT, Fritz (1960): Die volkswirtschaftliche Bedeutung des Verkehrssystems, Verkehrswissenschaftliche Forschungen 1, Berlin.

WAGNER, Hans-Günther (1993): A New Road in the Sahel of Mali - Does it Improve Food Security?, in: THIMM, Heinz-Ulrich und Herwig HAHN (Ed): Regional Food Security and Rural Infrastructure, International Symposium in Gießen/Rauischolzhausen May 3-6, p. 223-231.

WATANATADA, Thawat et al (1988): The Highway Design and Maintenance Standards Model, The World Bank, Washington.

WILSON, George W. (1973): Towards a Theory of Transportation and Development, in: HOYLE, B.S., Transport and Development, London.

World Bank (1994): World Development Report 1994: Infrastructure and Development, Washington D.C.

ZACHCIAL, Manfred (1985): Überlegungen zu einer adäquaten Verkehrsplanung in Entwicklungsländern, in: KLATT, Sigurd (Hrsg): Perspektiven wissenschaftlicher Forschung, Festschrift für Fritz Voigt zum 75. Geburtstag, Berlin.

Makete Field Study

AMANI, H.K.R. (1990): Policies to Promote an Effective Private Trading System in Farm Products and Farm Inputs in Tanzania, Tanzanian Economic Trends, Vol. 4 No. 3 October 1991 and Vol. 4 No.4 Jan. 1991, p 36-54.

AYRE, Michael and Christina MALMBERG CALVO (1988): Report on Testing and Development of Low Cost Vehicles, ILO Geneva.

BAGACHWA, M.S.D and T.L. MALYIAMKONO (1990): The Second Economy in Tanzania, Dar Es Salaam.

172

BAGACHWA, M.S.D, MBELLE A.V.Y. and Brian van ARKADIE (ed.) (1992): Market Reforms And Parastatal Restructuring in Tanzania, Dar Es Salaam.

BARWELL, Ian and Christina MALMBERG CALVO (1987): Report of the First Village Survey, Vol.1 and Vol. 2, ILO, Geneva.

BARWELL, Ian and Christina MALMBERG CALVO (1989): The Transport Demand of Rural Households: Findings from a Village Travel Survey, ILO Geneva.

BARWELL, Ian and Peter HARRISSON (1989): Draft Report on Escarpment Survey carried out in October 1988, IT Transport, Ardington 1989.

BIERMANN, Werner and Jean-Marc FONTAINE (1987): Bauern und Bürokraten, Die Krise des tansanischen Transformationsmodells, in: Peripherie No.28, p.19-40.

BOOTH, David, LUGANGIRA, Flora, MASSANJA, Patrick, MVUNGI, Abu, MWAIPOPO, Rosemarie, MWAMI Joaquim and Alison REDMAYNE (1993): Social, Economic and Cultural Change in Contemporary Tanzania, Report to SIDA, Stockholm..

BRYCESON, Deborah (1990): Food Insecurity and the Social Division of Labour in Tanzania, 1919-85, Oxford.

CALVO, Javier (1988): Transport Services in Makete District, ILO Geneva.

CHIWANGA, Meshack E., MILLER, Steven and Andres WIEDERKEHR (1992): Makete Integrated Rural Transport Project, Tripartite Terminal Evaluation, ILO Geneva.

COLLIER, Paul, RADVAN, Samir and WANGWE, Samuel and Albert WAGNER (1990): Labour and Rural Poverty in Rural Tanzania. Study prepared for the ILO, Oxford.

DIERKS, Christian (1995): Landwirtschaftlicher Wandel unter den Bedingungen einer Strukturanpassung am Beispiel des Makete Distriktes in Tansania, Diplomarbeit, Karlsruhe.

DIXON-FYLE, Kanyham and Irene FRIELING (1990): Paths in Rural Transport, ILO Geneva.

FRIELING, Irene and D. Letea MCHOAVU (1991): The donkey as a pack animal in Makete District, The MIRTP Donkey Programme, 1988-1990, ILO/MIRTP, Makete.

HOWE, John (1987): Initial Synthesis of Makete Integrated Rural Transport Project, Project Data Base, ILO CTP66, Geneva.

HOWE, John and Elias TSEGGAI (1985): Makete Integrated Rural Transport Project, Preparatory Mission, ILO Geneva.

Howe, John (1983): Conceptual Framework for Defining and Evaluating Improvements to Local Level Rural Transport in Developing Countries, ILO Geneva.

JENNINGS, Mary (1992): Study of the constraints on Women's Use of Transport in the Makete District, Tanzania, ILO Geneva.

Makete Integrated Rural Transport Project: Progress Reports. ILO Geneva.

MHALILA, Hans Mwanamhalala (1990): Constrained Rural Labour Participation in a Decentralised Planning Process: A Case Study from Makete District 1984-1989, Institute of Social Studies, The Hague.

STATISTISCHES BUNDESAMT (1989): Länderbericht Tansania, Wiesbaden.

STRANDBERG, Tom (1993): Makete Integrated Rural Transport Project, in: Appropriate Technology, No.1 June, p.6-8

TANZANIAN ECONOMIC TRENDS, Vol. 6, No.1 April 1993 and No.2 July 1993, Quarterly Review of the Economy, edited by: The Economic Research Bureau of the University of Dar Es Salaam.

Appendix

Table of Contents

Tanzania: Main Economic Indicators

Indicator	Year	
Calorie supply (Percentage of need)	1985	100 %
Life expectancy at birth	1987	53 Years
Population growth rate	1978-88	3.2 % (3.8 %)*
Growth rate of urban areas	1980-1990	10.8 %
% Population in urban areas	1985	22.3 %
Population density	1989	27.5 Inh/km^2
Inhabitants per hospital bed	1985	548
Literacy rate (>15 Years)	1985	85 %
GNP/Capita	1986	250 $
Per capita income	1989	130 $
Share of agriculture on GDP	1987	53.1 %
Share occupied in agricultural sector	1987	82 %
Share foodcrops grown for subsistence		70 %
External trade: Share Processed products	1981	11 %
External trade: Share agricultural products		75 %
Share second economy		30 %
Cars per 1000 Inhabitants	1987	3
* Estimation according to population census 1988 (Hofmeier 1993, p. 178)		

Location of the Makete District in Tanzania

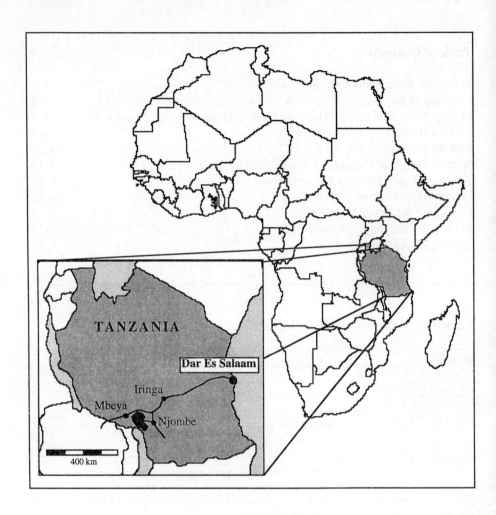

Makete Integrated Rural Transport Project: Objectives and Results

Objective	Output	Results	Realisation	Education	Sustainability	Remarks
Promotion of Donkeys	144 donkeys und 120 panniers sold	Amount of donkeys in Makete increased by 74 %	Three donkey centres constructed, manual for panniers developed	Donkey training	Subsidies for donkeys and panniers	Panniers not used, donkeys only used for transport of crops
Production and promotion of wheelbarrows	58 sold, 76 used for road works; 47 given away	181 wheelbarrows in use	Development of a construction manual	Training of carpenters	No wheelbarrow produced, because demand to little.	Only used for road construction or commercial activities
Upgrading of local footpaths	27.3 km of footpaths improved	Makete counts more than 500 km of footpaths	Unpaid: 1586 days paid labour: 1144 days	Two foremen and 14 gang leaders trained	Villages continue to maintain the paths	Very positive feedback from population
Upgrading of roads and tracks	40.5 km of feeder roads and 11 km of district roads improved: = 51.5 km	Total district network 679 km	Unpaid labour: 32683 days paid labour: 21345 days	Training of 7 foremen, 10 gang leaders, manual (labour-based construction)	Support was only given on request from village	
Capacity building of a road maintenance unit	see above: road improvements		Equipment for labour based methods supplied, Criteria for prioritisation developed	14 Foreman and 1 road inspector trained in labour based construction	Only in self help or if financed by district or by communal taxes	Regional and District authorities often do not fulfil financial promises
Improvement of district workshop	Spare parts supplied, regular maintenance of district vehicles	Default of payments could not be stopped		Staff trained	Financial sustainability since take-over by district council not given	Proposition: Privatisation of workshop
Management consultancy for district transport service	District bus repaired	Objectives not fulfilled, vehicles often not in working order	Condition of roads make bus service during rains impossible	Training programmes not conducted	Bus service is financially not viable	Proposition: Sell of broken down vehicles to finance maintenance
Repair of motorised and promotion of hand driven grinding mills	25 motorised mills repaired, hand operated mills promoted	37 villages have improved grinding mills	Working Mills 1989: 37 1992: 55 Not working: 1989: 44 % 1991: 61 % 1992: 50 %	16 Seminaries conducted, 6 mechanics trained	Financial viability often no given (subsidies by churches)	Maintenance by private operating mechanics recommended. Training in bookkeeping necessary.
Strengthening of planning capacity of district Council	Several seminaries and training programmes conducted	Awareness on the local level is enhanced			Rural Transport is partly institutionalised on the national government level	Rural Travel & Transport is part of the Second Integrated Roads Programme of the World Bank

Source: MIRTP: Full Evaluation Report October 1992

MAKETE INTEGRATED RURAL TRANSPORT PROJECT

HOUSEHOLD INTERVIEW QUESTIONNAIRE I

Interviewer's Name: . . . .   Village: . . . .
Interview Number: . . . .

Note:	Before starting the interview, explain the aim of the survey. The households have been selected **at random** for the interview. The interviewee should have no worries or concerns about why he or she has been selected.

PART A: HOUSEHOLD BASE DATA

1.   HOUSEHOLD COMPOSITION

1.1   Total number of people *presently living* in the household:
(Exclude temporary visitors and persons, who are regularly absent.)

Age	Male	Female
Children (<16)		
16-45		
> 45		

1.2   Number of household members with primary school education . . . .
Number of household members with secondary school education . . . .

1.3   Present head of household: 1. Male [ ]   2. Female [ ]

1.4   Main occupation of present head of household: (tick one)
[ ] 0. No Occupation,   [ ] 4. Businessman (Shop owner, Trader etc.)
[ ] 1. Farmer,   [ ] 5. Fundi
[ ] 2. Village Chairman   [ ] 6. Other
[ ] 3. Other employee (Teacher, secretary, extension officer, etc.)

2.   HOUSEHOLD POSSESSIONS (IN WORKING ORDER)
[ ] 1. Kerosene Stove   [ ] 4.   Sewing Machine
[ ] 2. Kerosene Lamp   [ ] 5.   Tin Roof
[ ] 3. Radio

3.   SOURCES OF CASH INCOME
Identify the main source of cash income for the household (tick one)
[ ] 1. Sale of Agricultural Produce   [ ] 7. Timber
[ ] 2. Sale of Livestock   [ ] 8. Artisan
[ ] 3. Sale of Casual Labour in the Village   [ ] 9. Trading
[ ] 4. Sale of Casual Labour outside Village   [ ] 10. Brewing
[ ] 5. Regular Paid Employment   [ ] 11. Other . . . .
[ ] 6. Cash Remitted by Relative

4.   HOUSEHOLD EXPENDITURE
Estimate of household cash expenditure *in the last 4 weeks*:
1. Food	. . . . .Tsh
2. Consumer goods (Household items, clothes, tools etc.)	. . . . .Tsh
- of which produced in Makete	. . . . .Tsh
- of which produced in Tanzania	. . . . .Tsh
- of which imported to Tanzania	. . . . .Tsh
3. Medical Expenses	. . . . .Tsh
4. Village Contributions/Schoolfees	. . . . .Tsh
5. Social Occasions	. . . . .Tsh
6. Beer and Refreshments	. . . . .Tsh
7. Payments to Relatives	. . . . .Tsh
8. Transport	. . . . .Tsh
9. Other Items	. . . . .Tsh
10.Amount bartered	. . . . .Tsh

A-4

PART B: TRANSPORT ACTIVITIES

5.   MEANS OF TRANSPORT:

5.1   Which means of transport in working order does your household possess?

Means of Transport	Number in working order	Number not in working order
Donkey		
Wheelbarrow		
Bicycle		
Animal Drawn Cart		
Motor-Vehicle		
Other Vehicles		

> **If the household possesses any donkeys, wheelbarrows or bicycles (in working order) fill out the Questionnaire II after finishing this Questionnaire I**
> **Only ask the questions 5.2 and 5.3 if no means of transport are owned**

5.2   Which of the following means of transport would be *most useful for the transport needs* of your household? For what price would you buy your desired means of transport?

Preferred Vehicle	Willingness to pay for preferred vehicle [Tsh]
1. Wheelbarrow	
2. Bicycle	
3. Donkey	
4. Animal Drawn Cart	

5.3   Why did you not purchase your most preferred vehicle? (tick one)
[ ]   1. too expensive
[ ]   2. can not purchase it in Makete
[ ]   3. do not know how to take care or repair it
[ ]   4. other (specify)...

6.   TRANSPORT ACTIVITIES

How are the following transport activities *usually* done?

Purpose/ Destination	For all households				Only if *not* walking	
	Name of Place	Number of Trips	Walking time (one way)	Means of Transport	Travel Time (one way)	Who goes?
Water						
Firewood						
Village Center						
Grinding mill						
MCH Clinic						
Dispensary						
Hospital						
First Market outs. Village						
2nd Market outs. Village						
3rd Market outs. Village						
Other Place outs. Village						
Other Place outs. Village						

Number of Trips: How many persons are travelling per day or week or month or year
Walking time: Walking time means the time used *to walk one way* to the mentioned place.
Means of Transport: Fill in the means of transport used (see instructions)
Travel Time   Write down the actual travel time for a one-way trip using the mode of transport.
Who goes?   Which member of the household usually travels? (see instructions)

7. USE OF IMPROVED FOOTPATHS

7.1 Do members of your household use any footpath (*not* road), which had been improved? Yes/No
If no, continue with question 8.

7.2 If yes, what is the mayor change after the improvement? (tick several)

[ ] 1. There has never been a real advantage.
[ ] 2. The improvements have already disappeared
[ ] 3. No advantages in the rainy season
[ ] 4. We can reach places, which we could not reach before
[ ] 5. We can use other means of transport (eg. bicycle) on the path
[ ] 6. Safety is better
[ ] 7. Faster travelling
        8. If yes, how much is the time saved per one way trip?

Purpose			
Time saved			

8. USE OF GRINDING MILLS

8.1 How does the household mainly grind its flour?   (tick one)
1. Grind all its flour traditionally   [ ]
2. Grind all its flour at home with a hand grinding mill   [ ]
3. Grind all its flour elsewhere with a hand grinding mill   [ ]
4. Use a motorised grinding mill   [ ]

8.2 If the answer is 4:
How much is ground at one time?....................................
Costs for grinding..Tsh

8.3 If the answer is 1, 2 or 3:
Why don't you (always) use a motorised grinding mill?   (tick one)
1. No grinding mill existent   [ ]
2. Mill too far away   [ ]
3. Mill often not in working order   [ ]
4. Grinding too expensive   [ ]
5. Other reasons..   [ ]

PART C: AGRICULTURE

9. CROP PRODUCTION

9.1 For each plot of land cultivated last twelve months obtain the following information:

Plot	1	2	3	4	5	6	7	8	9	10
Total Area										
Walking time										
Plot	11	12	13	14	15	16	17	18	19	20
Total Area										
Walking time										

9.2 Seasonal Crop Production Activities

Season	Clearing, Culti-vation, Planting	Weeding	Harvesting
Duration of the Working Season	weeks	weeks	weeks
Number of trips			
Means of Transport used			

9.3 Purchase of Farm Inputs in the last twelve months.

Input	Weight purchased	Means of Transport
Fertiliser		
Seeds		

10. CROP HARVESTING AND MARKETING

10.1 List the crops harvested and marketed in the last twelve months

	Weight harvested	Weight Marketed	Price [Tsh]
Pyrethrum			
Sorghum			
Maize			
Wheat			
Finger Millet			
Irish Potato			
Sweet Potato			
Beans			
Peas			
Other Vegetables			
Bananas			
Peaches			
Other Fruits			
Ulanzi			
Other			
TOTAL			

10.2 How did you transport the crops from the field?

Crop harvested	Weight transported	Means of transport used	Costs in Tsh (if hired transport)
Total weight		Cross check with total of question 10.1	

10.3 Marketing of Crops in the Last twelve Months?

Crop marketed (question 10.1)	Place of marketing	Weight marketed	Mode of Transport	Costs for Transport (Tsh)
	Total weight			

Calculate the total weight marketed and check with total amount marketed in question 10.1
Check if all mentioned places of marketing are listed in question 6?

10.4 Other Products Marketed
(except big animals: cattle, donkeys, pigs, sheep, etc)

Product	Place of marketing	Weight marketed	Mode of Transport	Costs (Tsh)
	Total weight			

Fill out the questionnaire II only for the households owning donkeys, bicycles or wheelbarrows?

11. DONKEYS

11.1 Purchase of Donkeys
    1. Number of female Donkeys   ....
    2. When was the last donkey purchased   ....
    3. At what price?   ....Tsh
    4. Number of donkeys dying in the last 12 months   ....
11.2 Costs for Donkeys last 12 months?
    1. Veterinary care / medicine   ....Tsh
    2. Additional fodder   ....Tsh
    3. Shelter / Fence   ....Tsh
    4. Pannier   ....Tsh
    5. Other costs   ....Tsh
11.3 How often do you use the donkey?   ....times/month
    1. Transport of own goods   ....
    2. Transport of persons from household   ....
    3. Lending or renting out to other households   ....
    4. Ploughing   ....
    5. other uses..   ....
11.4 If the donkey is rented out to other households
    1. Number of donkeys   ....
    2. Payments received last twelve months for renting: ....Tsh
11.5 Loading of the donkey:

Purpose	Destination	Weight loaded per	How many trips	Number of
1				
2				

12. WHEELBARROWS

12.1 Purchase of Wheelbarrow
    1. When was the last wheelbarrow purchased?   ....
    2. Was it new?   Yes/No
    3. At what price?   ....Tsh
    4. Type: 1. Wood   [ ]   2. Metal   [ ]
12.2 Was it necessary to repair the wheelbarrow   yes/no
    If yes, how often since purchase?   ....
        Which part was repaired? ....
        Costs   ....Tsh
12.3 How often do you use the wheelbarrow?   ....times/month
12.4 Load carrying

Purpose	Destination	Weight loaded per wheelbarrow	How many trips with wheelbarrow
1			
2			

13. BICYCLE
13.1 Purchase of Bicycle
    1. When was the last bicycle purchased?   ....
    2. Was it new?   0.No   1. Yes   2. Self made
    3. At what price?   ....Tsh
13.2 Was it necessary to repair the bicycle   yes/no
    If yes, how often since purchase?   ....
        Which part was repaired? ....
        Costs   ....Tsh/
13.3 How often do you use the bicycle?   ....times/month
13.4 Load carrying

Purpose	Destination	Weight loaded per bicycle	How many trips with
1			
2			

Makete Household Survey 1994

Survey 1994	Unen-amwa	Madi-hani	Uten-gule	Kidope	Bulo-ngwa	Ihela	Mpan-gala	Ngoje	Ngo-nde	Mata-mba	Total
Persons per HH	5.3	4.2	4.6	6.2	5.2	5.1	4.0	5.1	4.5	4.5	4.9
Female Adults/Male	1.15	1.00	0.82	1.23	1.07	1.35	1.12	1.09	1.20	1.14	1.13
Children	2.6	2.1	1.9	3.0	2.5	2.9	1.7	2.2	2.1	2.0	2.3
Persons >45	1.0	0.3	0.9	0.7	0.8	0.9	0.6	0.9	0.4	0.6	0.7
Primary Education	39%	35%	52%	45%	43%	40%	50%	53%	52%	51%	46%
Secondary Education	5%	0%	7%	1%	2%	1%	2%	4%	1%	2%	2%
Female headed HH	24%	7%	27%	5%	15%	14%	10%	6%	16%	12%	13%
Main Occupation of Head of Household											
Farmer	90%	93%	93%	82%	89%	76%	90%	88%	87%	88%	87%
No occupation	0%	0%	7%	0%	1%	0%	3%	0%	0%	1%	1%
Village Chairman	0%	0%	0%	0%	0%	0%	0%	0%	0%	0%	0%
Employee (Teacher,Secr..)	5%	7%	0%	5%	4%	10%	0%	6%	6%	4%	5%
Businessman	0%	0%	0%	0%	0%	0%	0%	0%	6%	3%	1%
Fundi	5%	0%	0%	14%	5%	14%	7%	6%	0%	4%	6%
Other	0%	0%	0%	0%	0%	0%	0%	0%	0%	0%	0%
Household Possessions in Working Order											
Kerosene Stove	10%	0%	7%	0%	4%	5%	0%	0%	3%	1%	3%
Kerosene Lamp	71%	73%	53%	41%	59%	62%	37%	29%	35%	35%	48%
Radio	52%	33%	40%	45%	44%	52%	30%	18%	32%	28%	38%
Sewing Machine	14%	7%	7%	0%	7%	5%	0%	6%	13%	6%	6%
Tin Roof	43%	13%	47%	36%	36%	48%	30%	35%	19%	27%	33%
Sources of Cash Income											
Sale of Agricultural Products	90%	80%	93%	86%	88%	38%	77%	76%	77%	77%	77%
Sale of Livestock	0%	0%	0%	5%	1%	0%	0%	0%	0%	0%	1%
Sale of Casul Labour in the Village	0%	7%	0%	0%	1%	5%	0%	0%	0%	0%	1%
Sale of Casul Labour outside the Village	0%	0%	0%	0%	0%	0%	0%	0%	0%	0%	0%
Regular Paid Employment	5%	7%	0%	0%	3%	14%	0%	0%	6%	3%	4%
Cash Remitted by Relatives	0%	0%	0%	5%	1%	14%	13%	6%	10%	10%	7%
Timber	0%	0%	0%	0%	0%	5%	0%	0%	0%	0%	0%
Artisan	5%	7%	7%	5%	5%	24%	10%	6%	0%	5%	8%
Trading	0%	0%	0%	0%	0%	0%	0%	6%	6%	4%	2%
Brewing	0%	0%	0%	0%	0%	0%	0%	0%	0%	0%	0%
Other	0%	0%	0%	0%	0%	0%	0%	6%	0%	1%	1%
Expenditure last month (US$ 1994)											
Total	29.65	37.98	43.58	34.47	35.68	29.98	17.70	20.75	22.55	20.36	28.00
Estimated Barter	0.37	1.54	3.60	0.39	1.28	0.07	0.00	0.00	0.53	0.22	0.65
Total excluding Barter	29.28	36.44	39.97	34.08	34.39	29.91	17.70	20.75	22.02	20.14	27.35
Food	4.78	3.85	6.44	6.80	5.54	5.96	3.55	3.94	4.06	3.85	4.82
Local Consumer Goods	0.00	0.00	0.00	0.60	0.18	0.35	1.00	0.86	0.99	0.99	0.56
National Consumer Goods	4.18	3.05	5.24	4.32	4.21	5.19	3.85	4.47	4.84	4.43	4.40
Imported Consumer Goods	1.42	1.85	2.65	1.51	1.79	4.37	2.01	3.08	1.90	2.22	2.29
Medical Expenses	7.38	3.36	3.16	2.59	4.22	3.47	1.91	0.89	2.65	1.98	3.12
Fees/Taxes	2.94	3.86	3.75	2.96	3.30	1.02	0.86	1.22	0.69	0.87	1.92
Social Occasions	2.55	0.83	6.47	6.68	4.25	5.81	0.88	1.20	1.50	1.18	3.05
Alcohol/Soft Drinks	1.60	1.92	1.13	5.28	2.68	1.02	0.96	1.14	1.00	0.99	1.72

Survey 1994	Unen-amwa	Madi-hani	Uten-gule	Kidope	Bulo-ngwa	Ihela	Mpan-gala	Ngoje	Ngo-nde	Mata-mba	Total
Transfers to Relatives	0.83	1.57	10.26	1.49	3.12	1.45	0.13	2.38	0.26	0.70	1.81
Transport	3.50	3.28	0.77	1.18	2.20	0.68	0.56	0.98	0.74	0.70	1.34
Other Expenditure	0.09	12.87	0.10	0.67	2.89	0.58	1.99	0.59	3.41	2.23	2.32
Households possessing IMT in Working Order											
Donkeys	0.0%	0.0%	0.0%	0.0%	0.0%	0.0%	8.0%	5.4%	0.0%	4.2%	1.9%
Wheelborrows	0.0%	0.0%	0.5%	0.0%	1.0%	0.0%	1.3%	0.0%	0.0%	0.5%	0.3%
Bicycles	0.9%	1.3%	2.1%	0.4%	0.9%	3.6%	3.3%	8.1%	5.1%	5.0%	2.7%
Desired Means of Transport, if no IMT Possessed											
No IMT desired	4.8%	0.0%	0.0%	4.8%	2.9%	5.0%	3.7%	7.7%	4.0%	4.6%	3.9%
Wheelborrow	4.8%	21.4%	35.7%	0.0%	12.9%	0.0%	0.0%	0.0%	0.0%	0	5.8%
Donkey	9.5%	7.1%	28.6%	42.9%	22.9%	10.0%	77.8%	46.2%	4.0%	43.1%	29.7%
Animal Drawn Cart	4.8%	0.0%	0.0%	9.5%	4.3%	0.0%	0.0%	7.7%	0.0%	1.5%	2.6%
Bicycle	76.2%	71.4%	35.7%	42.9%	57.1%	85.0%	18.5%	38.5%	92.0%	50.8%	58.1%
Willingness to pay for desired IMT (US$ 1994)											
Wheelborrow	1.93	8.37	5.47		6.21						6.21
Donkey	6.76	19.31	14.96	11.8	12.43	5.79	21.74	9.65	28.96	19.23	16.15
Animal Drawn Cart	19.31			19.31	19.31			7.72		7.72	16.41
Bicycle	19.79	17.57	16.6	29.82	21.09	16.14	21.24	33.18	21.48	22.95	20.9
Why was no IMT purchased?											
Wheelborrow											
Too Expensive		66.7%	80%		66.7%						66.7%
Maintenance Problems	100%		20%		22.2%						22.2%
Other		33.3%			11.1%						11.1%
Donkey											
Too Expensive	100%	100%	75.0%	66.7%	75.0%	50.0%	84.2%	100%	100%	88.5%	81.8%
Not Available in Makete				33.3%	18.8%	50.0%	10.5%			7.7%	13.6%
Other			25.0%		6.3%		5.3%			3.8%	4.5%
Bicycle											
Too Expensive	93.8%	90.0%	100%	75.0%	89.7%	82.4%	100%	100%	100%	100%	92.0%
Not Available in Makete				12.5%	2.6%						1.1%
Maintenance Problems	6.2%				2.6%						1.1%
Other		10.0%		12.5%	5.1%	17.6%					5.8%
Use of Grinding Mills											
Usual Way of Grinding											
Traditonally	0%	7%	0%	0%	1%	0%	0%	0%	0%	0%	1%
Handgrinding home	52%	13%	53%	29%	38%	10%	0%	0%	0%	0%	17%
Handgrinding neighbour	5%	0%	20%	38%	17%	0%	0%	0%	0%	0%	7%
Motorised Grinding Mill	43%	80%	27%	38%	46%	90%	100%	100%	100%	100%	76%
Why is no motorised Mill used?											
No Mill Existent	17%	0%	9%	0%	8%	0%	0%	0%	0%	0%	8%
Mill too far away	58%	100%	73%	0%	44%	0%	0%	0%	0%	0%	43%
Mill not in Working Order	0%	0%	0%	7%	3%	0%	0%	0%	0%	0%	3%
Grinding too expensive	25%	0%	18%	93%	46%	100%	0%	0%	0%	0%	48%

Survey 1994	Unen-amwa	Madi-hani	Uten-gule	Kidope	Bulo-ngwa	Ihela	Mpan-gala	Ngoje	Ngo-nde	Mata-mba	Total
Agricultural Production											
Fields											
Number of Plots	6.5	7.4	8.5	9.0	7.8	8.1	5.5	5.2	5.7	5.6	6.9
Total Size of Fields (acres)	4.3	5.2	7.9	8.8	6.6	4.9	3.3	4.0	4.5	3.9	5.2
Average Distance to the Fields [km]	3.6	4.3	4.1	3.9	4.0	4.1	3.6	2.3	3.2	3.1	3.6
Purchase of Fertiliser											
% HH purchasing fertiliser	5%	7%	7%	0%	4%	86%	50%	94%	100%	79%	48%
Weight/ (HH purchasing fertiliser).	2	50	1	0	18	110	107	139	147	135	125
%HH walking	100%	100%	100%		100%	100%	86%	87%	100%	94%	95%
%HH using Wheelb.											
%HH using Donkey							14%	7%		5%	4%
%HH using Bicycle								7%		1%	1%
Purchase of Seeds											
% HH purchasing Seeds	14.3%	7%	0%	0%	6%	14%	10%	0%	15%	10%	9%
Weight/ (HH purchasing Seeds)	4	10	0	0	6	27	13	0	12	13	14
%HH walking	100%	100%			100%	100%	100%		100%	100%	100%
Harvesting of Agricultural Products											
All Products [t]	1.72	2.25	1.57	2.64	2.08	2.05	4.01	3.13	2.38	3.17	2.57
Crops [t]	1.41	2.14	1.38	2.44	1.86	1.31	3.05	1.98	1.76	2.30	1.99
Ulanzi [t]	0.31	0.11	0.20	0.13	0.19	0.65	0.97	1.23	0.64	0.89	0.56
Transport from the Field											
Products transp. fr. Field [t]	1.72	2.20	1.42	2.64	2.03	1.91	2.17	2.63	2.04	2.22	2.10
Tkm "	6.2	10.6	6.3	9.9	8.2	7.6	7.6	5.8	6.7	6.9	7.5
% by Walking	95%	100%	100%	87%	95%	100%	86%	84%	99%	89%	92%
% by Donkey							5%	13%		6%	3%
% hired Donkey							5%			2%	1%
% by Bicycle								2%	1%	1%	
% hired Motor Vehicle							2%	2%		1%	
% by Hired Porters	5%			12%	3%		2%			1%	2%
Marketing of Agricultural Products											
All Products [t]	0.47	0.82	0.27	0.58	0.53	0.41	2.67	1.20	0.97	1.67	1.04
Crops [t]	0.38	0.80	0.21	0.35	0.42	0.20	2.09	0.62	0.75	1.24	0.77
Ulanzi [t]	0.08	0.02	0.06	0.03	0.05	0.21	0.58	0.61	0.23	0.45	0.25
Revenue All products [$]	46.77	35.07	39.47	64.00	48.06	27.37	113.13	99.53	145.14	122.60	79.39
Revenue Crops [$]	44.30	34.60	37.70	48.30	43.20	21.08	96.00	79.20	128.70	106.70	68.23
Crop Marketing											
Field	0%	1%	14%	0%	2%	0%	40%	4%	4%	27%	20%
Home	44%	7%	16%	16%	20%	29%	14%	35%	6%	14%	16%
Village	0%	1%	0%	2%	1%	3%	8%	0%	13%	8%	6%
Street	0%	0%	0%	0%	0%	0%	30%	0%	0%	20%	14%
External	56%	91%	69%	82%	77%	68%	8%	61%	77%	31%	43%

Survey 1994	Unen-amwa	Madi-hani	Uten-gule	Kidope	Bulo-ngwa	Ihela	Mpan-gala	Ngoje	Ngo-nde	Mata-mba	Total
Means of Transport for Crop Marketing											
Tons transported	0.22	0.73	0.15	0.30	0.33	0.14	0.94	0.38	0.67	0.71	0.48
% by Walking	100%	100%	100%	88%	96%	100%	24%	72%	100%	61%	73%
% by Wheelbarrow	0%	0%	0%	0%	0%	0%	0%	0%	0%	0%	0%
% by Donkey	0%	0%	0%	0%	0%	0%	6%	0%	0%	3%	2%
% Hired Donkey	0%	0%	0%	0%	0%	0%	8%	0%	0%	4%	2%
% by Bicycle	0%	0%	0%	0	0%	0%	0%	0%	0%	0%	0%
% Hired Motor Vehicle	0%	0%	0%	0%	0%	0%	19%	28%	0%	13%	9%
% by Hired Porters	0%	0%	0%	12%	4%	0%	43%	0%	0%	20%	14%
Marketing of Other Products											
Field	0%	100%	0%	0%	3%	20%	0%	8%	0%	2%	4%
Home	100%	0%	100%	24%	48%	7%	2%	0%	3%	2%	10%
Village	0%	0%	0%	65%	42%	52%	68%	21%	9%	43%	43%
Street	0%	0%	0%	0%	0%	0%	15%	53%	16%	26%	19%
External	0%	0%	0%	11%	7%	22%	15%	18%	72%	27%	23%
Means of Transport to Market (Other Products)											
Tons transported	0.00	0.00	0.00	0.18	0.05	0.15	0.59	0.53	0.21	0.43	0.24
% transp. by walking				100%		100%	100%	100%	100%	100%	
Marketing of All Agricultural Products											
Field	0%	3%	11%	0%	2%	10%	31%	6%	3%	21%	16%
Home	54%	7%	35%	19%	26%	18%	12%	18%	5%	11%	15%
Village	0%	1%	0%	27%	9%	28%	21%	10%	12%	17%	16%
Street	0%	0%	0%	0%	0%	0%	27%	25%	4%	21%	16%
External	46%	89%	54%	54%	63%	44%	10%	41%	76%	30%	38%
Means of Transport											
Tons transported	0.218	0.73	0.15	0.47	0.39	0.29	1.53	0.91	0.89	1.14	0.72
% by Walking	100%	100%	100%	92%	97%	100%	53%	88%	100%	75%	82%
% by Wheelbarrow	0%	0%	0%	0%	0%	0%	0%	0%	0%	0%	0%
% by Donkey	0%	0%	0%	0%	0%	0%	4%	0%	0%	2%	1%
% Hired Donkey	0%	0%	0%	0%	0%	0%	5%	0%	0%	2%	2%
% by Bicycle	0%	0%	0%	0%	0%	0%	0%	0%	0%	0%	0%
% Hired Motor Vehicle	0%	0%	0%	0%	0%	0%	12%	12%	0%	8%	6%
% by Hired Porters	0%	0%	0%	8%	3%	0%	27%	0%	0%	12%	10%
Transport Activities											
Water Collection											
Trips/annum	1373	1144	1022	1244	1215	1025	840	1031	918	913	1055
Distance [km]	1.2	1.8	1.9	0.9	1.4	1.8	1.5	1.8	2.1	1.8	1.6
Time	855	1010	920	576	816	915	541	914	934	779	811
Tonnes	24.7	17.2	18.4	18.7	20.0	18.5	15.1	18.6	16.5	16.4	18.2
Tkm	30.8	30.3	33.1	17.3	27.1	33.0	19.5	32.9	33.6	28.0	28.2
% HH Walking	95%	100%	100%	100%	99%	100%	100%	100%	100%	100%	99%
% HH by Bicycle	5%				1%						1%

Survey 1994	Unen-amwa	Madi-hani	Uten-gule	Kidope	Bulo-ngwa	Ihela	Mpan-gala	Ngoje	Ngo-nde	Mata-mba	Total
Firewood Collection											
Trips/annum	280	327	392	475	372	337	206	180	131	171	276
Distance [km]	5.2	4.9	3.8	6.0	5.1	5.2	3.8	4.0	8.0	5.5	5.3
Time	397	344	385	806	507	451	204	168	266	221	370
Tonnes	7.0	8.2	9.8	11.9	9.3	8.4	5.2	4.5	3.3	4.3	6.9
Tkm	39.7	36.9	38.5	80.6	51.4	45.1	20.4	16.8	26.6	22.1	37.3
% HH Walking	100%	100%	100%	100%	100%	100%	100%	100%	100%	100%	100%
Village Centre											
Trips/annum	255	201	187	198	213	208	330	127	114	200	206
Distance [km]	1.7	2.7	1.5	1.6	1.9	1.2	1.1	1.6	2.0	1.6	1.6
Time	142	208	157	153	162	141	134	103	104	115	138
% HH Walking	100%	100%	100%	100%	100%	100%	100%	94%	93%	97%	99%
% HH by Bicycle								6%	3%	3%	1%
Grinding Mill											
Trips/annum	42	41	29	81	51	31	21	26	26	24	36
Distance [km]	5.4	9.5	11.6	1.6	6.2	4.9	0.9	1.5	1.7	1.4	3.7
Time	127	188	158	69	129	71	8	17	20	15	71
Tonnes	0.8	0.8	0.5	1.6	1.0	0.7	0.4	0.5	0.5	0.5	0.7
Tkm	10.2	15.0	12.7	5.3	10.2	6.1	0.7	1.3	1.6	1.2	5.6
% HH Walking	100%	100%	100%	100%	100%	100%	100%	94%	100%	99%	100%
% HH using Donkeys								6%		1%	1%
Trips to the Fields											
Trips/annum	199	386	288	347	300	150	139	244	225	196	235
Distance [km]	3.6	4.3	4.1	3.9	4.0	4.1	3.6	2.3	3.2	3.1	3.6
Time	327	909	666	594	597	369	231	278	352	290	429
Tonnes	1.7	2.2	1.4	2.6	2.0	1.9	2.2	2.6	2.0	2.2	2.1
Tkm	6.2	10.6	6.3	9.9	8.2	7.6	7.6	5.8	6.7	6.9	7.5
% HH Walking	100%	100%	100%	100%	100%	100%	100%	94%	100%	100%	100%
% HH by Bicycle								6%			
Trips to MCH Clinic											
Trips/annum	6	8	4	11	7	8	7	6	7	7	7
Distance[km]	3.1	2.8	1.3	5.8	3.8	1.1	2.0	1.4	2.8	2.2	2.7
Time	10	11	3	30	15	4	8	4	10	8	10
% HH Walking	100%	100%	100%	100%	100%	100%	100%	100%	100%	100%	100%
Trips to Dispensary											
Trips/annum	23	0	16	15	14	0	10	8	7	8	10
Distance [km]	7.2	15.0	1.5	9.1	6.5	0.0	4.2	4.0	12.0	7.2	6.9
Time	65	1	9	64	40	0	18	16	47	29	30
% HH Walking	1.00	100%	100%	94%	98%	no data	100%	93%	88%	94%	97%
% HH by Bicycle									7%	12%	6%	3%
% HH Using Other Means				6%	2%						1%

Survey 1994	Unen-amwa	Madi-hani	Uten-gule	Kidope	Bulo-ngwa	Ihela	Mpan-gala	Ngoje	Ngo-nde	Mata-mba	Total
Trips to Hospital											
Trips/annum	9	11	4	9	8	19	2	3	6	4	8
Distance [km]	8.7	6.9	12.0	10.5	9.3	4.5	14.9	9.7	13.4	12.9	9.5
Time	40	34	24	45	37	43	8	17	41	23	31
% HH Walking	100%	100%	100%	95%	98%	95%	75%	71%	87%	82%	92%
% HH by Bus							13%		13%	10%	4%
% HH Other Means				5%	2%	5%	12%	29%		8%	4%
All Trips to all Health Facilities											
Trips/annum	38	19	24	34	30	27	19	17	20	19	25
Distance [km]	6.8	5.3	3.3	8.4	6.6	3.5	4.6	4.2	9.1	6.5	6.5
Time	115	46	36	140	92	47	34	40	98	61	72
Internal Marketing											
Trips/annum	0.0	0.3	0.0	8.0	2.5	5.7	32.6	21.4	7.5	20.2	10.9
Time	0.0	0.2	0.0	3.2	1.0	1.7	9.2	8.5	3.7	6.9	3.8
Tonnes	0.00	0.01	0.00	0.16	0.05	0.11	0.65	0.45	0.15	0.40	0.22
tkm per annum	0.00	0.02	0.00	0.25	0.08	0.14	0.73	0.68	0.30	0.55	0.30
External Marketing											
Trips/annum	11	36	7	16	17	9	13	24	37	25	20
Time	27	62	20	58	42	11	50	60	116	79	55
Tonnes	0.22	0.73	0.15	0.31	0.34	0.18	0.25	0.49	0.74	0.50	0.39
tkm per annum	2.15	4.96	1.62	4.66	3.37	0.90	4.00	4.80	9.32	6.29	4.39
Trips to External Markets											
Trips/annum	108	86	93	169	119	62	56	92	79	73	91
Distance [km]	8.2	8.8	11.7	12.3	10.2	5.4	6.1	7.7	12.7	9.2	9.2
Time	453	425	534	1049	644	186	186	348	486	341	450
Mode of Transport to 1st market											
% HH Walking	100%	100%	100%	100%	100%	100%	100%	100%	100%	100%	100%
Mode of Transport to 2nd market											
% transp. by walking	100%	100%	100%	100%	100%	100%	93%	100%	86%	93%	97%
% HH Bicycle									14%	5%	2%
% HH Other Means of Transport							7%			2%	1%
Mode of Transport to 3rd market											
% HH Walking	100%	100%	100%	100%	100%	100%	-	100%	100%	100%	100%
Other Trips outside the village											
Trips/annum	16	11	0	50	22	17	67	49	34	50	34
Time	65	138	10	154	112	36	103	89	97	98	93
% HH Walking	70%	60%		70%	60%	50%	83%	73%	58%	70%	64%
% HH Bicycle									8%	3%	2%
% HH Bus	30%	40%	100%	30%	40%	50%	13%	27%	34%	25%	33%
% HH Other Means of Transport							4%			2%	1%
Total Transport Activities											
Trips/annum	2310	2214	2035	2606	2324	1863	1711	1788	1554	1665	1970
Time	2416	3131	2856	3390	2948	2183	1347	1875	2263	1828	2346
Time(including other trips)	2481	3269	2866	3544	3060	2219	1450	1964	2360	1926	2439
Tonnes	34	29	30	35	33	30	24	27	23	24	29
tkm per annum	89	98	92	118	100	93	53	62	78	65	83

A-14

Makete Household Survey 1986/87

Survey 1986/87	Unen-amwa	Madi-hani	Uten-gule	Kidope	Bulo-ngwa	Ihela	Mpan-gala	Ngoje	Ngo-nde	Mata-mba	Total
Persons per HH	5.3	4.2	5.2	4.5	4.8	4.9	4.45	4.9	4.7	4.8	4.8
Female Adults/Male	1.47	1.33	1.32	0.96	1.3	1.38	0.97	0.96	1.18	1.1	1.2
Children	2.69	1.63	2.82	2	2.3	2.15	1.72	2	2.29	2.1	2.2
Female headed HH	25%	19%	20%	17%	20%	28%	14%	17%	26%	21%	21%
Main Occupation of Head of Household											
Farmer	94%	94%	75%	100%	90%	95%	100%	100%	94%	97%	94%
No occupation	0%	0%	0%	0%	0%	0%	0%	0%	0%	0%	0%
Village Chairman	0%	0%	0%	0%	0%	0%	0%	0%	0%	0%	0%
Employee(Teacher,Secr..)	6%	6%	20%	0%	8%	5%	0%	0%	0%	1%	4%
Businessman	0%	0%	5%	0%	1%	0%	0%	0%	3%	1%	1%
Fundi	0%	0%	0%	0%	0%	0%	0%	0%	0%	0%	0%
Other	0%	0%	0%	0%	0%	0%	0%	0%	3%	1%	1%
Household Possessions in Working Order											
Kerosene Stove			15%		4%	5%	5%	9%	10%	7%	6%
Kerosene Lamp	94%	75%	95%	44%	77%	72%	27%	39%	19%	39%	53%
Radio	31%	44%	55%	6%	34%	39%	36%	17%	16%	26%	29%
Sewing Machine			15%		4%		0%	0%	0%	0%	2%
Tin Roof	44%	19%	40%	11%	29%	33%	36%	22%	0%	22%	24%
Main Source of Cash Income											
Sale of Agricultural Products	88%	87%	60%	89%	80%	61%	90%	96%	60%	77%	78%
Sale of Livestock	0%	0%	0%	5%	1%	0%	0%	4%	7%	3%	2%
Sale of Casul Labour in the Village	0%	0%	5%	0%	1%	6%	0%	0%	0%	1%	1%
Sale of Casul Labour outside the Village	0%	0%	5%	0%	1%	0%	0%	0%	3%	1%	1%
Regular Paid Employment	6%	7%	25%	0%	10%	0%	0%	0%	7%	2%	6%
Cash Remitted by Relatives	6%	0%	0%	0%	1%	6%	10%	0%	7%	5%	4%
Timber	0%	0%	0%	0%	0%	22%	0%	0%	0%	5%	2%
Artisan	0%	7%	5%	0%	3%	6%	0%	0%	3%	2%	2%
Trading	0%	0%	0%	5%	1%	0%	0%	0%	0%	0%	1%
Brewing	0%	0%	0%	0%	0%	0%	0%	0%	13%	3%	2%
Other	0%	0%	0%	0%	0%	0%	0%	0%	0%	0%	0%
Agricultural Production											
Fields											
Number of Plots	2.7	2.8	3	2.9	2.9	4.8	2	2.3	1.9	2.7	2.69
Total Size of Fields (acres)	6.8	7.7	7.1	8.8	7.6	8	10.1	6.9	7.7	8.1	7.92
Purchase of Fertiliser											
% HH purchasing fertiliser	25.0%	25.0%	10.0%	6.0%	16%	67.0%	82.0%	100%	87.0%	85%	56%
Purchase of Seeds											
% HH purchasing Seeds	31.0%	19.0%	40.0%	28.0%	30%	33.0%	9.0%	9.0%	32.0%	18%	25%
Harvesting of Crops											
Crops [t]	0.8	1.2	1.3	1	1.1	2.2	1.6	1.8	1.5	1.6	1.45
Crops transp. from Field [t]	5.6	7.5	6.6	6.1	6.4	18.3	8.2	8.6	3.7	6.5	7.77
Means of Transport											
% Walking	100%	100%	100%	100%	100%	100%	100%	100%	100%	100%	100%

A-15

Survey 1986/87	Unen-amwa	Madi-hani	Uten-gule	Kidope	Bulo-ngwa	Ihela	Mpan-gala	Ngoje	Ngo-nde	Mata-mba	Total
Marketing of agricultural Products											
Crops [kg]	139	195	179	128	159	182	678	558	239	465	305
Other Products [kg]	no data	no data	no data	no data	no data	no data	187	84	851	425	
Total Revenues from Marketing Activities											
All Products [$ 1994]	no data	no data	no data	no data	no data	no data	77.02	116.00	70.92	87.06	54.60
Crops [$ 1994]	23.85	26.50	25.11	32.98	27.19	21.73	73.81	114.27	49.33	76.47	49.33
% marketed in village	8%	46%	76%	87%	56%	48%	99%	88%	83%	89%	71%
% marketed externally	92%	54%	24%	13%	44%	52%	1%	12%	13%	9%	29%
Tkm	1.3	0.6	0.9	0.3	0.8	0.7	0.1	1.5	1.6	1.1	0.93
Means of Transport for Crop Marketing											
% by Walking	100%	100%	100%	100%	100%	86%	100%	100%	100%	100%	98%
% by Donkey						14%					
Transport Activities											
Water Collection											
Trips/annum	800	765	840	655	765.9	765	711	894	675	750	759
Distance [km]	2.48	1.32	2.32	1.6	2.0	3.32	1.08	1.92	1.8	1.6	1.95
Time/a [hours]	975	690	630	537	703.5	1329	440	926	639	664	754
kg/trip	18	15	18	15	16.6	18	18	18	18	18.0	17.41
Tonnes/annum	14.4	11.5	15.1	9.8	12.8	13.8	12.8	16.1	12.2	13.5	13.24
Tkm/annum	43.9	31.1	31.7	25.3	32.9	59.8	22	46.3	30.4	32.6	35.72
HH Walking	100%	100%	100%	100%	100%	100%	100%	100%	100%	100%	100%
Firewood Collection											
Trips/annum	140	200	165	210	178.1	205	166	135	114	136	161
Distance [km]	5.2	3.6	8.8	6.4	6.2	7.2	5.2	7.6	9.6	7.7	6.99
Time/a [hours]	222	140	353	501	313.2	404	279	372	521	404	366
kg/trip	25	25	25	25	24.9	25	25	25	25	25.3	25.09
Tonnes/annum	3.5	5	4.1	5.2	4.4	5.1	4.2	3.4	2.9	3.4	4.04
Tkm/annum	16.8	15.9	33.3	30.9	24.9	33.1	26.3	31.3	33.8	30.8	28.56
HH Walking	100%	100%	100%	100%	100%	100%	100%	100%	100%	100%	100%
Village centre (Village Office + Village shop)											
Trips/annum	257	145	148	162	178	145	93	94	73	85	131
Distance [km]	2.68	2.04	1.88	1.8	2.1	1.52	1.04	1.08	2.72	1.7	1.86
Time/a [hours]	345	148	140	146	194	110	48	51	99	70	126.3
HH walking	100%	100%	100%	100%	100%	100%	100%	100%	100%	100%	100%
Grinding Mill											
Trips/annum	36	27.6	42	61	42.3	43.2	43.4	35.5	46.2	42	42
Distance [km]	8.4	6.4	2	4.2	5.1	7.6	1.2	4.8	8.4	5.2	5.41
Time/a [hours]	164	67	31	77	83.4	174	24	86	192	110.2	105.97
kg/trip	20	20	20	20	20.0	20	20	23	26	23.3	21.50
Tonnes/annum	0.72	0.55	0.84	1.2	0.8	0.86	0.87	0.83	1.18	1.0	0.91
Tkm/annum	16.4	6.7	3.1	6.2	7.9	17.4	2.4	10.1	24.6	13.7	11.66
HH Walking	100%	100%	100%	100%	100%	100%	100%	100%	100%	100%	1.00

Survey 1986/87	Unen-amwa	Madi-hani	Uten-gule	Kidope	Bulo-ngwa	Ihela	Mpan-gala	Ngoje	Ngo-nde	Mata-mba	Total
Trips to the Fields											
Trips/annum	169	314	213	217	225	440	479	609	419	493	374
Distance [km]	5.6	4.8	4.4	4.8	4.9	6.4	4	4	2	3.2	4.26
Time/a [hours]	487	740	457	504	538	1409	964	1213	425	820	766
Tonnes/annum	0.8	1.2	1.3	1	1.1	2.2	1.6	1.8	1.5	1.6	1.45
Tkm/annum	5.6	7.5	6.6	6.1	6.4	18.3	8.2	8.6	3.7	6.5	7.77
HH Walking	100%	100%	100%	100%	100%	100%	100%	96%	100%	99%	0.99
HH using Donkeys								4%		1%	1%
Trips to MCH-Clinic											
Trips/annum	6.7	5.2	4.2	6	5.5	6.7	4.4	3.1	4.3	4.0	4.92
Distance [km]	9.6	6.8	2	6.8	6.2	7.6	3.2	1.6	2.8	2.6	4.63
HH walking	100%	100%	100%	100%	100%	100%	100%	100%	100%	100%	100%
Trips to Dispensary											
Trips/annum	21	18.4	31.8	12	21.1	10.7	9.3	17.2	17.3	14.9	17.04
Distance [km]	12	7.6	2	7.2	7.0	7.6	3.6	4	14	7.9	7.51
HH walking	100%	100%	100%	100%	100%	100%	100%	100%	100%	100%	100%
Trips to Hospital											
Trips/annum	2	2.4	0.9	1.1	1.5	2.4	0.1	0.6	1	0.6	1.20
Distance [km]	10	7.6	14.8	10	10.8	7.6	22.8	26.8	16	21.2	15.33
Time/a [hours]											
HH Walking	100%	100%	100%	88%	97%	100%	33%	73%	97%	71%	85%
HH using Bus							57%	27%		25%	12%
HH using Other Means of Transport				12%	3%				3%	1%	2%
All Health Facilities											
Trips/annum	30	26	37	19	28	20	14	21	23	19	23
Distance [km]	11	7	2	7	7	8	4	4	12	7	7
Time/a [hours]	167	98	42	80	94.7	69	26	40	126	70.6	80.55
Internal Crop Marketing											
Trips/annum	0.50	4.50	6.80	5.60	4.4	4.40	33.60	24.60	9.90	21.4	12.35
Distance [km]	3.2	3.7	1.9	2.7	2.8	2.4	1.6	2.0	4.5	2.9	2.81
Time/a [hours]	0.40	4.20	3.30	3.80	2.9	2.6	13.40	12.30	11.10	12.1	7.20
kg/trip	22.2	20.0	20.0	19.6	20.5	20.5	19.9	19.9	20.2	20.0	20.26
Tonnes/annum	0.01	0.09	0.14	0.11	0.1	0.09	0.67	0.49	0.20	0.4	0.25
Tkm/annum	0.02	0.21	0.20	0.19	0.2	0.14	1.30	1.20	1.10	1.2	0.64
External Crop Marketing											
Trips/annum	6.4	5.3	2.1	0.8	3.5	4.7	0.5	3.3	2.0	1.9	2.90
Distance [km]	16.4	9.9	34.1	25.5	22.3	11.7	7.2	17.2	31.2	19.9	19.99
Time/a [hours]	26.3	13.1	17.9	5.1	15.6	13.8	0.9	14.2	15.6	10.8	13.14
kg/trip	19.8	20.8	19.0	20.8	20.1	20.2	20.0	20.3	20.0		
Tonnes/annum	0.13	0.11	0.04	0.02	0.1	0.10	0.01	0.07	0.04	0.0	0.06
Tkm/annum	1.3	0.6	0.9	0.3	0.8	0.7	0.1	0.8	0.8	0.6	0.67

Survey 1986/87	Unen-amwa	Madi-hani	Uten-gule	Kidope	Bulo-ngwa	Ihela	Mpan-gala	Ngoje	Ngo-nde	Mata-mba	Total
Trips to 1. Market											
Trips/annum	25.8	32.7	39.4	23.3	30.4	35.6	52.1	79.5	63.1	64.6	47.0
Distance [km]	10.8	4.4	13.6	10.8	10.2	9.2	5.2	8	15.4	10.2	10.06
HH walking	100%	100%	100%	100%	100%	100%	100%	100%	100%	100%	100%
Trips to 2. Market											
Trips/annum	15	10	33	21	20	13	12	37	8	18	18
Distance [km]	8.0	21.6	23.6	14.4	17.0	16.0	13.2	9.2	11.2	11.2	14.16
HH walking	100%	100%	100%	100%	100%	100%	100%	100%	100%	100%	100%
Total Trips to Markets											
Trips/annum	40	43	73	44	51	48	64	117	71	82	65
Time/a [hours]	206	199	597	153	299.6	310	144	283	534	343	321
Other Trips within District											
Trips/annum	12	69	42	32	38	31	30	106	12	45	41
Other Trips outside District											
Trips/annum	1.0	0.5	2.0	0.5	1.0	1.5	7.2	11.4	4.5	7.3	4.0
Total Transport Activities											
Trips/annum	1,492	1,600	1,570	1,407	1515	1,708	1,642	2,051	1,449	1684	1616
Time/annum	2,593	2,099	2,271	2,007	2244	3,821	1,939	2,998	2,563	2504	2540
Tonnes/annum	19.6	18.5	21.5	17.3	19.3	22.1	20.2	22.7	18.0	20.0	20.0
Tkm / annum	84.0	62.0	75.8	69.0	73.1	129.4	60.2	98.3	94.4	85.3	85.0

Source: BARWELL /MALMBERG 1989

Annual Transport Patterns of Households in Makete 1994

1994	Water	Fire-wood	Village centre	Grin-ding Mill	Fields	Health Facili-ties	Interna l Crop market.	Extern. Crop market.	Exter-nal Market	Other places	Total
Trips/annum	1055	276	206	36	235	25	11	20	91	34	1970
Distance [km]	1.6	5.3	1.6	3.7	3.6	6.5	-		9.2	-	-
Time/a [hours]	811	370	138	71	429	72	3.8	55	450	(93).	2346
Tonnes/annum	18.2	6.9	-	0.7	2.1	-	0	0.4	-	-	28.5
Tkm/annum	28.2	37.3	-	5.6	7.5	-	0.3	4.4	-	-	83.3
1986/87											
Trips/annum	759	161	131	42	374	23	12	3	65	45	1616
Distance [km]	1.9	7.0	1.9	5.4	4.3	7.1	2.8	20.0	-	-	-
Time/a [hours]	754	366	126	106	766	81	7	13	321	-	2540
Tonnes/annum	13.2	4.0	-	0.9	1.5	-	0.2	0.1	-	-	20.0
Tkm/annum	35.72	28.56	-	11.66	7.77	-	0.64	0.67	-	-	85.02
Absolute Changes since 1987											
Trips/annum	296	114	75	-6	-139	2	-1	17	26	-10	354
Distance [km]	-0.3	-1.7	-0.2	-1.7	-0.7	-0.6			-	-	
Time/a [hours]	57	5	12	-35	-337	-8	-3	42	129	-	-195
Tonnes/annum	5	3	-	0	1	-	0.0	0	-	-	9
Tkm/annum	-7.5	8.7	-	-6.1	-0.2	-	-0.3	3.7	-	-	-1.7
Relative Changes since 1987											
Trips/annum	39%	71%	58%	-14%	-37%	7%	-12%	572%	39%	-23%	22%
Distance [km]	-16%	-24%	-12%	-32%	-16%	-9%					
Time/a [hours]	8%	1%	9%	-33%	-44%	-10%	-48%	318%	40%		-8%
Tonnes/annum	37%	71%		-21%	44%		-12%	568%			43%
Tkm/annum	-21%	30%		-52%	-3%		-53%	559%			-2%

A-18

Traffic Survey Matamba-Chimala Road

Road traffic from Matamba to the Lowland

	Wednesday 15.6.94	Thursday 16.6.94	Friday 17.6.94	Saturday 18.6.94	Average
Trucks	8	6	3	5	6
Tractors	0	1	0	3	1
Four wheel drive	4	5	4	6	5
Total Motor Vehicles	**12**	**12**	**7**	**14**	**11**
Passengers	**27**	**33**	**15**	**48**	**31**
Potatoes [t]	0.0	1.0	0.0	8.5	2.4
Ulanzi [t]	10.1	9.6	6.0	9.5	8.8
Total Tonnes	**10.1**	**10.6**	**5.98**	**18.02**	**11.2**

Utengule - Ng'yekye Footpath

	Uphill			Downhill			Up and down		
	Men	Women	Total	Men	Women	Total	Men	Women	Total
Thur 26 May 1994	19	20	39	20	76	96	39	96	135
Fri 27 May 1994	107	179	286	151	276	427	258	455	713
Sat 28 May 1994	24	25	49	11	19	30	35	44	79
Thur and Fri 1994	126	199	325	171	352	523	297	551	848
Total 1994	150	224	374	182	371	553	332	595	927
Wed 19 Oct 1988			9			20			29
Thur 20 Oct 1988			4			31			35
Fri 21 Oct 1988			160			210			370
Sat 22 Oct 1988			26			14			40
Mon 24 Oct 1988			14			8			22
Tue 25 Oct 1988			8			5			13
Thur and Fri 1988			164			241			405
Total 1988			221			288			509
Change Thur +Fri			98%			117%			109%

Madihani - Ng'yekye Footpath

	Uphill			Downhill			Up and down		
	Men	Women	Total	Men	Women	Total	Men	Women	Total
Thur 26 May 1994	1	3	4	14	16	30	15	19	34
Fri 27 May 1994	76	123	199	80	97	177	156	220	376
Sat 28 May 1994	5	7	12	3	1	4	8	8	16
Thur and Fri	77	126	203	94	113	207	171	239	410
Total	82	133	215	97	114	211	179	247	426
Thur 20 Oct 1988			2			29			31
Fri 21 Oct 1988			66			134			200
Total			68			163			231
Change 1988-1994			199%			27%			77%

System Model Equations:

Income & Expenditure
Income(t) = Income(t - dt) + (Revenues - Disp_Income - Inputs) * dt
INIT Income = 73
INFLOWS:
Revenues = Other_Income+Net_Market_Revenue
OUTFLOWS:
Disp_Income = Income-Inputs
Inputs = Fertiliser*0.1345+Costs_IMT
Costs_IMT = Debt_Service/4180 + Share_Bicycle*3.74 + Share_Donkey*4.34
        + (1-Credit_Level)/Credit_Level*Disbursement/4180
Gross_Market_Revenue = Production-156
Growth_Income = Income/delay(Income,1)*100-100
Net_Market_Revenue = Gross_Market_Revenue - Gross_Market_Revenue/76.34*(1-Share_Internal)
        User_Charge - Gross_Market_Revenue/76.34(1-Share_Internal)*VOC
Other_Income = 56.7+Imp_Income+0.1*delay(Disp_Income,1)

Production
Fertiliser(t) = Fertiliser(t - dt) + (Δ_Fertiliser) * dt
INIT Fertiliser = 1
INFLOWS:
Δ_Fertiliser = (Net_Market_Revenue *0.1/0.1345*Diffusion_Faktor
        - delay (Net_Market_Revenue*0.1/0.1345*Diffusion_Faktor,1))*Imp_Fertilizer
Labour(t) = Labour(t - dt) + (Δ_Labour) * dt
INIT Labour = (164.72/9.294/Land^0.3724)^(1/0.4404)*6
INFLOWS:
Δ_Labour = 1/6*Diffusion_Faktor*Disposable_Time
Land(t) = Land(t - dt) + (Clear_Land) * dt
INIT Land = 4.355
INFLOWS:
Clear_Land = Labour/271 - Land
Diffusion_Faktor = if (time<6) then time/6 else 1
Growth_Prod = production/delay(production,1)*100 -100
Production = 9.294*Land^0.3724*Fertiliser^0.0499*(Labour/6)^0.4404
        *(1+Share_Donkey*0.5654+Share_Bicycle*0.3352)

Transport Sector
Dist_Field = 0.14 * Land + 2.89
Load = Share_Bicycle*0.04*0.4 +Share_Donkey*0.06*0.8+(1-Share_Bicycle*0.4-Share_Donkey*0.8)*0.02
Other_Time = 1858-Imp_other_Time-Share_Bicycle*203
Share_Internal = 0.12*Disp_Income/Gross_Market_Revenue
Time_Fields = Labour/6*Dist_Field * 2 / 4
Time_Market = Tkm_Market /Load /2
Tkm_Market = Gross_Market_Revenue / 76.34* (Share_Internal * 1.6 + (1 - Share_Internal) * Dist_Mark)
Trans_Time = Other_Time+Time_Market+Time_Fields

Time Budget
Disposable_Time(t) = Disposable_Time(t - dt) + (- Δ_Time) * dt
INIT Disposable_Time = 5000 - Trans_Time - Labour
OUTFLOWS:
Δ_Time = Δ_TransTime+Δ_Labour
Δ_TransTime = Trans_Time-delay(Trans_Time,1)

Credit System IMT

Credit System IMT

Bicycles(t) = Bicycles(t - dt) + (Purchase_Bicycle - B_paid) * dt
INIT Bicycles = 0
 TRANSIT TIME = 5
 ENTRANCE CAPACITY = ∞
INFLOWS:
Purchase_Bicycle = IMT_Fund_Start*WTP_Bic*2508-delay(IMT_Fund_Start*WTP_Bic*2508, 1)
 +Out_of_Order
OUTFLOWS:
B_paid = CONVEYOR OUTFLOW
Bicycles_paid(t) = Bicycles_paid(t - dt) + (B_paid - Out_of_Order) * dt
INIT Bicycles_paid = 0
 TRANSIT TIME = 5
 ENTRANCE CAPACITY = ∞
INFLOWS:
B_paid = CONVEYOR OUTFLOW
OUTFLOWS:
Out_of_Order = CONVEYOR OUTFLOW
Donkeys(t) = Donkeys(t - dt) + (Purchase_Donkey - Dpaid) * dt
INIT Donkeys = 0
 TRANSIT TIME = 5
 ENTRANCE CAPACITY = ∞
INFLOWS:
Purchase_Donkey = IMT_Fund_Start*WTP_Donk*1254-delay(IMT_Fund_Start*WTP_Donk*1254, 1)+Death
OUTFLOWS:
Dpaid = CONVEYOR OUTFLOW
Donkeys_Paid(t) = Donkeys_Paid(t - dt) + (Dpaid - Death) * dt
INIT Donkeys_Paid = 0
 TRANSIT TIME = 5
 ENTRANCE CAPACITY = ∞
INFLOWS:
Dpaid = CONVEYOR OUTFLOW
OUTFLOWS:
Death = CONVEYOR OUTFLOW
IMT_Credit_Fund(t) = IMT_Credit_Fund(t - dt) + (Debt_Service - Disbursement) * dt
INIT IMT_Credit_Fund = 0
INFLOWS:
Debt_Service = delay((Donkeys*Annuity_Donk + Bicycles*Annuity_Bic)*0.8,1)
OUTFLOWS:
Disbursement = Purchase_Bicycle*Credit_Bic+ Purchase_Donkey*Credit_Donk
Annuity_Bic = If (Credit_Level=0) then 0 else
 If (Credit_Level=0.25) then 5.13 else
 If (Credit_Level=0.5) then 10.26 else
 If (Credit_Level=0.6) then 12.32 else
 If (Credit_Level=0.7) then 14.37 else
 If (Credit_Level=0.75) then 15.4 else
 If (Credit_Level=0.8) then 16.42 else
 If (Credit_Level=0.9) then 18.48 else 0
Annuity_Donk = If (Credit_Level=0) then 0 else
 If (Credit_Level=0.25) then 6.10 else
 If (Credit_Level=0.5) then 12.21 else
 If (Credit_Level=0.6) then 14.65 else
 If (Credit_Level=0.7) then 17.09 else
 If (Credit_Level=0.75) then 18.31 else
 If (Credit_Level=0.8) then 19.53 else
 If (Credit_Level=0.9) then 21.97 else 0
Credit_Bic = Credit_Level*74
Credit_Donk = Credit_Level*88
Credit_Level = 0.75
Share_Bicycle = (Bicycles+Bicycles_paid)/4180
Share_Donkey = (Donkeys_Paid+Donkeys)/4180
Share_IMT = Share_Bicycle+Share_Donkey

Revenue_NonIMT = GRAPH(time)
> (0.00, 9.00), (1.00, 13.0), (2.00, 24.0), (3.00, 38.0), (4.00, 55.0), (5.00, 73.0), (6.00, 91.0), (7.00, 105), (8.00, 115), (9.00, 122), (10.0, 127), (11.0, 130), (12.0, 133), (13.0, 134), (14.0, 135), (15.0, 136), (16.0, 137), (17.0, 137), (18.0, 137), (19.0, 137), (20.0, 137)

WTP_Bic = GRAPH((74-Credit_Bic)/Revenue_NonIMT)
> (0.00, 1.00), (0.05, 0.915), (0.1, 0.8), (0.15, 0.723), (0.2, 0.615), (0.25, 0.523), (0.3, 0.462), (0.35, 0.4), (0.4, 0.369), (0.45, 0.331), (0.5, 0.262), (0.55, 0.215), (0.6, 0.2), (0.65, 0.185), (0.7, 0.131), (0.75, 0.092), (0.8, 0.077), (0.85, 0.062), (0.9, 0.046), (0.95, 0.031), (1.00, 0.015)

WTP_Donk = GRAPH((88-Credit_Donk)/Revenue_NonIMT)
> (0.00, 1.00), (0.05, 0.974), (0.1, 0.795), (0.15, 0.667), (0.2, 0.513), (0.25, 0.462), (0.3, 0.41), (0.35, 0.359), (0.4, 0.256), (0.45, 0.154), (0.5, 0.128), (0.55, 0.103), (0.6, 0.09), (0.65, 0.077), (0.7, 0.064), (0.75, 0.051), (0.8, 0.046), (0.85, 0.041), (0.9, 0.036), (0.95, 0.031), (1.00, 0.026)

Road Fund

Road_Fund(t) = Road_Fund(t - dt) + (Charges - Costs) * dt
INIT Road_Fund = 0
INFLOWS:
Charges = Gross_Market_Revenue*4180/76.34*(1-Share_Internal)*User_Charge
OUTFLOWS:
Costs = Road_Investment + Road_Maintenance - Road_Fund*0.08

Scenarios

Dist_Mark = IF(scenario = 1) then 33.2 else
> If (Scenario = 2 or scenario =4 or scenario = 5) then 9.5 else
> if (Scenario=3) then 1.6 else 0

Imp_Fertilizer = if (Scenario = 1) then 0 else 1
Imp_Income = if (scenario = 1 and time <1) then 0.96 else
> if (Scenario= 1 and time >= 1) then 0.06 else
> If (Scenario = 2 and time <1) then 17.36 else
> If (Scenario = 2 and time >= 1) then 0.99 else
> if (Scenario=3 and time <1) then 36.5 else
> if (Scenario=3 and time >= 1) then 2.52 else
> if (Scenario=4 and time < 1) then 33.6 else
> if (Scenario=4 and time >= 1) then 1.06 else
> If (Scenario= 5 and time <1) then 17.36 else
> If (Scenario= 5 and time >= 1) then 0.99 else 0

Imp_other_Time = If (Scenario=4 and time >=1) then 388 else 0
IMT_Fund_Start = If (scenario=5) then 1 else 0
Road_Investment = if (scenario=2 and time < 1) then 123019 else
> if (scenario=3 and time < 1) then 318075 else
> if (scenario=4 and time < 1) then 123019 else
> if (scenario=5 and time < 1) then 123019 else 0

Road_Maintenance = if (scenario=2 and time >= 1) then 7013 else
> if (scenario=3 and time >= 1) then 18072 else
> if (scenario=4 and time >= 1) then 7013 else
> if (scenario=5 and time >= 1) then 7013 else 0

Scenario = 5
User_Charge = If (scenario = 2 and Charge_on = 1) then 4.01 else
> If (scenario = 3 and Charge_on = 1) then 9.27 else
> If (scenario = 4 and Charge_on = 1) then 3.42 else
> If (scenario = 5 and Charge_on = 1) then 2.58 else 0

VOC = If (Scenario =1 and time >=1) then 0 else
> If (Scenario =2 and time >=1) then 15.18 else
> If (Scenario =3 and time >=1) then 19.15 else
> If (Scenario =4 and time >=1) then 15.18 else
> If (Scenario =5 and time >=1) then 15.18 else 0

Graphs & Tables
Charge_on = 0